RICHARD NIXON:

A Political and Personal Portrait

By EARL MAZO

HARPER & BROTHERS PUBLISHERS NEW YORK

To My Wife
RITA VANE MAZO

Author's Note

Nearly one thousand people have helped significantly in preparing this book. I am indebted to John Appleton of Harper & Brothers, who proposed, then edited it; to Robert J. Donovan, Chief of the New York *Herald Tribune* Washington bureau; to the Vice-President's Executive Secretary, Rose Mary Woods; to Jerry Voorhis, first victim of a Nixon campaign; to Paul Ziffren; to my wife, Rita, for teaching herself to type this manuscript without dropping any of her teaching, civic or family activities.

I am much obliged to the Vice-President, Thomas E. Dewey, Adlai Stevenson, Mrs. Hannah Nixon, Harold E. Stassen, Christian Herter, John Foster Dulles, Lyndon Johnson, John F. Kennedy, Sam Rayburn, William F. Knowland, Herbert Brownell, Jr., William P. Rogers, James P. Mitchell, and more than three hundred others who granted exhaustive interviews. I also wish to thank some five hundred individuals who provided useful information by mail or telephone.

Among friends I am grateful to Paul M. Butler, Meade Alcorn, Malcom Moos, Totton J. Anderson, Evelyn Chavoor, assistant to Mrs. Helen Gahagan Douglas, who made available the latter's files concerning her senatorial battle with Nixon, Robert H. Finch, Loie Gaunt, Herbert G. Klein, Roscoe Drummond, Irving Ferman, Robert E. Grayson, Guy Savino, William M. Blair, Gladwin Hill, Olive Montel, Pauline Tait, James E. Bassett, Earl Behrens, Jack Foisie, Larry Smyth, L. Richard Guylay, William Welch, John Harris, Harold G. Brown, Sam Zagoria, William G. Key, Ted Rogers, Pierre Salinger, Ethel Greenberg, Dan Vane, Charles Wingenbach and Robert Hansen.

Generous help was received from the Library of Congress, the libraries of the New York *Herald Tribune,* the *New York Times,* the Washington *Star,* the Washington *Post,* the *Christian Science Monitor's* Washington bureau, the Los Angeles *Times,* the Alhambra (California) *Post-Advocate,* the late Los Angeles *Daily News,* and the libraries of both Republican and Democratic National Committees.

EARL MAZO

RICHARD NIXON:

A Political and Personal Portrait

1

W<small>HEN</small> Sherman Adams telephoned to report that President Eisenhower was stricken again, he suggested that the Vice-President come to the White House immediately. A few minutes later in the Presidential Assistant's office Richard Nixon was informed that Eisenhower had probably suffered a stroke, but the extent of brain damage wouldn't be determined for twenty-four hours.

It was midafternoon November 25, 1957. For the third time in just over two years Nixon faced the possibility of having to succeed to the Presidency. But the tranquil spirit of Geneva that prevailed during the President's previous serious illnesses had given way to the Sputnik–Little Rock–Recession crises, and, as a result, Eisenhower later drew up a historic agreement empowering Nixon to assume complete presidential powers if necessary to assure the nation an active Chief Executive. The two-and-three-quarter-page agreement was written in letter form and layman's language by Eisenhower himself, with copies for Secretary of State John Foster Dulles and Attorney General William P. Rogers. No other President had given so much responsibility and power to his Vice-President.

For all his prominence and the millions of words that have been written and spoken about him, surprisingly little is known about Richard Milhous Nixon. In the political area, his point of greatest contact with the public, extremes of praise or vilification have been the general rule. Complexity of character is not unusual among important public men. But Nixon is singularly complex, a paradoxical combination of qualities that bring to mind Lincoln, Theodore

(1)

Roosevelt, Harry Truman and Joe McCarthy.

He is a fatalist, to the point of believing that whether he becomes president will depend more on "circumstances" than on anything he, his friends or his opponents do. Although he is the hardiest campaigner in the Republican party, he has an aversion to—and actually "shudders at the thought of"—campaigning. Many intellectuals see him as a know-nothing; yet two of his speeches were models for advocates of a Washington Fine Arts Center and his Law School dean considered him a "scholar."

Nixon is a practicing Quaker, at home with precepts of kindness to one's fellow man; yet, in fighting for votes, he has resorted to malignant innuendo such as the statement (made during the 1952 campaign) that "the only way to save America is to get rid of Trumanism, or Stevensonianism, or whatever *ism* with which you choose to tag the whole sorry mess." Considering his reputation as the party's hatchetman, the political fraternity, and the Republican leadership in particular, may be surprised to learn that Nixon regards as "silly" his National Committee's long and intensive drive to have the opposition called the "Democrat" instead of "Democratic" party.

It is generally conceded that if Nixon succeeds to the Presidency before the next election, he automatically will be the Republican nominee for the ensuing full term. Democratic National Chairman Paul M. Butler believes he will get the nomination in any case. "The first objective of our effort and attention is Nixon," said Butler. "He is our common target." The Democratic organization's Nixon files already have overflowed from the party headquarters at 1001 Connecticut Avenue in Washington to a nearby hotel. At the core of this burgeoning library of newspaper clippings, speeches, memoranda, and reports of various classifications is a large, ready-reference loose-leafed notebook, known to Democratic researchers as the "Nixophobia." (A less bulky comparison volume is the "Iklopedia.") The Nixophobia is filled with excerpts from Nixon speeches, and remarks he is said to have made in private conversations and confidential pep talks to party workers.

The threat from Democrats is of less immediate concern to Nixon,

(2)

however, than the great new challenge from New York within his own party. Before the 1958 election exposed Governor Nelson Rockefeller's extraordinary flair for vote getting, the Republican national organization, like the Democratic, was geared to a Nixon nomination, and happily so. In spite of the otherwise gloomy outlook, National Chairman Meade Alcorn and his fellows consoled each other with thoughts of peace and unity at the Republican Convention, while the Democrats squabbled furiously at theirs. The GOP brass, therefore, was understandably unnerved by postelection speculation that put Rockefeller rocketing ahead of Nixon. Qualified confidence in Nixon's nomination was subsequently restored, but the hope for an uncontested convention in which Republicans damned only the Democrats, instead of each other, was not.

While Nixon has always felt that getting the nomination will depend mostly on "circumstances at the time, not a man's ambition," his parallel belief is that "a man must be ready to take advantage of an opportunity when it is offered." Furthermore, nothing disgusts him so much as a politician who shuns responsibilities in a campaign—or in office—for fear of being considered controversial. "I don't know of any person in a leadership position who is worth his salt who isn't controversial," he says. "It's what you are controversial about that counts."

From the outset Democrats have made Nixon their principal target in the Republican administration. Although sometimes painful, it is an unequaled distinction for a vice-president. Nixon gained it, of course, by handling the administration's major assaults on its political opposition, a task normally performed by presidents. The battles often degenerated into gouging and name-calling. The extremes of feeling they have aroused is such that among partisans Nixon is regarded as either a giant or a pipsqueak. Two former candidates for the Presidency typify those divergent opinions. Thomas E. Dewey says Nixon knows more about "the sensitive areas of government relations in the world than any man who might be nominated [and is] the most logical, most widely experienced" contender. On the other hand, Adlai E. Stevenson declares, "I recoil at the prospect of Mr. Nixon as custodian of this nation's future."

(3)

That Nixon is often underrated indicates the extent to which he is unknown and misunderstood. At the height of the storm in 1952 over the "Nixon Fund," for instance, practically everybody thought he was through. The clamor for his scalp had become nonpartisan and an hour before the television program on which he was to explain it all Nixon was notified, in secret, that General Eisenhower and the General's campaign hierarchy thought he should resign as candidate for vice-president. The experts expected his talk to be a funeral oration. Instead, he gave one of the most noteworthy performances of its kind in American politics. He turned a sentimental discussion of his finances, his family and the origin of his children's dog, Checkers, into a counteroffensive against the Democrats— and, when it ended, his would-be Republican pallbearers stampeded for places on his bandwagon.

Nixon is a practical individual, careful to master details and alternatives; still he is at his best in a crisis. And, though there is no impetuosity in his make-up, the most precipitate action he ever took was also probably the wisest. He proposed marriage the day he met Pat Ryan. (She said "No," and a couple of years later changed it to "Yes.") The natural Nixon stands out more clearly winning friends on overseas tours than vote hunting at home. During a free hour of his autumn, 1958, visit to London he made an unscheduled handshaking tour that pleased the people he met and delighted Queen Elizabeth. (His report to the Queen that the people thought Prince Philip's was the best speech at a televised state function the night before gave her "quite a kick," according to Nixon, who knew she had been offended by an uncomplimentary assessment of her husband's effort in Randolph Churchill's newspaper column.)

"I never in my life wanted to be left behind," Nixon says, conceding that he was born ambitious—requisite for success in politics. So is energy—and also brains, courage, gall, cunning, persuasiveness, the bent for rationalizing and compromising, a healthy respect for realities, and a rapport with fate and luck. Nixon has them all, plus an array of characteristics that normally would be a drag on a politician. Basically he is shy and taciturn. He broods, abhors back-

(4)

slapping and gives the appearance of being a friendless "loner," a too-smooth and humorless perfectionist.

"I have a fetish about disciplining myself," Nixon says. He can swear like a sailor, but does it only among friends, mostly when it becomes necessary to open a safety valve on pent-up frustrations and anger. He dislikes social affairs, especially formal dinners, but has mastered his boredom. "I found when you get bored you get tired," he says. Nixon watches his diet carefully, figuring "the worst thing in the world is to eat heavy food when you have a lot of work to do." He is probably the fastest dresser in high office, with a record of eight minutes for formal clothes and two and a half for regular wear.

Nixon is a political craftsman. His instincts and training as a debater, practically since childhood, make him a forceful salesman. Nixon is also a bit of a dreamer. Some of his ideas would horrify friends and amaze others. While he is, essentially, a practical operator, fully aware of the perils which often keep aspirations from becoming realities, Nixon considers himself a "radical" when it comes to the goals he would set for the country. (His definition of "radical" being the "opposite of conservative.")

Since early youth Nixon has earned his own way and made his own decisions. He has known much happiness and an exceptional amount of success. But there also has been great sadness, and emotional wrenches in his public life of which only intimates were aware. Once during the 1952 presidential campaign he dictated a telegram resigning from the ticket. There were times since when he resolved to quit politics for good at the first opportunity. Nixon has only a few intimate friends. He has an obsession about the separation of his private and his public life, and no one outside his family is a personal confidant.

Harold E. Stassen, of all persons, was his first political mentor and offered him the vice-presidential nomination on a Stassen ticket. Nixon and Nelson Rockefeller became good friends and supported each other consistently in White House fights when Rockefeller was a member of Eisenhower's first administration. Typical of the relationship was a note the present New York Governor sent to Nixon following a National Security Council meeting in November, 1955,

(5)

at which there was a particularly intensive argument over the budget for overseas programs. "You were superb," said Rockefeller. "You have no idea what your understanding, integrity, courage and leadership mean to so many of us." Senator John F. Kennedy is another potential opponent for the Presidency with whom Nixon has been very friendly. They came to Congress together in 1947 and served on the House Labor Committee that wrote the Taft-Hartley Labor Law. During a luncheon at which they were on the same platform for the first time in years, Nixon slipped the potential Democratic nominee the following note: "Jack—I wish I were sitting with you on the labor hearings. I'm sure we could come up with something better than in 1947!"

In a way, Nixon also is a fan of Harry Truman's, despite the insults they have traded. He admires Truman's courage and, in fact, has more in common with him than either would admit. Both love to play the piano. Each is his party's toughest campaigner, has plenty of guts, and is notably loyal to party and friends. They also share the unhappy experience of having failed once in a business.[1]

Although a vice-president has no executive responsibilities, Nixon took at face value Eisenhower's suggestion that he keep abreast of everything a president should know. As a result, he has raised the Vice-Presidency to a full-time legislative-executive operation. His influence has grown steadily and he has become a strong man—in some respects, *the* strong man—in the administration. Eisenhower hasn't referred to him as "my boy" for a long time. During the second term, particularly, Nixon has participated in most major administration decisions. It was his idea, for instance, to have Ambassador Robert G. Murphy go as special envoy to the Middle East during the Lebanon crisis.

Nixon disagrees with Eisenhower on several major issues. He expresses his views and presses for their acceptance at Cabinet and National Security Council meetings and in private conferences with

[1] The Washington *Post* contrasts the campaigning techniques of Truman and Nixon as being "the difference between a warmhearted fellow who plows into a fist fight for the sheer joy of it and the grim-minded fellow who charges in with a pipe wrench."

the President and other administration leaders. But, in so far as he is concerned, the arguments end once Eisenhower makes a policy decision. Eisenhower has had occasion to point up that loyalty to Nixon's critics, including Stassen.

On January 7, 1955, while Democrats were protesting about Nixon's tactics in the 1954 campaign and parading a "Chamber of Smears" labeling him "the All-American Boy Demagogue," Sherman Adams told Nixon in a note: "It would have warmed your heart to have heard the President extoll your virtues last night to his White House Stag Night guests. He said your effectiveness was measured by the volume of your criticism, which indicated to him that you have made a deep mark on the opposition, and indeed, upon the country." Adams' handwritten message was on State of New Hampshire stationery, left over from his tenure as governor. Eisenhower had sent the Vice-President three letters of encouragement and approval during that campaign, which developed into the most vituperative and enervating of Nixon's career.

Nixon became a nationally controversial figure late in 1948 when, as a junior member of the Un-American Activities Committee, he pushed the investigation of Alger Hiss. The Hiss case soon developed into the issue of Communists-in-Government, which became the mid-twentieth-century version of the Party-of-Treason shibboleth Republicans had used to their great political advantage for three decades after the Civil War. It was called "The Bloody Shirt" in those days; now it became known as "McCarthyism." Rightly or wrongly, Nixon was identified with everything said by all Republican orators who taunted Democrats with this issue.

Actually, Nixon was more precise than his colleagues. His charges, when examined carefully, and in toto, were practically always accurate from a strictly technical viewpoint. But this was no angels' carnival. It was what *seemed* to be said that paid off, not the intricate lawyerlike interweaving of facts and qualifications. Nixon did not exactly call Secretary of State Acheson a "pink," for instance. But he did refer to "Acheson's color blindness—a form of pink eye toward the Communist threat in the United States."

Politicians were not averse to hyperbole before Nixon. But not

(7)

many in modern times handled it so resourcefully. Take, for example, his much-debated manipulation of the word "traitor." In 1954 he charged that "real Democrats are outraged by the Truman-Acheson-Stevenson gang's defense of Communism in high places"; and Truman, Stevenson and Acheson were "traitors to the high principles in which many of the nation's Democrats believed." Was that nothing more than an appeal for the votes of "real Democrats," as the Republicans insist? Or was it slick juggling, meant to highlight "traitor" and "Communism in high places"?

Did Nixon deliberately associate the heinous words with major figures in the party that Senator Joseph R. McCarthy was baldly accusing of twenty years of treason?

Nixon was always a fast man on the uptake. He reached a peak of nimbleness, however, in his retort to Stevenson's assertion that Nixon represented "McCarthyism in a white collar." That, declared Nixon, was an attack on the working people. "What Mr. Stevenson calls me is unimportant," he stated, "but I resent his typically snide and snobbish innuendo towards the millions of Americans who work for a living in our shops and factories."

Nixon's role as the bayonet of Republican offensives was hardly calculated to endear him to Democrats. Since it was politically unhealthy to attack Eisenhower during his first six years in office, Nixon drew all the fire. Truman sized him up as an "s.o.b."; Roger Kent, the Democratic chairman of his home state, insisted "he would double-cross and destroy the reputation of anybody if it seemed to serve his interest"; Congressman Celler, the veteran New York Democrat, called him "a naïve, inept, maladjusted Throttlebottom"; the New Republic, a liberal weekly, described him as the administration's "trapdoor, escape hatch and hygienic flush"; and Adlai Stevenson conjured up visions of a "Nixonland—a land of slander and scare, of sly innuendo, of a poison pen, the anonymous phone call and hustling, pushing, shoving—the land of smash and grab and anything to win." The Democratic campaign handbook for 1958 contained a section called "Nixon." It opened with an excerpt from a column by Walter Lippmann, assessing the Vice-President as a "ruthless partisan . . . [who] does not have within his

(8)

conscience those scruples which the country has a right to expect in the President of the United States."

Among old-line Democrats few have taken a more definite position with regard to Nixon than Speaker of the House Sam Rayburn. Mister Sam, who sits with the Vice-President when Congress meets in joint session, has privately referred to his colleague as "that ugly man with the chinkapin eyes." He was much annoyed at an unexpected House resolution praising Nixon for his "courage" in South America. It passed unanimously. Mister Sam became doubly annoyed when a fellow Texan, Lyndon Johnson, next day led the entire Senate to the airport to welcome the Nixons. This, Johnson explained, was a compromise to avoid paying more formal tribute; Senator Charles E. Potter had been persuaded to drop his resolution congratulating the Nixons on their dignity and courage.

Passionate Republicans never hated Franklin Roosevelt and Harry Truman more than partisan Democrats have hated Richard Nixon. For a time his name was a bad word in certain Republican circles as well, and some considered it politically dangerous to associate with him. Governor Dewey, an old hand at dealing with campaign invective, told Nixon at the 1956 Republican Convention: "I don't see how you take it."[2]

Nixon insists that the record of his campaigns would show that he questioned the judgment but never the loyalty of Democratic opponents and party leaders. A memorandum prepared by his office for distribution among Republican leaders urges that charges against him of unfair campaigning tactics be considered "in terms of the official Democratic Party estimate of Nixon's value to the Republicans."

While the determination of Democratic leaders to defeat Nixon is unanimous, burning hatred of him is not. A number of the party's major personalities, including Senator Johnson, trust and think very highly of him, professionally, and a few are personal friends.

---

[2] Nixon's enemies are a mild bunch compared with those of Martin Van Buren, the Vice-President under Andrew Jackson. Van Buren found it necessary once to preside over the Senate with a brace of pistols on his desk. He was later elected president.

(9)

Senator George A. Smathers, chairman of the Democratic Senate Campaign Committee, would "do anything to get a Democrat elected President, except to go out and slander Nixon." One of the half dozen most powerful Democratic leaders has said, confidentially: "I'd like to have him in my party."

Some of the legends that have become standard props in stories about Nixon are true. Others are based on falsehoods or misunderstandings, and many are a hodgepodge of fact and fiction. Individuals expressing the most extreme opinions, favorable and otherwise, are often the least familiar with Nixon, the man and his politics. What one sees in him depends on who is looking. To Herblock, the Pulitzer Prize-winning cartoonist for the Washington *Post*, he has a hard, criminal face and a stout, sloppy body. When, for variety, he draws Nixon as a sleek, fat cat, Herblock says he assures the complaining cat lovers that he intended no offense to them or their cats. Jim Berryman, the Pulitzer Prize-winning cartoonist for the Washington *Star*, depicts Nixon as a clean-cut young statesman and sees him "as a very high type of American who would make a good, positive President."

General Lucius D. Clay, an influential friend of Eisenhower, says "Nixon is unquestionably going to be the leader of the Conservative forces"; Senator Kenneth Keating, of New York, a middleground legislator, considers Nixon "pretty much my brand of Republican"; and Arthur S. Flemming, Secretary of Health, Education and Welfare, who has observed Nixon at about three hundred Cabinet and National Security Council meetings, regards him as "a genuine, progressive Republican."

Notwithstanding his tough exterior, the cold disregard with which he seems to slough off attacks and his frequent references to Truman's dictum—"If you can't take the heat, get out of the kitchen" —Nixon is painfully sensitive to what he considers unwarranted criticism. But he is less so now than he was on becoming vice-president. That is one way he has changed over the years. There has also been a tempering of his outlook in general. When Adlai Stevenson said in a 1954 campaign speech that the American economy was shrinking while the Soviet economy was growing, Nixon accused him of "spreading pro-Communist propaganda." Four years later, however, Nixon told the Newspaper Publishers Association that Americans should ponder the "sobering fact [that] the Soviet economy is growing faster than ours."

One thing about which there can be no differences is the fact that Richard Nixon has been one of the luckiest public figures in American history. None can match his experience of having been saved by a mob that tried to kill him during his good-will tour of South America. (On his visit to the United States eight months later Soviet Deputy Premier Anastas I. Mikoyan, ignoring the fact that it was a Communist-inspired attack, lauded Nixon for "standing up to them like a rock.") There have been other curious and dramatic incidents in his life, starting with a headlong fall from a buggy when he was three. Nixon's father narrowly missed becoming an oil millionaire, and at one time or another Nixon almost became a frozen orange juice promoter, a Wall Street lawyer, an FBI agent, a college president, dean of a law school, president of one of California's largest corporations. He might still be a career member of the House of Representatives. From his earliest years, an undisturbed portrait of Richard Nixon presents many unexpected features.

2

Nixon has managed to stand out in one way or another for a good part of his life. He was the first child born in Yorba Linda, a farming village thirty miles inland from Los Angeles. (Next day there was a partial eclipse of the sun.) Nixon's father, whose wide-ranging talents included carpentry, built the family homestead alone, except for the fireplace.[1] The small frame house, perched on a knoll above a deep irrigation ditch bordering the lemon grove from which the elder Nixon tried to coax a livelihood, was difficult to heat. Hot wind blasts from the California desert normally scorched Yorba Linda by day. But its nights were often cold, particularly in January and February. When the town was cold, the Nixon house was very, very cold. The family dressed in the kitchen, huddled around the cooking stove, and the children played close to the living-room fireplace. But on the night of January 9, 1913, the whole house was warm and comfortable, especially the tiny alcove that served as master bedroom. Francis A. (Frank) Nixon had a collection of stoves operating in tandem with the fireplace, and he pulled aside the curtains that separated the alcove from the living room so the heat would flow into the room where his second son, Richard, was to be born. Mrs. Henrietta Shockney, a practical nurse who helped with the delivery, still marvels at the "even temperature." The Nixons were a pleasant family, easy to

[1] The house now is occupied by the janitor for the elementary school. But the townspeople and school board dedicated it as a "historic site" on Nixon's forty-sixth birthday, January 9, 1959. When they can find another home for the janitor, the house will be used for "historic purposes."

work with, she says. The father harnessed his excitement that night by fussing around with the stoves. Harold, the baby's four-year-old brother, carefully avoided getting in anyone's way, and Mrs. Elmira Milhous, the grandmother, fulfilled her role as matriarch without pestering doctor or nurse.

Nurse Shockney recalls Richard as a "roly-poly, good-natured" infant with brown eyes and brown hair. The first characteristic that impressed Mrs. Nixon was her new son's "decided voice." To Grandmother Milhous the resonant "yowl" meant the boy would be a preacher or a lawyer.

Richard took his spankings without a whimper. He was a willing helper around the house when the chores were "men's work." But before submitting to tasks associated with girls, like washing the dishes, he would draw the blinds tight to shut the world out from his humiliation. Richard was unlike his contemporaries around Yorba Linda only in that he was an avid newspaper reader when they were starting with picture books, and he preferred daydreams to anything else on earth. The great joy of his early boyhood centered on a spurline of the Santa Fe Railroad. There were toughness, vigor and unbendable firmness in the smooth steel tracks that stretched beyond sight in both directions and at one point were just across an irrigation ditch and a roadway from the Nixon house. Long freight trains rumbled past at all hours. The Nixon homestead shook and the throbbing stirred in Richard visions of faraway places. In his fantasies the ugly, noisy freighters were spotless passenger mainliners with the sure hand of Engineer Nixon on the throttle. "The train whistle was the sweetest music I ever heard," he recalls.

Naturally he aimed to become a railroad man. His determination was reinforced by the practical prospect of making money and achieving social status. "The best-off man in town was an engineer who ran the Santa Fe train from Los Angeles to Needles," Nixon says. "Every time I saw him or heard his name I thought that being a railroad engineer was an awfully good job to have."

Nixon stuck by his railroading dreams until he was practically in high school. His mother hoped he would become a musician or, if not that, a preacher. He had never seen a real live lawyer when

(13)

he switched ambitions. From his newspaper reading he developed a fascination for the law. Lawyers seemed to be involved in all the intriguing doings of government. In elementary school he became a star debater and orator and once or twice overheard an adult say "Dick is a born lawyer." There was also his tenth birthday present from Aunt Edith—a large volume on American history, which he read and reread and practically memorized. The book glorified non-military heroes, all of whom appeared to be lawyers.

Finally, there was the Teapot Dome Scandal. Nixon's father, who might have been an oil millionaire with better luck,[2] became increasingly livid over each new disclosure in the sensational theft of government oil reserves through the connivance of principals in President Harding's administration. His diatribes against "crooked politicians" and "crooked lawyers" dominated the family conversation for weeks and provoked 12-year-old Richard to abandon the romance of railroading for a more idealized road to greatness.

His mother was the first to be told of the decision. She recalls that the boy declared, "I will be an old-fashioned kind of lawyer, a lawyer who can't be bought." Donald, the third Nixon boy and Richard's junior by two years, believes his brother "made up his mind to political life then and there, whether he realized it or not.

"Dick was always reserved," Donald says. "He was the studious one of the bunch, always doing more reading while the rest of us were out having more fun." In eighteen years as a student he ran for many offices and lost only one election. It was the first and last time he ever underestimated the opposition. At stake was the student body presidency of Whittier High School. For years the contest for the position had been between the political machines of the junior and senior classes, controlled by their respective faculty

[2] The elder Nixon tried his hand at running a trolley car, working as a carpenter, and operating an orange and then a lemon ranch before settling down with a gasoline station in 1922. Two good sites for the station were available to him. They were two miles apart. After much deliberation he chose the East Whittier site over one at Santa Fe Springs. A year later oil was discovered on the Santa Fe property. The very first well was a 25-barrel-a-day gusher. It has been difficult for the Nixons to forget altogether how close they had been to becoming rich.

advisers. Though he had just transferred from Fullerton High School, the senior class organization nominated Nixon; the junior class group nominated a friend, Roy Newsome. The campaign was progressing according to form when a venturesome boy named Robert Logue defied tradition by entering the race as an independent. On top of that, while Nixon and Newsome stuck by the practice of relying on their respective "machines," Logue made a vigorous personal campaign. He electioneered at recess, shook all the student hands he could reach, and produced banners and literature urging one and all to "Stop, Think and Vote for Bob Logue."

Logue won. "He had something new," says Nixon. "He deserved to win. There were no hard feelings."

In the storied format of poor but honest folks, Nixon's parents gave their five boys each a name, a religion, a political identification, and the basis for a way of life. "Allowances" and "spending money" were unheard of. The honorableness of hard work was emphasized as a matter of necessity. Richard began to earn his way as soon as he was big enough to hire himself out as a part-time farm laborer. He was ten or eleven, and picking beans was his first specialty. ("It was awfully hard work, I can tell you.") Over the years the boy's main work was in the general store his father opened after the lemon grove failed. He pumped gasoline, culled rotten potatoes and apples, delivered groceries, and on entering college he became manager of the vegetable department and bookkeeper. There were many outside jobs to supplement the income. One, as handyman and sweeper in a packing house, caused young Nixon sixteen weeks of misery. The boy tended to motion sickness, even in automobiles, and the whirling, churning and hammering of the packing-house machinery nauseated him.

A season as janitor at a public swimming pool was more pleasant, as were two stints of three weeks each as barker for the wheel of chance at the "Slippery Gulch Rodeo" in Prescott, Arizona. Nixon barked for the legal front of the concession, where the prizes were hams and sides of bacon, which was a "come on" for a back room featuring poker and dice. Pay was based on total concession earnings, front and back. Nixon earned $1 an hour the first year, quite

(15)

a windfall for a 14-year-old. The next was a depression year, and his pay fell to 50 cents.

What with jobs, school and studies, sixteen-hour workdays were commonplace for Nixon before he was sixteen years old. They still are. "I can't do anything about it," he told me. "I still have to learn to pace myself."

A buggy accident in which he was almost killed happened near his home in Yorba Linda. "We had taken my aunt to the train at Placenta," his mother recalls. "I held Donald, the baby, in my lap and drove the buggy. I couldn't handle both boys because Richard, then three, was too lively. So a little neighbor girl came along to hold him."

As the buggy rounded a steep curve along the bank of the irrigation ditch, Richard outsquirmed his young guardian and fell into the road. The heavy wheel grazed his scalp before Mrs. Nixon could stop the horse. Blood spurted from a gash that stretched clear across the top of his head, a little to the left of center. The nearest hospital was twenty-five miles away, too far for a dash by buggy. The Quigley family owned the only automobile in town. It was nearby and available. The doctor told Nixon's mother later that Richard reached the hospital emergency room just in time to save his life. The ugly scar is still there—from above the forehead to the neck— hidden by hair always parted on the right.

Nixon has been susceptible to illnesses of one kind or another since that childhood experience. When he was four he nearly died of pneumonia. During his senior year at high school he had a severe attack of undulant fever. His temperature rose to 104 degrees every day for over a week. He was absent much of that school year, but he managed to graduate with honors, maintain his four-year "A" average in Latin and win the oratorical contests and debates he entered, and also to take the Harvard Club of California Prize awarded annually to the school's outstanding all-around student. The prize was a biography of Dean Briggs. "I thought he was remarkable then and I still do, and I got a great opinion of Harvard from that book," Nixon says.

Nixon's ancestry dates back almost as far as one can in North America. A kinsman of his mother came to Delaware from Wales in 1690. The first Milhous, a Quaker, left County Kildare, in Ireland, for the religious freedom of Chester County, Pennsylvania, in 1729. His father's line on this continent began when James Nixon landed at Brandywine Hundred, Delaware, from Ireland in 1753. The family's roots and branches spread through the nation's history. One forefather crossed the Delaware with General Washington and survived a dozen battles of the Revolution. Another is buried on the Civil War battlefield at Gettysburg. The Nixons and the Milhouses followed the frontier—to western Pennsylvania—to Ohio—to Indiana—and then to California. Generation after generation they were mostly farmers. Also among them were preachers, teachers, and a few merchants. None before Richard became known outside his community, but quite a few achieved local prominence.

On his father's side, Nixon's forebears were tough, strait-laced, Bible-pounding Methodists. His mother's family were devout and gentle Quakers. They tolerated violence only to save bodies and souls—mainly those of runaway slaves. Grant Smith, an aged resident of Columbus, Indiana, says the countryside where he lives is filled with descendants of slaves rescued by one of the most effective underground railroad operations in the nation. It was run, at their peril, by the Milhouses and fellow Quakers in southern Indiana.

Nixon's father and his mother's parents emigrated to southern California for reasons of health. But the family is unusually long-lived. The ancestor who landed in 1690 passed away at age 105. Nixon's Great-grandmother Milhous lived to ninety-six, and his Grandmother Milhous, to ninety-four.

Whittier, California, was first among the places that markedly affected Nixon. He grew up there. Washington, D.C.—the Washington he knew for a few months in 1942 as a minor bureaucrat in an entangled war agency—was second. It set and hardened much of his political philosophy.

Whittier was a tranquil town of orange and avocado groves, unostentatious homes and Quaker purity when the Nixons moved there from nearby Yorba Linda in 1922. The very reason for Frank Nixon's choice of Whittier foretold for it a much less tranquil future, however. The elder Nixon sought to open a gasoline station.

He felt the area's biggest build-up of auto traffic would be along East Whittier Boulevard, so he set his family and his gasoline pumps up on one of its barren corners.

A leader of the Society of Friends had chosen the Whittier townsite because it was the least likely place in southern California to attract mainline railroads and the noise and bustle of industry and commerce that would spring up at a maddening pace in the wake of good transportation facilities. But that was in 1887. The broad meadow abutting the Puente Hills, with a view of the Pacific in the distance, epitomized the tranquillity of Quaker living. Los Angeles was a safe thirteen miles away. How was the founder of the new Quaker mecca in California to know that someday there would be automobiles?

Nixon's mother, Hannah Milhous, came in an early wave of emigrants from Butlerville, Indiana. In the family caravan were her parents, grandmother, eight brothers and sisters, the cows and horses, and a freight car of lumber, doors, windows and miscellaneous building material that her father feared would not be available in the California "wilderness."

Nixon's father happened upon Whittier much later. It was after the turn of the century, in fact, and he was searching for sunshine and warmth to ease a gnawing pain in his feet. The severe frostbite he suffered while running an open-vestibule trolley in Columbus, Ohio, had gone, but the agony remained.

Frank Nixon was motorman of a trolley in frost-free southern California when he met Hannah Milhous in February, 1908. They were married four months later, and Frank became a Quaker. Their first son, Harold, was born in 1909. Then came Richard, in 1913; Donald, in 1914; Arthur, in 1918; and Edward, in 1930. Harold and Arthur have died. Donald now is employed by a California milk company, after having tried unsuccessfully to establish a chain of drive-in restaurants which featured a triple-decker sandwich called the "Nixonburger." Edward is a Navy pilot.

Several men and women influenced Nixon's early development. Lewis Cox, his seventh-grade teacher, impressed on him more forcefully than anyone else, for instance, "the importance of fighting hard all the time and working hard all the time." Fundamentally, however, his family intimates see Richard Nixon as a composite of his father, mother and grandmother.

Nixon recalled in one of our conversations that his grandmother "had a big house on the Boulevard and every year at Christmas and usually once during the summer we had a family reunion. She kept the family together through the years. She was a prolific letter writer. On birthdays she composed rhymes and couplets and sent them to us. She used the 'plain speech' [thee and thou] exclusively. My mother used the plain speech in talking with her and her sisters, but never with the children. So with us, the children, we don't use it at all.

"My grandmother set the standards for the whole family. Honesty, hard work, do your best at all times—humanitarian ideals. She was always taking care of every tramp that came along the road, just like my own mother, too. She had strong feelings about pacifism and very strong feelings on civil liberties. She probably affected me in that respect. At her house no servant ever ate at a separate table. They always ate with the family. There were Negroes, Indians and people from Mexico—she always was taking somebody in."

The jutting jaw, thick eyebrows, tendency to jowls and upswept nose that caricaturists have made Nixon's trademark are actually the Milhous family imprint. The Vice-President's brothers have the same no-nonsense look, and Hannah Nixon is a small, dainty, gray-haired replica of her sons.

To his mother the Vice-President is "Richard," not "Dick." "We named him Richard, and he just seems like Richard to me, just as Donald is Donald, and Edward is Edward," she says. Furthermore, she recalls, Richard's standout qualification among the brothers was as a potato masher. "He never left any lumps," she said. "He used the whipping motion to make them smooth instead of going up and down the way the other boys did."

Hannah Nixon worked endless hours to help lift her family from its early poverty. When the boys were young, her day would begin before dawn, when she would get up to bake pies for sale that day in the store. Always the family would sit down to breakfast together. "That permitted us to say our prayers and Bible verses together each morning," she recalls. When the oldest boy, Harold, contracted tuberculosis, Mrs. Nixon took him to Arizona in the desperate hope that his lungs would heal in a drier climate. For two years she stayed at the nursing home with her ill son, and paid the board by scrubbing, cooking, tending the furnace and doing whatever else needed to be done there. Frank Nixon met the huge medical bill by selling half of the acre of land on which his store stood. It was a period of extreme hardship for the whole family. In Whittier the father, Richard and the other boys took turns preparing the meals—usually canned chili, spaghetti, pork and beans, soup, and at least half the menus consisted of either hamburgers or fried eggs. "Odd as it may seem, I still like all of those things," Nixon admits. "There were many mornings when I ate nothing for breakfast but a candy bar."

Meanwhile Arthur, the fourth son, became seriously ill, and a week or so later died of tubercular meningitis. He was seven. "It is difficult at times to understand the ways of our Lord," Mrs. Nixon confided to a neighbor after the funeral, "but we know that there is a plan and the best happens for each individual."

The long stay in Arizona did not cure Harold of tuberculosis, and he and his mother had to return to Whittier. Harold was given the downstairs bedroom, the one his parents had occupied. One morning he asked Richard to drive him into town so he could buy a birthday present for his mother. He selected an early-model electric mixer, and smiled at the thought of all the elbow bending it would save her when she baked angel food cake. Richard took Harold back to the house, then headed for school, fifteen minutes away. A message awaited him in the classroom. "Come home," it said. "Your brother has died."

"My mother still has the old-fashioned cake mixer," says Nixon.

Much of Richard Nixon's early life centered at the East Whittier Friends Meeting House—the Quaker church—where he and his

(20)

family attended one form of service or another four times on Sunday and several times during the week. Richard played the organ at the meeting house and taught Sunday school. His high school principal says he was "a self-starter . . . a fighting Quaker." Dr. Albert Upton, professor of English and drama at Whittier College, says, "The Dick I knew so well in college was not what I would call a militant Quaker. He was just a typical American Quaker." Merton G. Wray, a schoolmate of Nixon's in high school and college and now a Whittier attorney, says, "I cannot reconcile his massive retaliation policy in politics and as a public official with what I understand of the Quaker philosophy and of their fellowship of reconciliation." Wray, who was often an opponent of Nixon's in speaking contests during their school days, adds, "Since high school Nixon has had an uncommon ability to take advantage of a situation before and after it develops. . . . His success is due to knowing what to do and when to do it, perfect timing in everything."

Nixon's brother Donald recalls that "Dick always planned things out. He didn't do things accidentally. . . . He had more of Mother's traits than the rest of us. He wouldn't argue much with me, for instance, but once, when he had had just about as much of me as he could take, he cut loose and kept at it for a half to three quarters of an hour. He went back a year or two listing things I had done. He didn't leave out a thing. I was only eight, and he was ten, but I've had a lot of respect ever since for the way he can keep things in his mind."

Nixon was seventeen when he entered Whittier College, a small Quaker institution with exacting standards. Within a month he was part of a cabal that formed a new student fraternity, The Orthagonians, or Square Shooters, to compete with The Franklins, a long-established group that had a reputation for being highbrow and favoring the town's wealthier families. Franklins always wore black ties to school functions and when posing for photographers. The Orthagonians, most of whom couldn't afford evening clothes, adopted slouch sweaters and open, tieless collars as their trademark. Nixon composed the club song. He collaborated in writing its first play, a shocker entitled *The Trysting Place,* and was its director

(21)

and male lead. Needless to say, he was elected first president of the Orthagonians, his freshman status notwithstanding. Furthermore, he was elected president of the freshman class almost unanimously, and won a place on the college Joint Council of Control, all during that first, flashy month as a college student.

During his sophomore year Nixon represented Whittier in more than fifty debates, winning the bulk of them, including a match with the national champions. The topic was Free Trade. Nixon was for it. Debating and oratory were Nixon's specialties. But he worked much harder—and with considerably less success—at trying to make the football team. A classmate recalled that "Dick had two left feet. He couldn't co-ordinate. But, boy, was he an inspiration. He was always talking it up. That's why the chief [the coach] let him hang around, I guess. He was one of those inspirational guys." Another schoolmate recalls that he and other members of the team would always scuffle over the right to sit next to Nixon at the meal served the football players before each game. The main course was always steak, and Nixon invariably was "too tensed up" to eat. "I always tried to grab the seat so I could eat my steak and his too," said the teammate.

Dr. Paul S. Smith, then professor of history and politics and now Whittier president, tells of the enthusiasm with which Nixon devoured a ten-volume history of America. Its emphasis was on Lincoln. The professor said he dared to give such an advanced assignment only to two students—Nixon and Leonidas Dodson, now professor of history and archivist at the University of Pennsylvania. At that stage of his college career Nixon also learned French and took to reading the classical French philosophers.

"As a young student Dick had the uncommon capacity to brush aside the façades of a subject and get to the heart of it," says Dr. Smith. "He always completed on half a page what would take a normal 'A' student two pages. He also perfected a skill he was developing, perhaps unconsciously, as an undergraduate. He has a fantastic capacity to communicate with people eye to eye, shoulder to shoulder."

Dr. Albert Upton said he twinged when he saw pictures of

Nixon weeping on the shoulder of Senator Knowland at the Wheeling, West Virginia, airport after General Eisenhower had come to greet him in the wake of his telecast about the Nixon Fund during the 1952 campaign.

"I taught him how to cry," said Dr. Upton, "in a play by John Drinkwater called *Bird in Hand*. He tried conscientiously at rehearsals, and he'd get a pretty good lump in his throat and that was all. But on the evenings of performance tears just ran right out of his eyes. It was beautifully done, those tears."

In his senior year Nixon was elected president of the student body. Since graduating he has been awarded an honorary degree at Whittier and the college is preparing to establish "The Richard M. Nixon Chair of Public Affairs" as a major department. But the students remember him best for two accomplishments: one dealing with dancing and the other with the annual bonfire. It was Richard Nixon who junked the blue-nose regulation that forbade dances at Whittier by convincing the hierarchy—the trustees, preachers, faculty and rich alumni—that students would either dance under honorable auspices on the campus or go to "dens of iniquity in Los Angeles." He secured a place for himself high in the annals of Whittier bonfires when he was a junior. He was chairman that year of the traditional undergraduate escapade—the annual bonfire on a mound of earth called Fire Hill. The custom was for everyone in the student body to pile things for burning on the allotted site, for days, with the chairman tossing on the last item. The chairman provided the crown for the heap, and his status as a leader of men was judged over the years by the style and size of the country privy he could purloin for that purpose.

Normally the bonfire was topped by a one-holer. Occasionally a really superior chairman would drag in a two-holer. In 1933 Richard Nixon established a record that still stands. He produced a four-holer.

William Brock, one of Nixon's Orthagonian fraternity brothers, says that bonfire was the hottest thing that ever happened at Whittier. Brock is an electrical engineer in Pasadena, and a Democrat. He is a Negro, and was a football star. "I remember Dick as being a lot better player than he's given credit for," says Brock. "He was little, but he had more fight and spunk than the big man."

Brock said he sticks by Democratic candidates in elections, except when Nixon runs. "And I get really mad when I hear Democrats or anybody accuse him of bigotry. That sort of thing is fantastic. Dick was my buddy in college many years before he or anybody else figured him to become a politician. He was one of the fellows who got me into the Orthagonians."

Nixon graduated from Whittier in 1934. The New Deal had already generated some cautious hope—but no jobs. Nixon was among the fortunate few who didn't need one. All he wanted was a law school where you could get by without money, and by happy coincidence a school across the continent, in Durham, North Carolina, was looking for bright students on whom to spend its newly acquired abundance. James Buchanan Duke, the tobacco multimillionaire named for the pre-Civil War Democratic President, had left a huge endowment to Trinity College. The austere little Methodist institution took its benefactor's name, becoming Duke University, and then adopted his mode of living.

Nixon applied for one of the law scholarships available to high-honor college men throughout the country. In a letter of recommendation Dr. Walter F. Dexter, then the Whittier College president, wrote: "I believe Nixon will become one of America's important, if not great leaders."

Nixon got a full tuition scholarship and a National Youth Administration job which paid 35 cents an hour. There were forty-four students in his class from thirty-seven states, practically all scholarship students. To develop high standards for the school, Duke offered fewer scholarships to the second- and third-year students than to the first-year students. That also developed strenuous competition. "In those depression years few families found it easy to raise tuition money," says Acting Dean E. R. Latty. "Richard Nixon demonstrated his superior legal ability by maintaining his scholarship for his entire three years." He also became a member of the Order of Coif, the national scholastic fraternity for honor law students.

(24)

A month or so after matriculation he was studying late one night in the library. His mind wandered from the book—to his homesickness, the seven courses he was determined to master that semester, the troubles ahead if he did not achieve a high enough average to keep his scholarship. William Adelson, an upperclassman who happened by, asked him, "What's wrong?"

"I'm scared," said Nixon. "I counted thirty-two Phi Beta Kappa keys in my class. I don't believe I can stay up top in that group."

"Listen, Nixon, you needn't worry," said Adelson, a high honor man himself. "The fact that you are studying so late yourself shows you don't mind hard work. You've got an iron butt, and that's the secret of becoming a lawyer."

None of Nixon's friends in law school expected he would go into politics. Basil Whitener, a tall, backslapping North Carolinian, the number one politico in the class and now a Democratic congressman from the North Carolina hill country, told me: "Nixon was not outward, but seemed shy. He was friendly in a quiet way. He was no smiler then; quite the contrary. Like most others, I figured he would wind up doing a wonderful job in a big law firm, handling securities or other matters that need the attention of a scholar, not a politician."

Nixon's ambition was to join a "great" law firm. During the Christmas holidays of 1936 he and two fellow seniors—Harlan Leathers and William Perdue—went job hunting in New York. They applied at practically all the well-known law offices: Donovan, Leisure, Newton and Lombard; Root, Clark, Buckner and Ballentine, now Dewey and Ballentine, with former Governor Dewey of New York as senior partner; Coudert Brothers, of which the prominent Democrat Thomas K. Finletter is a senior partner; Davis, Polk, Wardwell, Gardiner and Reid, which was headed by the late John W. Davis, Democratic candidate for president in 1924; Millbank, Tweed, Hope and Webb; Lord, Day and Lord, of which Herbert Brownell, Jr., was then a member and is now a senior partner; and others.

Leathers landed a place with Millbank, Tweed. Perdue wound up with a large oil corporation of which he is now vice-president.

(25)

Nixon got only an "iffy" response from the Donovan firm. His highest hope was to find a place with Sullivan and Cromwell, of which John Foster Dulles was senior partner. Nixon recalls that he was attracted more by the "thick, luxurious carpets and the fine oak paneling" of the Sullivan and Cromwell reception room than by the possibility of being a low-echelon associate of Dulles, however.

"If they had given me a job," he told me, "I'm sure I would have been there today, a corporation lawyer instead of Vice-President."

Nixon classified himself as "liberal" in college, "but not a flaming liberal." Like many law students of that period, his public heroes were Justices Brandeis, Cardozo and Hughes, then the Supreme Court's progressive minority.

Through his three years at law school Nixon's morale rose and sank to peaks and valleys that are characteristic of him even today. Friends gave him the nickname "Gloomy Gus" because he would sometimes complain, "I'll never learn the law; there is too much of it," at the very time his grades were highest. Years later, during the 1952 presidential campaign, when he delivered the television speech about the "Nixon Fund" that reversed national sentiment in his favor, Nixon at first adjudged his performance a flop.

The depression had not eased up much by 1937. As graduation drew near, Nixon decided to apply for a job with the FBI. "The FBI looked very good to a young lawyer wanting work that year," he recalls. On May 3, 1937, Dean H. Claude Horack wrote J. Edgar Hoover: "Sometime ago you suggested that I might refer to you any exceptional young man who has an interest in the work of the Federal Bureau of Investigation. I have such a man in mind who is to graduate in June . . . Richard Nixon, one of the finest young men, both in character and ability, that I have ever had the opportunity of having in my classes. He is a superior student, alert, aggressive, a fine speaker and one who can do an exceptionally good piece of research when called upon to do so. His position with his fellows is shown by the fact that he is this year president of the Duke Bar Association. . . ."

In June, when the FBI job had not materialized, Nixon decided to try his luck in his home town. He had to cram five months of detailed California law into two months of study. He did it successfully.

Meanwhile, there was the Duke graduation. His mother and grandmother, then eighty-nine, drove across the continent to be there. Witnesses say the pride those ladies felt showed through their Quaker composure. Only twenty-five of the forty-four students who started with the class graduated. Nixon stood third in the class scholastically.

Four months later he wrote Dean Horack that he had taken the FBI examination. "They have been investigating my character since that time," he added. "But unless my present prospects fall through, I shall not accept the job even if it is offered to me." Long afterwards Vice-President Nixon jokingly asked his friend J. Edgar Hoover why the FBI never came through with the job. The explanation was simply this: the FBI was preparing a form notifying him to report for duty when an unexpected appropriation cut forced the bureau to stop hiring.

3

W<small>HITTIER</small>, known as "Ye Friendly Town," was becoming a Los Angeles suburb and had grown to a population of about 25,000 when Nixon returned in 1937 to practice law. The founding Quakers and their progeny were already far outnumbered, but the quiet tone of the community had not changed. The Chamber of Commerce still boasted, justifiably, that Whittier "tolerates no establishments that may be an invitation to hoodlumism."

Nixon wore a sharply pressed blue serge suit his first day as a member of Wingert and Bewley, Whittier's oldest law firm. Before settling down at his own desk, however, he went after the years of accumulated dust in the firm's library. Mrs. Evelyn Dorn, a secretary who became a devoted friend, said he rearranged all the books —several hundred of them. "He took every one of them out, cleaned up all the shelves, and I think he even used some varnish on them."

When cases started coming to him, Mrs. Dorn says, he would work without letup. During particularly busy periods he would live on pineapple malts and hamburgers. At first Nixon was given all the firm's divorce cases. The intimacies confided to him by some clients would often cause him to blush. He became hardened to hearing these facts of marital life, but he cost Wingert and Bewley more fees than he earned because he saw to it that most of the prospective divorces ended in reconciliation. Later Nixon took to handling much of the legal work that he liked best—he became the firm's chief trial lawyer and he also became its specialist on estates and federal income taxes.

After he had become established he set up a branch office in nearby La Habra, a lawyerless community of 4,000. Nixon's office in La Habra was a desk in a real estate office, but he made a good enough impression to be chosen as the town attorney. Furthermore, his senior partner, Tom Bewley, the town attorney of Whittier, appointed Nixon as his assistant. "Dick's duties were to draft the ordinance and keep the Council happy," Bewley recalls. He also had to act as town prosecutor in police court and a sort of overseer of law enforcement. Whittier was dry then, but permitted wine to be sold with food in restaurants. A certain café became a public nuisance, it was said, because customers often drank too much and staggered out into the street. This was a sight Whittier's citizenry would not tolerate. Nixon posted the small police force in the vicinity of the café with orders to arrest for intoxication tests anyone who seemed to stagger. Within a week practically every customer had been picked up at least once. The café closed, and the owner moved his sinful trade to Los Angeles.

Nixon was not only a thorough police prosecutor, but also as a corporation and tax lawyer he impressed juries because, Bewley says, "he was more legalistic than dramatic in his courtroom manner." His first big civil case concerned an oil-gas lease. It was a complicated affair involving intricate and finely drawn points of law. Associates in the case say Nixon won it simply because he was more zealous than the opposition in researching every conceivable angle of the subject.

When his law practice had been safely established, Nixon branched out into business. The Whittier area had a particularly troublesome oversupply of oranges that year, so he and a group of local plungers decided to try to market them as frozen orange juice. The Citra-Frost Company was formed with Richard Nixon as president and attorney and a total of $10,000 of invested money in the bank. The product showed great promise. Two large shipping lines became interested and agreed to buy tons of it—if more satisfactory means of preserving and packaging it could be found.

"Dick worked his heart out on the thing," says Bewley. The Nixon company was preserving whole orange juice, not the condensed variety now available everywhere. The major problem was finding a container that would hold it and preserve it at the same time. Everything imaginable was tried from cartons and cans to cellophane bags. In trying to save the business until the container and preservative experiments might succeed, Nixon and his associates cut costs by picking and squeezing oranges themselves. The venture folded in a year and a half. A few disappointed investors blamed Nixon for the failure—and still vote accordingly.

Meanwhile Nixon had been elected president of the Whittier Alumni Association. The following year he was made a trustee of the college. He was twenty-six, the youngest member of the board, and already a leader of several civic and church groups in the community. He also conducted a course in practical law at the college, and when he was twenty-nine a movement was started to make him president of the college. There had been dissension on the board. A president had quit and left town. One of the biggest donors withdrew his support until "things are done right." Nixon became his choice at the behest of a young faculty group headed by Dr. Upton. Dr. Upton says Nixon would have become president if the war had not intervened. (He could have had the post after the war, too, but by then he was already committed to run for Congress.)

Nixon never had the time or the money as a young fellow to be a lady's man. A classmate in high school and college said she and the other girls admired him but thought "he was too intelligent to be much fun." He dated the daughter of the local police chief steadily before going east to law school, and at Duke he attended occasional dances as a stag. Shortly after his return to Whittier as a graduate lawyer, he met Pat Ryan.

It happened at tryouts for a Little Theater play. "I was a new teacher in Whittier, and they encouraged teachers to take part in all the local events in town, including the Little Theater which was quite thriving at the time," Mrs. Nixon recalls. "I wasn't too anxious, but this friend of mine decided that she would go down to try out for a part, so I went with her. In the meantime she had told Dick that this 'glamorous' new schoolteacher was going to be

(30)

in the play. Consequently, he just thought, 'Well, I'll go down and take a look.' So he went down too. I'm sure he didn't have time to be in any plays, because he was a struggling young lawyer, and he wouldn't necessarily want to come right back and start being in plays rather than getting down to business. So, I met him there at the Little Theater. He decided to take the part. I did too—not because of him, but because I was sort of pressured into it."

That very night Nixon proposed, and his wife said long afterwards, "I thought he was nuts or something. I guess I just looked at him. I couldn't imagine anyone ever saying anything like that so suddenly. Now that I know Dick much better I can't imagine that he would ever say that, because he is very much the opposite, he's more reserved.

"I admired Dick from the very beginning," Mrs. Nixon added. "I was having a very good time and wasn't anxious to settle down. I had all these visions of doing all sorts of things, including travel. I always wanted to travel."

Thelma Ryan was born in Ely, Nevada, two months after Richard Nixon was born. Her father, who worked in a mine, nicknamed her Pat. "There were accidents in the mines, so we moved out to California, and my father bought this little farm which we called a ranch [at Artesia, eighteen miles from Los Angeles]," Mrs. Nixon told me. "I was just a baby, so I don't remember Nevada. Of course, I've been back since. We all helped out on the ranch, and it was a good kind of life when you look back on it. It was truck garden. All irrigation. There was a lot to do. And I loved to be out of doors, so I worked right along with my brothers in the field, really, which was lots of fun. We picked potatoes; we picked tomatoes; we picked peppers and cauliflower. When I was real tiny I just tagged along. But when I got older I was able to do more. I drove the team of horses and things like that. We didn't have a tractor then. You had to use the horses for a number of things. For instance, when you went down rows of cauliflower you had to have a special cart with high wheels so that you didn't injure the cauliflower heads. I remember we used to take our produce over to ship, like the tomatoes were shipped, and we would ride up on top of the wagon. Things like that were the fun we had.

"The farm was ten and a half acres, but we were able to make a living on it. And, of course, all my friends lived on little ranches, as they are called there, too. Consequently, they did about the same things that we did. We also had the work horses which we rode. We thought that was great sport—to get on them and ride them bareback. All the fun that we had was more or less connected with our little farm there. Then we would raise peanuts. My father would put in just enough for family use. We would have a roast of peanuts in the yard, and all the children would come. My mother baked a lot. She was very good. She baked bread and cinnamon rolls and all sorts of things like that. I helped her too. I was the only girl home at the time. I have another sister, who was older and away. We used to eat up the whole baking. All the children used to play in the yard, 'Run, Sheep, Run' and all the other fun games, and we would get hungry and come in and eat up the whole baking.

"The school was a mile away. We walked a mile each way, to and from school."

Pat Ryan's mother died when she was twelve, and she took charge of the house. Her father died five years later, the year she graduated from high school. She worked in the local bank for a year. Then she drove east with relatives and had a job in a hospital near New York for a year or so before returning to Los Angeles to attend the University of Southern California.

"I took merchandising, and while I was in college I worked holidays and vacations at the Bullock-Wilshire store," she said. Her work schedule also included occasional bit parts in movies. "I was a good student, so I was able to miss classes and do this extra work in the movies," Mrs. Nixon recalled. "I was in quite a number of them, but mostly just in mob scenes. You would have to hunt real hard to find me, but I made quite a bit of money. I was in *Small Town Girl*. In *Becky Sharp* I had a little walk-on part and got $25. I just walked on, but at least I could be seen. I did have a line. I can't remember what it was though, because it was cut before it reached the screen. What I do remember about that movie is that I got $25 for it, rather than the usual $7. I made quite a bit of extra money that way. To earn the regular $7, you would have to stay out there (on the studio lot) for the whole day. I never thought of movies as a career because it seemed so very boring. It was those retakes and retakes, and you would see those stars going over and over and over about three words until you almost went mad. I did the extra bit playing only for the money. But I did all sorts of interesting things to earn a little extra money then, you know, secretarial work and other things because I was earning my way through school."

Pat Ryan graduated from the University of Southern California the year Nixon finished law school. Both were honor students. She wanted to become a buyer for a large store. "I had trained to be one and I loved that field of merchandising very much," she said, "but I was offered this job teaching. The pay was $190 a month, which was fabulous in 1937, and much more than was offered in the other field. So, you see, my coming to Whittier wasn't planned at all. I only went four years to college and the requirement was five years at that time to teach in high school. But I had a special credential because I had a great deal of business experience. Consequently, out of a clear sky I just decided to accept this teaching job because it would be a lot of fun and I received all this money, and I had great visions of those free summers when I could do what I wanted to. I really dreamed about those summer months. But now I've decided that the only reason that I accepted the teaching job was destiny. Through it I met Dick in his own home town."

At the high school she taught commercial subjects, was faculty adviser for the "Pep Committee," coached the cheerleaders, directed school plays, and became generally involved in most of the school and community activities. She also met most of the town's eligible bachelors and had a fine time. After the Little Theater tryouts, Nixon stopped dating anyone else. But not Pat. He hung around dutifully even when she had other dates and would drive her to Los Angeles, if she was to meet someone there, and wait around to take her home.

"I don't think that Dick had done a great deal of dancing, but he swung into it all right," Mrs. Nixon says. "We had a young group,

(33)

mostly my friends from college. He became part of that group when we dated. We liked to do active things like sports of different kinds. We were taking up ice skating. The artificial ice rinks had just opened up and it was the gay thing to do. But it was awful for Dick. He almost broke his head two or three times, but he still kept going.

"Our group used to get together often. Of course, none of us had much money at the time, so we would just meet at someone's house after skating and have food, a spaghetti dinner or something of that type, and then we would sit around and tell stories and laugh. Dick was always the highlight of the party because he has a wonderful sense of humor. He would keep everybody in stitches. Sometimes we would even act out parts. I will never forget one night when we did *Beauty and the Beast*. Dick was the Beast, and one of the other men dressed up like Beauty. This sounds rather silly to be telling it now, but in those days we were all very young, and we had to do home entertainment rather than go out and spend money. We used to put on funny shows. It was all good, clean fun, and we had loads of laughs."

Mrs. Nixon said, "There was no talk of politics or anything of that type" in those days. "I didn't even think in terms of that. He was doing well as a lawyer. He was well liked by everybody. He was always president of some group like the 20-30 Club and this, that and the other thing, so I knew that he would be successful in whatever he undertook."

Pat Ryan finally said "Yes" in the spring of 1940. Nixon brought her engagement ring on May 1 in a lovely May Day basket, and they were married June 21, 1940, at the Mission Inn, in Riverside. It was a fine wedding, Mrs. Nixon says, and after the ceremony "we just took off in our car . . . heading, generally, for Mexico City, but without any particular destination. We didn't have a trip outlined. We just went. We felt really splurgy. That's what we still like to do—to get in the car and ride off just to be going, without any particular destination. It is always a lot of fun . . . but because of television we can't go anywhere now without being recognized. It seems everybody has seen our faces on television. I had the girls at the beach one day and I looked a sight. They wanted ice cream, so we went up to this little corner drugstore. The minute I stepped out of the car, two elderly ladies said: 'Why, there is Pat Nixon.' I thought no one would recognize me, dark glasses, beach skirt and everything, but they did. We are even recognized at night. People blow their horns and wave to us. It gives you a good feeling—it always does with us—to have people be so friendly, so kind, to give us a cheery wave, to put the children up to the windows to look, and so forth . . . but then, too, it means no more private automobile trips."

The Nixons rented an apartment above a garage, and their circle of friends became the other young married folk of Whittier. Frequently they attended performances at the Los Angeles Opera. Often their group would get the same seats in the gallery, one of which was behind a post. They named it the "post seat" and proceeded to take turns using it. Jack and Helene Drown were their closest personal friends then—and still are. Drown practiced law, but now has a large magazine- and newspaper-distributing business in Los Angeles. Mrs. Drown was on the Whittier High School faculty with Mrs. Nixon.

Mrs. Nixon continued to teach after her marriage, and Nixon confided to a few intimates that he aimed sooner or later to get into a big city law practice. He kept looking over the field, quietly, and even during a brief trip to Cuba he spent a bit of his vacation time exploring the possibilities of establishing law or business connections in Havana.

Then the Japanese attacked Pearl Harbor. Nixon was determined to serve in the war effort but, considering his Quaker upbringing and family, it had to be done slowly. In January, 1942, he went to Washington and applied for a job in the tire-rationing section of the Office of Price Administration, the many-tentacled OPA bureaucracy which later was to become the butt of many Nixon attacks on the Democratic administration. Thomas I. Emerson, a member of the Yale University law faculty, was in charge. Emerson told John Harris, then Washington correspondent for the Boston *Globe*, "Dick Nixon came into my office without warning. My secretary had been making appointments for applicants. I don't recall that Nixon had any letter of introduction from anybody. He just walked in and said he had come to Washington to get in the war effort. I found he had a very good record at Duke and a good law practice in Whittier. He gave that up to enter the war effort. He was a nice-looking boy, seemed intelligent, and had an excellent record. He was obviously a person we could use. I gave him the job right then and there."

Nixon's immediate superior recalls he was "very quiet, self-effacing, conservative and competent. . . . He had a desk out in one of the open bays." His starting salary was $61 a week. By August, when he left to join the Navy, he had gotten two raises and was making $90. Nixon's six months as a minor government bureaucrat shattered some of his illusions, reshaped a bit of his political philosophy (and practically assure frequent efficiency drives in the government service if he becomes president).

"I came out of college more liberal than I am today, more liberal in the sense that I thought it was possible for government to do more than I later found it was practical to do," Nixon told me. "I became more conservative first, after my experience with OPA. . . . I also became greatly disillusioned about bureaucracy and about what the government could do because I saw the terrible paper work that people had to go through. I also saw the mediocrity of so many civil servants. And for the first time when I was in OPA I also saw that there were people in government who were not satisfied merely with interpreting the regulations, enforcing the law that Congress passed, but who actually had a passion to GET business and used their government jobs to that end. These were of course some of the remnants of the old, violent New Deal crowd. They set me to thinking a lot at that point." In the OPA, Nixon said, he learned firsthand how "political appointees at the top feathered their nests with all kinds of overlapping and empire building."

As a lawyer Nixon was entitled to a direct commission in the military service, so he joined the Navy as a lieutenant, junior grade.[1]

---

[1] He was promoted to full lieutenant a year later. In October, 1945, he became a lieutenant commander and in June, 1953—six months after he had taken office as vice-president—he was raised to full commander in the Naval Reserve. He is now on the inactive list of the Reserve.

After routine training he was shipped to New Caledonia and detailed to the Naval Air Transport organization, known as SCAT. Lester Wroble, a Navy friend and now vice-president of a paper company in Chicago, says Nixon earned a three-pronged reputation at their first war theater outpost, a place called Green Island. With supplies and materials wheedled out of visiting naval craft he set up what became known as Nixon's Hamburger Stand, where officers and men supplemented their less appetizing service rations without charge; from time to time he got hold of various items not on the government issue list, like bourbon whiskey, priceless to the men, and shared everything with all hands; and Nixon also became known as the only sane and sensible poker player in the South Pacific. Nixon's Quaker upbringing excluded card playing as an unnecessary frivolity, and gambling as a sin. (He never smoked, either, until the war, when he took to puffing an occasional cigar. Now he lights a cigar when it seems to be the thing to do at a banquet or a ceremonial occasion, and about once a month he actually smokes one.) "I played bridge in law school for the first and last time," he said. "I never knew what poker was until I joined the Navy." When he was a member of the House and a senator, he played a few times with fellow congressmen. Since becoming vice-president he has joined only one game, however, because he has not had the time for more. There was plenty of time for poker during his Navy days, particularly on Green Island.

The Green Island games ran to high stakes, as they did at other lonely outposts around the world. Wroble remembers one pot of $1,100. But Nixon steered clear of the wild hands. "Dick never lost, but he was never a big winner," said Wroble. "He always played it cautious and close to the belt. If you stood behind him or were kibitzing, he had no prejudice and was not superstitious about showing you his hole card. He seemed always to end up a game somewhere between $30 and $60 ahead. That didn't look like showy winnings, but when you multiplied it day after day after day, I'd say he did all right."

Wroble and other wartime friends say that what they recollect most clearly about Lieutenant Nixon is that "he was one guy who knew where he was going." "Most of us had big, grandiose schemes," said Wroble. "Dick's plans were concise, concrete and specific." He was a good lawyer before the war and he intended to be a better and more successful one after it.

Since then Nixon sometimes has wished he had renewed his law practice instead of going into politics. He believes his family would have been far better off financially if he had. He worries, for instance, that he may not be able, now, to save adequately for his children's education. "I came to Washington twelve years ago with $10,000 in government bonds, my GI life insurance, a 1946 Ford, furniture, $14,000 worth of life insurance," he said. "Today I have an equity in a $75,000 house; we have a lot invested in furniture [the family is better and more expensively clothed and its living standard is considerably higher], but my net worth today is pretty small"—very much less than it would have been, he thinks, if he had gone back to his law practice after the war or even into some other career.

Nixon's current financial status is this: "I own no stocks or bonds, which was the same situation when I came to Congress [in 1946]. The only real property I have an interest in is the house in which I live on Forest Lane, in Washington. The purchase price was $75,000, and I have a $50,000 mortgage on it with interest at 5 per cent. In addition to that, we have only that amount of money in the bank which is necessary for current expenses. I have my retirement which I contribute to on the same basis as members of the Senate. [He pays $218.75 a month and will be eligible for a pension of about $15,000 a year when he is sixty.] I have increased my life insurance, but I have increased it in what you call term insurance. On this basis you get far more coverage for your money, but get nothing back unless you die. [His family is protected with $39,500 in ordinary life insurance, including the GI policy, which he kept, plus about $50,000 in term insurance with private companies and a $40,000 Senate group insurance policy.] The only other things I have are a 1955 Oldsmobile, our furniture, and what one columnist likes to refer to as 'the fabulous gifts' I have received on my trips around the world. I own no real estate other than my house. I don't own a lot, a piece of land any place. My wife owns nothing. We live actually on the basis that we spend everything that we get in. That is the way it has to be if I am to do my job properly."[2]

While the net-worth breakdown in dollars and cents shows him to be only a little better off, relatively, after a dozen years of an exceptionally successful political career, Nixon says he regards himself—the knowledge and personal potential he has piled up—the really important investment he has made for his family. "The only thing is, the health angle could ruin it," he adds. "If anything happens to you physically, at this age, I would have only a short time to get around it. That's perhaps the major risk I am taking at the present time—the one in health. It's the gamble."

While some Whittier residents were never particularly friendly to Nixon, he had no enemies in his home town before he got into politics. A prominent figure in the local Democratic organization insists now, for instance, that Nixon used "unfair tactics" to beat him in an elementary school oratorical contest thirty years ago. Another schoolmate, who says he was shocked by the "methods" Nixon used in defeating Congressman Jerry Voorhis in 1946, told me: "Real Quakers look at men with a level eye. Dick Nixon doesn't." A close friend of his in high school and college said, "There was never anything ruthless about Dick when we were growing up. If it was a fair fight, anything went . . . but not anything dirty. That's why I could never understand the positions he took in campaigns. I gathered that probably it was a matter of political advice that people gave him . . . because Dick knew that a lot of us who are liberal are not Communists, in fact we are anti-Communists." After he was elected vice-president a citizens group blocked the City Council's plan to name a new street for Nixon, and several Whittier College seniors protested so angrily when he was invited to deliver the 1954 Commencement Address that a separate receiving line

[2] The Vice-President's gross salary is $35,000 a year, plus a nontaxable $10,000 expense allowance. Nixon gets his check the last day of every month. After all the deductions—including $485 for federal income taxes—his monthly take-home pay is $2,202.09.

(39)

was provided after the ceremonies for those who preferred not to shake Nixon's hand.

The election returns every time he has run for office bear out the consensus in Whittier that the town is for Richard Nixon. In his first election, that of 1946, Whittier gave Nixon a majority of 5,727 to 2,678 over incumbent Congressman Voorhis, who was quite popular and highly regarded in the community. Four years later in the primaries to nominate candidates for senator, twice as many Whittier Democrats voted for Nixon as voted for Congresswoman Helen Gahagan Douglas, a bona fide Democrat, and in the general election that fall Nixon carried the town by a majority of 9,187 to 2,198. The vote in Yorba Linda that year was 504 for Nixon and 92 for Mrs. Douglas.

4

BEFORE the war, when the state assemblyman from his district was appointed a judge, Nixon considered running for the vacancy. Someone else was endorsed by the Republican party leaders, however, and his only campaign venture was in the 1940 presidential election when he made some speeches locally for Wendell Willkie. Nixon recalls harboring "no grandiose ambitions" in the political field. "I wanted to enter the law, but I wasn't a youngster who wanted to be President of the United States," he says. "Even in college political battles as such never appealed to me, but I always seemed to get dragged into them to run for some office or another."

Mrs. Nixon remembers distinctly that "there was no talk of political life at all in the beginning" either before or after their marriage. When opportunity was offered Nixon to run for Congress, she adds, "I didn't feel strongly about it either way. . . . I felt that a man had to make up his mind what he wants to do, then after he made it up, the only thing that I could do was to help him. But it would not have been a life that I would have chosen."

Nixon registered as a voter in 1938. He was twenty-five, and had missed four voting years. But his job as assistant city attorney of Whittier was a political plum, so to speak, and therefore he had become, in effect, a politician. But it was the late fall of 1945 before he went into politics in earnest.

Whittier and its environs, then the 12th Congressional District of California, was stanch Republican territory. Yet in 1936 it

(41)

elected a Democrat for Congress, and kept re-electing him. Jerry Voorhis, the Congressman, was mild mannered, conscientious, likable and extremely popular. He was respected by fellow Congressmen and the press corps in Washington. He worked hard at his job, answered his mail promptly, dealt with personal problems of his constituents on an eagerly nonpartisan basis, and when Congress was not in session he seldom passed by opportunities to be guest teacher of Sunday-school classes or to address church and civic groups. Furthermore, the Congressman faithfully remembered births, anniversaries, and other happy occasions in his district. And, of course, that kept his name in the minds of many voters. In short, Jerry Voorhis was a smart politician.

As was customary for candidates in the crazy quilt of California politics, Voorhis always sought both the Democratic and the Republican nomination. He never ran as an out-and-out, partisan Democrat. In fact, the word "Democrat" rarely appeared in his advertisements and other paraphernalia (just as the word "Republican" almost never showed up on the material of his opponents). Several Republican organization leaders were among Congressman Voorhis' loyal supporters. This galled other rock-ribbed Republicans because, well known to the party faithful, Voorhis was no ordinary Democrat. He was raised in well-to-do circumstances, and that made him all the more sensitive to the woes of the poor. After graduating Phi Beta Kappa from Yale, he took a factory job at 39 cents an hour, worked as a freight handler in a railroad yard, where he saw two fellow workers killed for lack of adequate safety equipment, toured Europe, where he witnessed hunger everywhere, and then, after failing to get a job in a southern textile mill, and working awhile on a Ford assembly line, he married and with financial help from his father, opened a school and home for orphaned boys. In the mid-twenties Voorhis was a LaFollette Progressive. Then he became an active Socialist. And in the early depression years he embraced the "End Poverty in California" program of Upton Sinclair and ran for assemblyman on the ticket which Sinclair headed for governor. By 1936 Voorhis had become a bona fide Democrat and ran for Congress as a follower of Franklin D. Roosevelt. Although he grew increasingly conservative in Congress and became an energetic foe of Communism, his record as a whole was bitter medicine for most stalwart Republicans. Worst of all to them was his espousal of co-operatives and a Voorhis plan for altering the monetary system. They called the latter a "funny-money scheme."

When all else failed, the Republican hierarchy in California turned to the 1940 census for salvation. Since the legislature was Republican, the plan was to gerrymander Voorhis and several other Democratic congressmen out of office simply by redefining their districts. Two communities which Voorhis normally carried by a ratio of 5-1 were sliced from his district. Even so, Voorhis was re-elected in 1942 by a 13,000 vote majority and again in 1944, for a fifth term, by the same impressive margin. Other Democrats also survived the gerrymander. Therefore, in 1945, Republican professionals agreed to let complaining amateurs try their hand. These, most of them successful business, industrial and professional figures, traced the trouble to low-grade candidates, known in the trade as "turkeys." It was decided to form a Fact-Finding Committee of leading citizens in each troublesome district. This committee would interview potential candidates, weed out the perennials and the misfits, and support with all available resources "sound-thinking, articulate, and respected" individuals, preferably newcomers. Murray M. Chotiner, a resourceful Beverly Hills lawyer-politician whose enterprises included a public relations firm, was designated by the party organization to help the amateurs. Chotiner had masterminded several exceptionally successful campaigns for Republicans, including Governor Earl Warren, and later was to become Richard Nixon's political manager.

Meanwhile the citizen fact-finders in the 12th District bestirred themselves well ahead of schedule. In the late spring of 1945—a full year and a half before the target election—a group met in Arcadia. Stanley Barnes, an attorney who has since been appointed to the United States Circuit Court of Appeals, as chairman and Frank E. Jorgensen, a vice-president of the Metropolitan Life Insurance Company, were the spark plugs. Later, to assure unity,

(43)

leaders of various regular Republican party organizations were added to the committee in time to hear the first aspirants for nomination. As might be expected, none of the eight applicants were satisfactory. In fact, Jorgensen and his group already knew the man they wanted. He was Walter Dexter, a former president of Whittier College who had become California's superintendent of education. To run for Congress Dexter would have had to resign his state position and, as Jorgensen recalls, "he couldn't afford to risk the financial loss that would result if he was not elected." Dexter therefore suggested one of his former students, Richard M. Nixon, whom he described as one of the most promising young men he had ever known. Jorgensen and two associates, Boyd Gibbons and Rockwood Nelson, drove over to the Nixon grocery store to make inquiries. Frank and Hannah Nixon were more than willing to talk about their oldest living son. They noted that a good friend in town, Herman L. Perry, manager of the local Bank of America branch, also had mentioned that their son would be an ideal candidate.

Perry telephoned Nixon in Baltimore, where he was renegotiating Navy contracts while awaiting release from the service. Nixon flew to California, and on December 4, 1945, he formally accepted the fact-finding committee's endorsement in a letter to Roy O. Day, district Republican chairman. It was evident from his letter that the 32-year-old Nixon was eager to be out of uniform and running for office. "I am going to see Joe Martin and John Phillips and try to get what dope I can on Mr. Voorhis' record," he wrote, in part. "His 'conservative' reputation must be blasted. But my main efforts are being directed toward building up a positive, progressive group of speeches which tell what *we* want to do, not what the Democrats have failed to do." The neophyte politician advised Day to "bring in the liberal fringe Republicans. We need *every* Republican and a few Democrats to win. I'm really hopped up over this deal, and I believe we can win."

In January Nixon was released from active duty, and he came west with a satchelful of ideas and a set of electioneering pictures from which he learned a fundamental political truth. It was that the great majority of veterans had been enlisted men for whom a politician campaigning in the uniform of an officer held little attraction. The photographs were thrown out, and the simple words "Dick Nixon" or just "Nixon" replaced "Lieutenant Commander Richard M. Nixon" on proposed literature. Nixon began his active campaign immediately. Shortly thereafter the Nixons' first daughter, Patricia, was born, and within three weeks Mrs. Nixon left the child with her mother-in-law and joined her husband.

Murray Chotiner was the principal professional member of Nixon's campaign organization. Chotiner was Senator Knowland's southern California campaign manager, in itself a full-time job. Roy Day retained him as publicity director for Nixon, on the side, at a fee of $500.

Voorhis and Nixon took advantage of California's peculiar cross-filing system to become candidates for the nominations of both parties. But, while Nixon worked at it energetically, Voorhis sent word that he was very busy looking after the people's welfare in Washington and therefore could not spare the time to campaign in the spring primaries. As usual, that was fine strategy. Voorhis won the Democratic nomination, got a substantial vote in the Republican primary, and gained the psychological advantage of beating Nixon by 7,000 votes in the over-all count. Normally this would have meant sure victory in the November general election. But Nixon's morale went up when a Los Angeles political reporter pointed out that Voorhis' vote, 53.5 per cent of the total, was quite a drop from 1944, when he polled 60 per cent.

"Keen political observers . . . thought we ran a darn fine race, and this was the best Republican primary showing in years," Nixon wrote Chairman Day. "Frankly, Roy, I really believe that's true, and it is time some of the rest of the people began to realize it. All we need is a win complex and we'll take him in November."

The general election campaign flared up early in September, much like many others being fought throughout the country that year of meat and housing shortages, labor unrest and general post-war disenchantment. The Republicans were the "outs," and their battlecry was "Had enough?" The theme of the 12th District campaign followed the national pattern in most respects—that is, the incumbent Democrat was branded as a tool of Sidney Hillman's

CIO-Political Action Committee, a promoter of controls, and an enemy of free enterprise who would socialize America.

But the Voorhis-Nixon battle developed distinctive nuances of bitterness. The veteran Congressman had never before been confronted by a buzz-saw opponent, and the tenderfoot candidate had never before debated so totally for keeps. Both candidates electioneered on three fronts. Most exciting to them and the voters were five debates. Meanest of the three fronts was a battle of newspaper advertisements and statements. Most strenuous for the candidates were handshaking and coffee-hour tours.

While Voorhis believes, in retrospect, that he would have lost anyway, Nixon believes the turning point for him, as the underdog, was the first debate. "It was tough," Nixon says. "I was the challenger, and he was the experienced incumbent. Once that debate was over, I was on my way to eventual victory." Nixon went into the debates against the wishes of all his advisers except Chotiner. The others feared Voorhis was too experienced and Nixon too green. Chotiner insisted the gamble had to be taken because, at worst, Nixon would lose and, at best, he might strike the spark his campaign needed so badly.

The first debate did just that—thanks to a Political Action Committee endorsement of Voorhis which is still the subject of controversy. There had been a small Nixon advertisement which declared, in part, "A vote for Nixon is a vote against the Communist-dominated PAC with its gigantic slush fund." Voorhis vigorously insisted he had not sought and didn't have the endorsement of the regional Political Action Committee of the CIO. At this Nixon leaped to his feet, drew a paper from his pocket, and read a report in which the Los Angeles chapter of the *national* Political Action Committee recommended that the national group endorse Voorhis. Nixon also read off the names of officers of the national organization's chapter who were also officers of the regional group. Then, dramatically, he thrust the paper at Voorhis.

Shortly afterwards Voorhis issued a long, poignant statement declaring that, while he cherished the support of labor, he didn't have and didn't want the backing of the California CIO because "under present top leadership of the CIO in California, there is at least grave question whether the Communist Party does not exercise inordinate if not decisive influence over state and county organizations."

A few days later he telegraphed the national Political Action Committee demanding that it withdraw its "qualified indorsement" of him.

For the remainder of the campaign Voorhis expended much of his time and energy denying that he was the CIO's errand boy, while Nixon jabbed or punched, as the occasion demanded, with observations about "lip-service Americans" and high officials "who front for un-American elements, wittingly or otherwise, by advocating increasing federal controls over the lives of the people." In mid-October Nixon warned voters against being "fooled" by the "very conservative" tone Voorhis was adopting. "In the last four years, out of forty-six measures sponsored by the CIO and the PAC, my opponent has voted against the CIO and PAC only three times," declared Nixon. "Whether he wants it now or not, my opponent has the PAC endorsement and he has certainly earned it. It's not how a man talks, but how he votes that counts."

The PAC controversy reached its shrill peak three days before the election, when Republican campaign headquarters issued a statement in behalf of a former lieutenant governor accusing Voorhis of "consistently voting the Moscow-PAC-Henry Wallace line in Congress." The statement also mentioned "the insolence of Moscow in telling the American voter to elect PAC candidates, such as Mr. Voorhis," and it pronounced Candidate Nixon to be "a man who will talk American and at the same time vote American in Congress . . . and fight in and out of Congress to perpetuate American ideals and American freedom."

There were, of course, other issues in the campaign, and in the context of those times it is not unlikely that some were more decisive with voters than exchanges about the PAC. There was, for example, the veteran issue. Nixon pointed to his own wartime service (and indirectly to Voorhis' civilian status) in an often-repeated promise "to preserve our sacred heritage, in the name of

(47)

my buddies and your loved ones, who died that these might endure."
For his part, Voorhis referred to his opponent at times as "the
Lieutenant Commander" and the "subtlety" escaped no one.

As an "in," Voorhis was compelled to harp on only one positive
theme. It was that he had achieved seniority and experience and
to turn him out for a newcomer "wouldn't be good sense and would
be damaging to popular government in these critical days."

On the other hand, as an "out," with no record to defend, Nixon
was free to attack and promise at the same time. Thus he became
"thoroughly committed to a program of federal tax reduction" and
promised that a Republican Congress would solve the meat, housing
and controls problem.

(It was during this first campaign that Nixon developed the
knack of repeating verbatim questions asked of him from the floor.
It requires the vocal apparatus to operate on one track while the
thinking apparatus operates on another. Nixon does it to give himself time to think of the answer.)

Voorhis had 296 inches of campaign advertising and Nixon 162
inches, in the *Post-Advocate*, the daily newspaper of Alhambra,
largest city in the district. It is noteworthy that not one line in a
Nixon manifest mentioned the fact that he was a Republican, and
none of Voorhis' alluded to his membership in the Democratic
party.

Nixon won by a vote of 65,586 to 49,994, and was one of seven
Republicans to unseat incumbent Democrats in California. All
told, the Republicans picked up fifty-five House seats and won
control of the Eightieth Congress. In reflecting on the campaign
twelve years later Nixon said the race was, in effect, a contest between a well-known New Dealer and a conservative Republican.
"Voorhis lost because that district was not a New Deal district," he
said. "Our campaign was a very honest debate on the issues."[1]

---

[1] Six years after the election, when Nixon was running for vice-president, a
story in the *New Republic* stated that there had been anonymous telephone calls
accusing Voorhis of Communism. Nixon insists he had never before heard of
such calls. Voorhis says several people told him they had received the calls, but
he didn't know their source. It is possible that some or all of the calls were
designed to hurt Nixon as well as Voorhis by making him appear guilty of
vicious tactics.

(48)

At the same time Voorhis offered this opinion: "I'm frank to say that I felt a little bit this way: I had been the Congressman ten years. I'd done the best I could. And I really felt if the voters wanted to throw me out, by golly, okay. I'm afraid this was on my mind the whole time, to some extent. I hated a fight like that, especially because of its effect on my family."

On the whole, Nixon's record in Congress was a moderate one. During his first two-year term 91 per cent of his votes conformed with Republican party policy, according to a survey by the non-partisan *Congressional Quarterly*. In his second term it was 74 per cent. After the campaign, becoming a freshman congressman was tame stuff, and Nixon admitted to "the same lost feeling that I had when I first went into the military service." Nixon requested assignment to the Labor Committee and, although he did not ask for it, he was also placed on the Un-American Activities Committee. One of his first specific jobs concerned civil rights. At the request of Adam Clayton Powell, Democratic Congressman from Harlem, he was made a member of a five-man subcommittee which had one mission: it was to answer immediately anything said by Congressman John Rankin, the vehement racist from Mississippi. His work on the Herter Committee, whose reports led to the Marshall Plan, has been particularly significant for Nixon. As the only freshman representative on it, he visited Europe and learned something of America's international responsibilities. He was a leading proponent of the Herter program in Congress and, surprisingly, in his own isolationist district—which nominated him later in both Democratic and Republican primaries. Nixon considers his service to the Herter Committee the most important of his Congressional career.

At the outset Nixon's favorite work was as a member of a small subcommittee that drafted the Taft-Hartley Labor Law. That was where he became quite friendly with a freshman Democrat from Massachusetts named John F. Kennedy. Nixon and Kennedy were on opposite sides of the Taft-Hartley question, and in the spring of 1947 they went to McKeesport, Pennsylvania, to debate the issue. (Nixon still considers Kennedy "a good personal friend" and says, "I have a very high regard for him as an able senator and campaigner; he's very attractive and formidable." Kennedy does not now reciprocate those feelings. In fact, his attitude toward Nixon is that he would like very much to run against him for president.)

Meanwhile Nixon's interest in the Un-American Activities Committee was not very great. But it warmed up on August 3, 1948, when Whittaker Chambers, a former Communist, listed among his one-time fellow conspirators a man named Alger Hiss.

5

ALGER HISS was first mentioned to Nixon in February, 1947, a few weeks after his arrival in Washington as a congressman. A colleague had introduced him to the Rev. John F. Cronin,[1] a newcomer to Washington from Baltimore, where he was professor of philosophy and economics at St. Mary's Seminary. Father Cronin had been helping to organize labor unions, and he became so alarmed at the extent of Communist infiltration in war plants that he took time off from his teaching to make an intensive study of Communist party activities. That led him to Washington, where he ran across all the names and episodes that subsequently became familiar to the public through Congressional hearings— Alger Hiss, Elizabeth Bentley, and the whole litany. The information was not at all difficult to come by, and Father Cronin was startled by the apparent indifference of responsible officials. It was on his mind when he met Congressman Nixon, and he talked about it.

Nixon was interested. But he had other interests—too many, in fact, for a fledgling legislator. It was a year and a half before the incidents Father Cronin had discussed were aired by the House Un-American Activities Committee. On July 31, 1948, Elizabeth Bentley, who said she had been a courier for a Communist spy ring, was the first to testify. Afterwards a man she named as part of the apparatus contradicted much of what she said. That led to the calling of Whittaker Chambers, a confessed former Communist who

[1] One of several nonpolitical friends with whom Nixon has occasional long discussions.

(51)

had become a senior editor of *Time* magazine. Although Chambers had shown no inclination to co-operate with the committee, its members felt he might corroborate some of the Bentley testimony. Chambers had been interrogated by the FBI five years before. But the information he provided was in the files of the Justice Department. Since Justice was an agency of the Executive Department, its files ostensibly were not available to the Congressional committee.

In 1939, after breaking with the Communist party, Chambers had gone to Assistant Secretary of State A. A. Berle, Jr., with his story of government employees with whom he had operated as a Communist party member from 1934 to 1937. This information was known indirectly to the House committee. But in January, 1948, two of its investigators got practically nowhere in an effort to convince Chambers that he should repeat it to them.

Nevertheless, Chambers was summoned before the committee on August 3. The story of his testimony and of the people he named as associates in his Communist party activities is well known. But additional material has become available from a memorandum Nixon prepared when a friend urged that he set down privately any otherwise unrecorded facts about the case, and also his impressions, while they were still fresh in mind. Nixon saw Chambers for the first time in the committee counsel's office before the session. "He impressed me as being extremely shy and reticent, and also as if what he was doing was being done because he thought he should, rather than because he wanted to." The committee heard Chambers in executive session. "He was not a crackpot and was, in fact, a very responsible person, at least as far as his background was concerned," Nixon wrote in his memorandum. The session then was made public—and, though Chambers spoke softly and had to be prodded repeatedly to raise his voice, he produced his list of names clearly enough for them to be speeded into headlines and over airwaves.

For Nixon, who was to make of the Hiss investigation a phenomenal political success, the high spot of Chambers' testimony came toward the end of his prepared statement. When Chambers said he knew the consequences of what he was doing but felt that duty to his country compelled him to do it, Nixon recalled, "His voice broke and there was a pause of at least fifteen to twenty seconds during which he attempted to gain control of his emotions before he could proceed.

"This one incident was to have a considerable bearing upon my own attitude toward him because I did not feel that it was an act. . . . On the contrary, I felt he indicated deep sincerity and honesty."

Alger Hiss, the most important name uttered by Chambers, asked the committee immediately for an opportunity to deny the charge, and it agreed to hear him August 5. Chambers hadn't impressed all the committee members as favorably as he had Nixon, and there was considerable anxiety.

The year 1948 brought a presidential election. Truman, Dewey, and their forces were warming up for September. The Communist issue hadn't yet been tried nationally as a campaign weapon and, since the Soviet Union had so recently been America's ally, there was serious doubt as to whether Republicans would gain or lose by accusing Democrats of "softness" on Communism. In control of the Eightieth Congress, Republicans were running the committee now pointing a finger at Alger Hiss and others. And, although Hiss was not well known to subway straphangers, coal miners, or cotton pickers, he was highly respected in the government, and also in legal and diplomatic circles. Only the year before he had been appointed president of the Carnegie Foundation for International Peace at a salary of $20,000, which was $5,000 more than what was then paid Cabinet members and congressmen. The Carnegie board which hired him was composed of eminent men. Its chairman was John Foster Dulles, the Republican party's foremost expert on foreign affairs. Hiss had been principal adviser to the American delegation at the first United Nations General Assembly Session. Before that he had distinguished himself as secretary general of the conference in San Francisco which created the United Nations. Furthermore, he had accompanied the Roosevelt party to Yalta and had been executive secretary of the Dumbarton Oaks Conference in 1944. Hiss had graduated from Johns Hopkins University and

(53)

the Harvard Law School. After a year as clerk to Supreme Court Justice Oliver Wendell Holmes he practiced law briefly in Boston and New York; then, in 1933, he began his government career in Washington.

From the moment he walked into the Congressional hearing room on August 5, 1948, and raised his hand to be sworn, it was obvious to everyone that Alger Hiss was quite different from run-of-the-mill types that usually paraded before those microphones. Before the day was done, Nixon realized that this was his "first real testing." "Very few men get in the merciless spotlight of national publicity in a case that may make or break a party, or for that matter even a country," Nixon said twelve years later. "The Hiss case was a very rugged experience in some ways. Considering the amount of time I spent on it, it's as difficult an experience as I've ever had. From the standpoint of responsibility . . . the resourceful enemies I was up against . . . the battle day in and day out . . . the terrible attacks from the press, nasty cartoons, editorials, mail . . . and there was always a great doubt whether you are going to win and whether you are on the right side or not. I was convinced that I was."

When Hiss concluded his testimony, the general feeling in Washington was that the long-controversial Un-American Activities Committee had made its final blunder, and was finished. Hiss had impressed practically everyone with the implication that the committee had been duped into permitting Chambers to use it as a forum from which to slander people. Congressman Rankin, the crusty old Mississippi Democrat, was so moved that he left his seat to shake Hiss's hand. That morning President Truman declared at a White House press conference that Republicans had cooked up spy hearings "as a red herring to keep from doing what they ought to do" about inflation and the nation's other serious problems.

When the committee went into executive (secret) session that evening, "virtual consternation reigned among the members," Nixon noted. All, except Nixon, felt Hiss was telling the truth. F. Edward Hebert, a Democrat from Louisiana, suggested the Committee wash its hands of the case at once and send the files to the Attorney

General to determine whether Hiss or Chambers should be charged with perjury. Karl E. Mundt, a South Dakota Republican and acting chairman, suggested nervously that the committee develop a collateral issue at once to take itself off the spot. Nixon recorded that he and Robert Stripling, the committee counsel, insisted that "although we could not determine who was lying on the issue of whether or not Hiss was a Communist, we should at least go into the matter of whether or not Chambers knew Hiss." Nixon was of the opinion that "Hiss was a particularly convincing witness that day . . . the committee had no real facts to use as a basis for cross-examining him and consequently he was able to dominate the situation throughout." Nixon suggested that a subcommittee examine Chambers again, in executive session. Stripling said that could be done very easily in New York because a witness in the Elizabeth Bentley case lived there and the committee could go there purportedly to see into that matter.

Mundt fancied that solution, and wasted no time telling reporters outside the committee room that things were brewing in New York. A witness had been found there who might break the Bentley case wide open, he stated. Mundt refused even to hint as to the identity of the person to be questioned. The next day's headlines inevitably described him as "a mystery witness."[2]

In his memorandum Nixon noted: "The real mystery witness turned out, of course, to be Chambers, who on August 7 gave the information which eventually was to be responsible for breaking the Hiss case." In reply to questions Chambers had provided a mass of details about Hiss, the Hiss family, their hobbies and habits, and additional material that Nixon and other committee members were almost certain could be known only by someone who was as friendly with Hiss as Chambers said he had been. Representative Hebert still had doubts. And so did Representative John McDowell, a Pennsylvania Republican.

Nixon recorded several reasons for his skepticism about Hiss from the outset:

[2] The witness was, indeed, interrogated, but he pleaded the Fifth Amendment to all questions and thus shed no light on the Bentley case.

Hiss was much too smooth . . . much too careful a witness for one who purported to be telling the whole truth without qualifications. . . . I felt he had put on a show when he was shown a picture of Chambers . . . his statement "This might look like you, Mr. Chairman," seemed to me to be overacted . . . when I asked him who had recommended him for his government position, he attempted to keep the name of Frankfurter out of the testimony and this indicated to me he might be following a general practice of testifying apparently forthrightly and openly on all matters, but actually giving the committee what information he wanted to and refusing to give information which he did not want the committee to have. He was rather insolent toward me from the time that I insisted on bringing Frankfurter's name in, and from that time my suspicion concerning him continued to grow.

Furthermore, Nixon wondered about rumors which spread immediately "to the effect that Chambers had spent some time in a mental institution, was insane, was an habitual drunkard and a homosexual . . . it seemed to me that this was a typical Commie tactic and though, of course, Hiss might not have been responsible for it, I was convinced that at least we should look into the matter further. . . ."

Between the secret interrogation of Chambers and August 16, when Hiss was recalled, also in secret, Nixon and the committee staff tried to double-check all the new material Chambers had provided. Nixon wanted "to convince myself and other members of the committee that Chambers had at least made a *prima facie* case which required that we bring Hiss back to rebut it." The fact that two members were still skeptical was "probably quite a good thing because it kept the rest of us from going off half-cocked."

On August 10 Nixon visited Chambers at his farm at Westminster, Maryland. He said it was "mainly for the purpose of attempting to convince myself on the issue of whether or not Chambers, in speaking of Hiss, was speaking of a man he knew, or was telling a story which he had concocted." Two hours of conversation just about convinced him. The clincher came when Chambers walked to the porch with Nixon as the Congressman was leaving. "I was still trying to press him for any personal recollection which might help us in breaking the case," Nixon's memorandum reads on. "The conversation came around to religion and he said that Mrs. Hiss was a Quaker and that he also was a Quaker at the present time. I told him that I was a Quaker, and then suddenly Chambers snapped his fingers and said, 'Here's something I should have recalled before. Mrs. Hiss used to use the plain language in talking with Alger.' As a Quaker I knew that Chambers couldn't know such intimate matters unless he had known Hiss, although, of course, there was a possibility that some friend of Hiss' might have told him of this. He pointed out that Alger was a genuinely kind, intelligent individual. That was the reason that Chambers was attracted to him—probably because they were both in the movement for the very highest motives."

It was then that Nixon went to several outsiders for confirmation of his own judgment. One of the first was William P. Rogers, counsel for the Senate Investigating Committee, who had considerable experience in assessing the veracity of witnesses. Nixon told Rogers that if he found Chambers was not telling the truth he would admit the mistake and apologize to Hiss. On the other hand, if Chambers was right, his story had to be proved. Rogers agreed and, after reviewing the transcripts, said he felt the Chambers testimony was provable.

Bert Andrews, chief of the New York *Herald Tribune* bureau in Washington, was another to whom Nixon turned. In 1947 Andrews won a Pulitzer Prize for a story that exposed damage done to a government employee because of unfair security procedure. Like most newspapermen and public officials in contact with Hiss, Andrews regarded him highly as a public servant. When Dulles sought his opinion of Hiss before appointing him to the Carnegie Endowment presidency, Andrews gave a fine recommendation, as other prominent Washington correspondents had done. Andrews was amazed by Chambers' testimony. When he checked the hearing transcripts at Nixon's request he became as convinced as Nixon was that Chambers told the truth. He had the impression, however, that Chambers still had not told all he knew. Thereafter Andrews became an informal adviser to Nixon. Many months later, following Hiss's conviction for perjury, Nixon wrote the editor of the New York *Herald Tribune*: "As in all such cases, there were a number of people who deserve credit for the parts they played, but I know from first hand experience that Bert Andrews' name should be among the first when the credits are given for those who participated."

Christian Herter's advice was also sought and that of Foster Dulles, a foreign policy adviser to candidate Dewey. Charles J. Kersten, a Republican congressman from Wisconsin and a friend of Nixon's, recalls how Nixon received word that the Carnegie Foundation and several important men associated with it were preparing to come vigorously to Hiss's defense. "We talked in the caucus room of the old House Office Building at the end of a day's hearings of the House Labor Committee," Kersten said. "Dick decided to see Dulles immediately, and he asked me to go with him."

They visited Dulles at the Roosevelt Hotel in New York where Dulles had a suite in the Dewey campaign headquarters. With Dulles as foreign policy aides to Dewey were his brother, Allen Dulles, now director of the Central Intelligence Agency, Herter, and C. Douglas Dillon, a New York banker, later ambassador to France and undersecretary of state. Nixon brought along the transcript of testimony. The Dulles brothers read it very carefully, then discussed the matter with Nixon, well into the night.

"Hiss had a reputation at the time that was very high indeed," Secretary of State Dulles pointed out in an interview many years later. "Dick had gotten a lot of evidence, but it was clear he did not want to proceed with Hiss until people like myself had agreed that he really had got a case to justify his going ahead. Dick wanted to proceed cautiously, and he did not want to jeopardize a person's right."

As he reviewed the evidence Dulles walked back and forth in front of a fireplace in the large hotel room. He and Allen examined and re-examined sections of the transcript. "We went through the evidence to the end, and I told Dick that I thought it was a case that ought to be followed up," Secretary Dulles recalled. "I was greatly impressed. Many people in that position, who appeared to have something sensational, would go ahead. But Dick wanted to be careful about hurting reputations and sought the opinions of people who knew Hiss as to the weight of the evidence. It was the first time Dick and I had any intimate association. I formed a very high judgment of the sense of responsibility under which he operated."

When Hiss appeared before the committee again on August 16 and was questioned closely about the personal data Chambers had provided, Nixon saw practically every answer as a confirmation of Chambers—and his last doubts were cleared away. In a discussion that night with Bert Andrews, according to a note in his memorandum, he agreed "that it was best to have the confrontation [between Hiss and Chambers] at the earliest possible date before Hiss could build up his story."

Later, in his book *In the Court of Public Opinion,* Hiss asserted that he had requested and had been promised a face-to-face meeting with Chambers much earlier, and then, on August 16, had been told it would take place August 25. The committee staged the confrontation hurriedly on August 17, Hiss reasoned, to divert public attention from the fact that Harry Dexter White, a former assistant secretary of the treasury, who also had been named by Chambers, had died suddenly after being interrogated by the committee.

Nixon, in his memorandum, and Hiss, in his book, differ widely in their interpretations of the dramatic confrontation at the Commodore Hotel, New York, on August 17. According to Nixon, the scene was this:

The committee members and staff went up to Suite 1400, which consisted of a living room and a bedroom—I would imagine they rented for about $15 a day. The living room was decorated with Audubon prints. We had one of the investigators take Chambers to another room and keep him in readiness for the hearing. We then proceeded to set up the room.

When Hiss arrived, he obviously was very upset. He said that he had a dinner engagement and asked permission to make a call so that he could let them know how late he would be. We told him that the hearing would probably not take too long. On the previous day Hiss had been much less smooth than on August 5. Some of us seemed to sense that when Hiss brought up the name of George Crosley [a free-lance writer Hiss said he had known who looked like the photograph of Chambers] he was extremely glib. Now, when Hiss was seated, we told the investigator to go get Chambers. Chambers entered at Hiss's rear and walked behind him over to the davenport, where he sat down. Hiss did not once turn around to get a good look at the man he claims he did not know. Instead he looked at all times stonily straight ahead at the members of the committee.

From the record it appears that I had no reason to criticize Hiss for suggesting that Chambers be sworn. The record fails to show just how the incident occurred. Hiss actually interrupted me as I made the suggestion and of course his manner and tone were insulting in the extreme. By this time he was visibly shaken and had lost the air of smoothness which had characterized most of his appearances before. In fact, this hearing, I think for the first and probably the last time, showed the committee the real Hiss because, except for a few minutes at the beginning and for possibly a few minutes right at the end as he was leaving, he acted the part of a liar who had been caught, rather than the part of the outraged innocent man, which he had so successfully portrayed before then.

When Hiss and Chambers stood up to confront each other, they were not more than four or five feet apart. Incidentally, we put the windows down so as to keep the street noises out, but at the last minute we raised the blind so that there would be ample light when the two men saw each other. When Hiss asked Chambers to open his mouth so he could see his teeth, he took two or three steps toward him and I would say was about a foot from his face as he peered into his throat. When he asked to have Chambers open his mouth wider, he actually reached up with his hand and made a gesture of opening the fingers to indicate what he wanted Chambers to do. I would say that his hand was not more than six inches from Chambers' teeth. In fact, I wondered why Chambers didn't reach out and bite his finger.

When Hiss finally admitted that he knew Chambers, he did so in a very loud, dramatic voice as if he were acting in a Shakespeare play. In fact, he rose from his chair and pointed his finger. When he walked over toward Chambers at the time that he dared Chambers to speak where he could be sued, he actually shook his fist and gave the appear-

(60)

ance of one who was about to attack. But I was convinced it was purely a bluff. A staff member walked up behind him and actually touched only his clothes and asked him to sit down. Hiss wheeled on him as if he had stuck him with a hot needle in a sensitive spot, and shouted to take his hands off.

Chambers as contrasted to Hiss was very quiet throughout the hearing. He showed no fear when Hiss walked toward him. He was rather nervous, I would say, when he was reading [so Hiss might check his voice] but settled down as the hearing progressed, and after a time, I would say, he seemed secretly to be enjoying the situation. He was completely in command of himself throughout the proceedings.

At the conclusion of the hearing Hiss was completely unnerved, and my only regret is that we more or less agreed to let him go at an early hour so that he could make his appointment, because I feel that if we had continued to press him we might have gotten even more contradictions out of him, if not an actual break.

Nixon noted at this point that Hiss always insisted on having both the executive and the public session testimony before he would be interrogated at another hearing. On the other hand, Chambers did not want to see the transcripts and refused to have an attorney. Hiss, a lawyer himself, always insisted that an attorney sit by him.

In his book Hiss stated that the committee on August 16 had given him "a clear commitment in time and place for me to see Chambers face to face." This, he added, gave him an unwarranted sense of having accomplished something. "The committee's delay in bringing Chambers and me together and their substituted procedure of separate secret hearings proved far more damaging to me than I then realized," he wrote. "I had been concerned because the impression was being created that I had categorically denied ever having met the man Chambers by any name or under any circumstances. . . . By taking Chambers' testimony of August 7 in secret, where it could not be promptly corrected by me, and by characterizing all of his testimony as accurate, the committee created an impression that Chambers and I had had a close association, and that what one supposedly intimate friend did the other might be expected to do also. This might be called a theory of 'guilt by close association.' "

(61)

Hiss then traced the hurriedly called session of August 17 to Harry Dexter White. He noted that White was frequently applauded by the audience in the hearing room when he appeared before the committee a week before and denied the charges both Chambers and Elizabeth Bentley had made against him. White had sent a note to the Chair which said, "I am recovering from a severe heart attack. I would appreciate it if the Chairman would give me five or ten minutes rest after each hour."

At this the chairman snapped, "For a person who had a severe heart attack you certainly can play a lot of sports."

"Flying back from Washington after my testimony of the afternoon before," wrote Hiss, "I had had time to read the fully reported accounts of White's appearance and had been impressed by his courage in voluntarily facing, despite his illness, the ordeal of a public grilling in the circus-arena atmosphere of klieg lights and flashbulbs. I had found unpalatable the committee's badgering of a sick man and its implication that he was malingering in privately asking for an occasional intermission." The next morning, Hiss continued, a staff member called to say Congressman McDowell was to be in New York that afternoon and hoped to see Hiss for ten or fifteen minutes. During the day, Hiss recalls, he read in newspapers that White had died "having over the weekend suffered a further heart attack, presumably brought on by his exertions before the committee."

At nearly 5:30, Hiss related, McDowell called.

Instead of saying that he would be along soon, he rather surprised me by inviting me to come to the Commodore Hotel and then added that Nixon "and one other" were with him. At this point I felt quite sure that something more than a casual conversation was planned and that the manner in which the arrangements had been made had been deliberately less than frank. A colleague, Charles Dollard of the Carnegie Corporation, was still in his office, and I took the precaution of asking him if he would walk over to the Commodore with me to see what lay behind this slightly mysterious maneuvering. I was by now highly suspicious of the good faith of various members of the committee. Biased accounts in the morning papers of my testimony of the

(62)

day before were a plain and prompt repudiation of the protestations of secrecy by some members of the committee. I wanted at least one friend present who would be able to give his version of any further relations I might have with the committee.

We went to McDowell's hotel room and, as we entered, found that it was still in the process of being hastily converted into an improvised hearing room. McDowell and Nixon were there; Thomas arrived a good deal later. . . . Suddenly the connection between White's death and the hastily summoned hearings struck me. The impact of the press account of White's fatal heart attack was hardly favorable to the committee. . . . My experience with the committee up to this point led me to conclude that they had decided to meet the crisis of a bad press by a sudden and sensational move. . . .

When Chambers was ushered in, Hiss saw him as "short, plump, perspiring and very pale." Hiss added that "his appearance was certainly familiar, and I thought I saw Crosley in the added pounds and rumpled suit. But there was no expression, no spark of individuality as yet. I wanted to hear his voice and to see if he had Crosley's bad teeth before expressing my feeling that this was George Crosley. . . . Chambers did not meet my eye, but stared fixedly before him or up to the ceiling. He had given his name in a tight, rather high pitched, constrained voice, barely opening his mouth. This seemed evidently not the man's normal voice, nor could I see whether his front teeth were decayed. In response to my request that in speaking he open his mouth wider, he was able only to repeat his name, again in a strangled voice, through almost closed lips."

Finally, the session ended with a sharp exchange between Hiss and the chairman.

"I had followed the traditional forms long enough out of respect for the Office of Congressman and out of habit," Hiss wrote subsequently, in his book. "I had tried to get the Committee to follow the orderly procedure with which I was familiar. Now at the end of this hearing I wanted to make it quite plain that I resented the committee's callous and ruthless procedures. It helped, I felt, to clear the air in this fashion. As I told Mr. Dulles that evening in a telephone conversation, it was evident that the committee and I were now at war."[3]

The public hearing at which Hiss and Chambers were brought face to face was held on August 25. It produced the expected headlines and heightened the controversy over who was lying. But Nixon and the committee were aware that, for all their effort, there was still one big hole in the case. It was summed up in the word "Why?"

"The weak point in Chambers' story was that Chambers was unable to give a satisfactory explanation for what he talked about with Hiss and the other [Communist party] members of their group when he came down to see them each week [in the mid-thirties]," Nixon noted in his memorandum. "Chambers used to say that they discussed party policies, how to get new members for the ring, and so forth. Of course, the explanation was that his group was engaged in espionage, and although both Stripling and I discussed this possibility, we were not able to get any information from Chambers along that line."

Later Nixon added: "It now seems probable that the explanation for Chambers' letting out his story in bits was that he did not want to go into the espionage phase unless absolutely necessary, and he knew that the more of the story he told the more likely it was that a connection with the espionage activity would be established." The scene for that fatal phase was set on August 17 when Hiss dared Chambers to repeat his charge where he would not have Congressional immunity from a libel suit. On August 27 Chambers did just that on a radio program, "Meet the Press."

A month later Hiss sued. And it was that civil suit which led to Chambers' production of handwritten, typewritten and microfilmed copies of classified government documents which, he said, Hiss

[3] As a government witness at the Hiss perjury trial two years later Dulles testified that on August 18, a day after the confrontation, he suggested that Hiss resign as president of the Carnegie endowment organization to save the foundation from further embarrassment. Dulles stated also that he had told Hiss he would not be fired, however. When Hiss was indicted in December, 1948, he offered to resign, but the board granted him a leave of absence with full pay instead of accepting the resignation.

passed to him to be relayed to the Soviet Union.

There were still anxieties for Nixon and his colleagues before the case was closed. Once early in December the so-called "Pumpkin Papers"—microfilm Chambers had produced from a hollowed-out pumpkin—were thought to be fraudulent, because the first test indicated the film was new, and not eleven years old as it would have been if Chambers' story was authentic. Another, more careful test verified the authenticity of the film.

Nixon concluded his memorandum with a notation about the reason Chambers gave for finally turning over the documents:

He said that he had become convinced that unless he did he would never be able to convince anyone of the seriousness of his charges and of their truth. He said that Hiss' lawyers [in the libel suit] had questioned Mrs. Chambers rather ruthlessly and that also he had resented the implications which Hiss' people had been making that he was a homosexual and had been crazy and the like, but he said that when he made the decision in a period of Quaker meditation he tried to put these personal animosities out of his mind, and he felt that he had reached the decision and made it primarily because of the public interest which was involved.

Although Chambers was always very relaxed and confident in giving his testimony, I seemed to sense that after he finally decided to go into the espionage phase of the case, he talked as if a great load had been lifted from his mind, and he seemed very free and almost elated by what he had done.

On December 15, 1948, a federal grand jury in New York indicted Hiss for perjury in denying that he ever turned over government documents to Chambers. The first trial took five weeks, and ended inconclusively on July 8, with the jury deadlocked 8 to 4 for conviction. Nixon and three other members of the House Un-American Activities Committee accused Judge Samuel H. Kaufman of bias for Hiss and demanded that his fitness be investigated. The judge's "prejudice for the defense and against the prosecution was so obvious and apparent that the jury's 8 to 4 vote for conviction frankly came as a surprise to me," Nixon declared. He accused the judge of refusing, for political reasons, to permit two witnesses to

(65)

testify. "I think the entire Truman administration was extremely anxious that nothing bad happen to Mr. Hiss," he said. "Members of the administration feared that an adverse verdict would prove that there was a great deal of foundation to all the reports of Communist infiltration into the government during the New Deal days."

Congressman Emanuel Celler, a New York Democrat and chairman of the House Judiciary Committee, vigorously defended Judge Kaufman's conduct, but admitted that if impeachment proceedings were brought in the House he would disqualify himself since Judge Kaufman had been his law partner. No positive action followed against the judge.

On November 17, 1949, the second Hiss trial began before Judge Henry W. Goddard, and on January 21, 1950, Hiss was found guilty by the jury. Among the hundreds of messages received by Nixon was one in which Herbert Hoover stated: "The conviction of Alger Hiss was due to your patience and persistence alone. At last the stream of treason that existed in our government has been exposed in a fashion that all may believe."

With the conviction, the Hiss case became a major political asset to the Republican party, and to Nixon in particular. When he was nominated for vice-president in 1952, General Eisenhower introduced him to the National Convention as "a man who has shown statesmanlike qualities in many ways, but has a special talent and an ability to ferret out any kind of subversive influence wherever it may be found, and the strength and persistence to get rid of it."

From some of the speeches during the presidential campaign one might have thought that Alger Hiss was a candidate on the Democratic ticket. Nixon charged on several occasions and in several different ways that a Democratic victory would yield for America "more Alger Hisses, more atomic spies, more crises" instead of lasting peace. In a major campaign address, televised nationally from New York on October 13, 1952, Nixon reviewed the dramatic highlights of the Hiss investigation.

"We rented a room in the Commodore Hotel, Room 1400, incidentally, and in that room we called both Mr. Hiss and Mr. Chambers and asked them to give testimony as to whether or not one or the other could recognize each other," Nixon told his television audience. "Let me describe the room for you, because it is here that you can see the Communist conspiracy in action . . . twisting and turning and squirming . . . evading and avoiding. Imagine yourself in an ordinary hotel sitting room, with the windows to my back looking out on 42nd Street, a couple of chairs here . . . a small hotel sitting room in front of us . . . a chair here facing us for Mr. Hiss, and a lounge over there where Mr. Chambers was to sit."

As a climax Nixon produced some of the documents obtained from Chambers and declared that the Russians had been given hundreds like them "from Hiss and other members of the ring," which meant "that the lives of American boys were endangered and probably lost because of the activities of a spy ring." That shows what "just one man can do to injure the security of his country when he owes his loyalty not to his own government but to a foreign power . . . and again this case is a lesson, because we see the action of the administration in covering it up rather than in bringing Hiss to book many years sooner as they should have."

Nixon got to the principal point of his story at the last minutes of his half hour:

Mr. Stevenson was a character witness, or should I say a witness for the reputation, and the good reputation, of Alger Hiss. He testified that the reputation of Alger Hiss for veracity, for integrity, and for loyalty was good. . . . This testimony . . . was given after all these facts, this confrontation in which Hiss had to look into Chambers' mouth to identify him, after these papers came out of the pumpkin, after all of those facts were known . . . it was voluntary on Mr. Stevenson's part . . . it was given at a time when he was Governor of Illinois and the prestige of a great state and the Governor of the state were thrown in behalf of the defendant in this case. . . . It is significant that Mr. Stevenson has never expressed any indignation over what Mr. Hiss has done and the treachery that he engaged in against his country.

Then Nixon added:

Let me emphasize that there is no question in my mind as to the loyalty of Mr. Stevenson, but the question is one as to his judgment, and it is a very grave question. . . . In my opinion, his actions, his

(67)

statements, his record disqualifies him from leading the United States and the free nations in the fight against Communism at home and abroad; because, you see, the election of Mr. Stevenson would mean four more years of the same policy which has been so disastrous at home and disastrous abroad for America.

Ten days later Stevenson replied with an assertion that General Eisenhower and John Foster Dulles had been far closer to Alger Hiss than he, Stevenson, ever was. In a national broadcast he asserted that he was doing his duty as a citizen and as a lawyer in giving a deposition about Hiss's reputation as he had known it. He pointed out that Senator Taft, Senator Bricker and Congressman Joseph W. Martin, Jr., had attested in far more complimentary terms to the reputation of a Republican congressman from Ohio who recently had been convicted of unlawfully receiving political contributions from his employees. "It is obvious that my testimony in the Hiss case no more shows softness toward Communism than the testimony of these Republican leaders shows softness toward corruption," Stevenson said. "At no time did I testify on the issue of the guilt or innocence of Alger Hiss. As I have repeatedly said, I have never doubted the verdict of the jury which convicted him."

Stevenson spoke of Nixon as "the brash young man who aspires to the Vice-Presidency" and declared that if Nixon "would not tell, and tell honestly, what he knew of a defendant's reputation, he would be a coward and unfit for any office. The responsibility of lawyers to co-operate with the courts is greatest of all because they are officers of the court. And Senator Nixon is a lawyer."

Stevenson added:

I would suggest to the Republican "Crusaders" that if they were to apply the same methods to their own candidate, General Eisenhower, and to his foreign affairs adviser, John Foster Dulles, they would find that both these men were of the same opinion about Alger Hiss, and more so. . . . The facts are that the General and Mr. Dulles both demonstrated a continued personal faith in Alger Hiss in circumstances which imposed on them—as circumstances never did on me—the obligation to make a searching examination of his character and background.

In December, 1946, Hiss was chosen to be president of the Carnegie Endowment by the board of trustees of which John Foster Dulles was chairman. After Hiss was elected, but before he took office, a Detroit lawyer [whom Stevenson never named] offered to provide Mr. Dulles with evidence that Hiss had a provable Communist record. No such report or warning ever came to me. Under date of December 26, Mr. Dulles responded. Listen to what Mr. Dulles said: "I have heard the report which you refer to, but I have confidence that there is no reason to doubt Mr. Hiss' complete loyalty to our American institutions. I have been thrown into intimate contact with him at San Francisco, London and Washington . . . under these circumstances I feel a little skeptical about information which seems inconsistent with all that I personally know and what is the judgment of reliable friends and associates in Washington."

That, my friends, was John Foster Dulles, the General's adviser on foreign affairs. In May, 1948, General Eisenhower was elected to the board of trustees of the Carnegie Endowment at the same meeting at which Hiss was re-elected president and Dulles was re-elected chairman of the board. This was months after I had seen Hiss for the last time. I am sure the General would never have joined the board of trustees if he had any doubt concerning Hiss's loyalty.

After he had been indicted by the grand jury, Hiss tendered his resignation. . . . The board of trustees of which General Eisenhower was a member declined to accept his resignation and granted him three months leave of absence with full pay so that he might defend himself. . . . Alger Hiss, General Eisenhower and Dulles continued as fellow members of the board of trustees until after the conviction of Alger Hiss.

Before concluding his speech, Stevenson said, "I bring these facts to the American people," not to suggest that either Eisenhower or Dulles was soft toward Communists or even guilty of bad judgment, but "only to make the point that the mistrust, the innuendoes, the accusations which this 'Crusade' is employing, threatens not merely themselves, but the integrity of our institutions."

There were so many ramifications to the Hiss case that books already are being written about relatively small facets of it, and identical facts are being subjected to contradictory interpretations. It is obvious that the Hiss case was far more complex than its immediate political impact would indicate.

(69)

On reflection, Nixon says that "looking back, I suppose the great lesson of the Hiss case is the personal tragedies involved for both Hiss and Chambers. They came from very different backgrounds, but both of them were sensitive, very capable men. Intellectually, Chambers was superior to Hiss, but Hiss was no slouch when it came to brains. Both were, I think, sincerely dedicated to the concepts of peace and the concept of bettering the lot of the common man, of people generally. They were both idealists. Yet, here are two men of this quality who became infected with Communism, infected with it to the degree that they were willing to run the risk, as they did, of disgrace in order to serve the Communist conspiracy. The fact that this could happen to them, shows the potential threat that Communism presents among people of this type throughout the world."

Nixon all but dropped the word "Hiss" from his political lexicon after one of his earliest press conferences in the 1956 campaign when he praised Stevenson as being "forthright and direct," and acting "very creditably," in dissociating himself from an observation by Truman that Hiss had never been proved to be a spy or a Communist.

"Domestic Communism," Nixon says today, "is no longer a political issue. The danger has receded a great deal in the last few years, domestically, mainly because we have become increasingly aware of it. The Communists used to fool an awful lot of well meaning people who were not Communists. There is still a group, a small group that can be fooled."

But both Nixon and the Republican party were to work a tremendous amount of political mileage from the sturdy treads of the Hiss case—and for Nixon, this road started in 1950, when he ran for the Senate against Democratic Congresswoman Helen Gahagan Douglas.

6

NOTHING in the litany of reprehensible conduct charged against Nixon, the campaigner, has been cited more often than the tactics by which he defeated Congresswoman Helen Gahagan Douglas for senator. It is one of the most familiar stories of Nixon's political career, and the source of much dislike and mistrust of him. A searching study of that campaign, including a check of Mrs. Douglas' files in her New York apartment, reveals that the accepted account is only a fraction of what really transpired. It was indeed a ripsnorting campaign, overflowing with villains and political iniquity—or heroes and cagey maneuvers, depending on how one judges.

It began with a conflict of political ambitions—Nixon's, Mrs. Douglas', Senator Sheridan Downey's, and others'. The Democrats had regained control of Congress in the 1948 election and, although the Hiss case focused enough national attention on Nixon for him to be recognized by Capitol tourists, he now was not only a junior member but a junior in the minority party of the lower house. Nixon raised his sights to the Senate.

Challenging Republican Senator Knowland was out of the question. But California's other senator was a Democrat whose seat would be at stake in 1950. Senator Downey wanted a third term, and most people felt he probably would win it. It is an axiom of California politics that an incumbent enjoys a great advantage regardless of party, record or office, because practically a third of the voters almost always go for the name identified with the office.

Three senior Republicans coveted Downey's post. But they decided against risking the race. That left only Nixon. He was a sad but earnest underdog until his lucky star came through in the form of Mrs. Douglas' candidacy, which meant a showdown fight among the Democrats.

Though California had many more registered Democrats than Republicans, the latter frequently won state elections because left- and right-wing Democrats had habitually clawed each other so viciously in their party primary that the survivor, or nominee, was too weak and demoralized to campaign effectively in the general election. The encounter between the conservative Downey and the liberal Mrs. Douglas was destined to be a prize show.

Earlier, before the Republican picture had brightened, Nixon toured the state quietly to muster backing for his candidacy. Former President Herbert Hoover encouraged him. Senator Knowland offered his own "unqualified support" and that of the Oakland *Tribune*, his family's newspaper. Principal figures in a Stassen political organization, "California Volunteers for Good Government," also were enthusiastic. They endorsed Nixon ahead of schedule, almost upsetting his timetable.

But the small band of original supporters in his Congressional district were the principal holdouts. "We were against it," says Frank Jorgensen. "We thought Dick was firmly entrenched as a congressman, and there was too much risk in running for the Senate." Nixon called a meeting in his former law partner's office. Beforehand, he instructed Roy Day, local Republican chairman, to argue for his running for senator.

Day obliged. This provoked Herman Perry, the old banker and family friend, to shake his finger excitedly and accuse Day of being "nothing but a politician!" Perry pleaded with Nixon not to "sacrifice" himself. It was an emotional and inconclusive get-to-gether.

On November 3, 1949—a full year before the election—Nixon announced for senator. The issue, as he declared it, was "simply the choice between freedom and state socialism."

Much of his speech was directed at conservative Democrats. He has repeated it in one form or another during every campaign since. Nixon paid tribute to the Democratic party's record of distinguished service in the past. Then he said: "But today, nationally and in our own state of California, it has been captured and is completely controlled by a group of ruthless, cynical seekers after power—committed to policies and principles completely foreign to those of its founders." If they could see "the phony doctrines and ideologies now being foisted upon the American people," Thomas Jefferson and Andrew Jackson would "turn over in their graves. . . . Call it planned economy, the Fair Deal, or social welfare—but it is still the same old Socialist boloney, any way you slice it."

He also proclaimed his candidacy to be "a banner of freedom which all people, regardless of party, can follow."

Politicians treat California as two separate states. They electioneer through different campaign organizations in the south and in the north. Each of these normally has two sachems—a distinguished citizen, as a nonsalaried "chairman," and a professional operator, usually a public relations man, as "campaign manager." The star Republican professional in 1950 was Murray Chotiner. Beginning with Warren's election as governor, he had executed a dazzling run of Republican triumphs. Chotiner was engaged as Nixon's southern manager and also to oversee the whole campaign. A rapport developed between the two men and Chotiner became Nixon's closest political associate and campaign adviser. That relationship lasted until 1956 when Chotiner's name figured in a Congressional investigation of influence peddling. Chotiner is a Beverly Hills lawyer. His emergence as a national political figure was followed, as it is for most lawyer-politicians, by an influx of clients from beyond California's borders. One of Chotiner's new clients was a Philadelphia racketeer. Another was a clothing manufacturer accused of cheating the armed services. A third was a relatively small airline with an important case pending before a government agency. Nixon was in no way involved in Chotiner's private operations, but he was embarrassed. Chotiner became a political exile. Since then he and Nixon have resumed their personal friendship.[1] Nixon still

[1] Several knowledgeable Republicans in California believe their party's disastrous defeat in 1958 might have been averted if Senator Knowland had asked Chotiner to run his campaign, as he thought seriously of doing. Chotiner had managed Knowland's victory over Will Rogers, Jr., in 1946 and also the 1952 campaign which Knowland won by the biggest majority in California history.

(73)

considers Chotiner the ablest campaign technician in America. Chotiner, in turn, respects Nixon as a master campaigner but admits he was the hardest candidate of all to manage. Nixon insisted on perfection, says Chotiner, which is impossible in the heat of a political battle, and he couldn't cure himself of a tendency to try to do everything. Chotiner recalls a showdown during the 1950 race for senator. "I had to tell him: 'Dick, you can either be the candidate, or the manager. You can't be both. A candidate's job is to think and to speak. You just go out and make speeches and get votes, and let us make the other mistakes.'"

The only way a Republican could win, Nixon had told friends, was with "a fighting, rocking, socking campaign." At the outset in 1950 all the rocking and socking was done by the Democrats— on each other. In the warmup, Mrs. Douglas accused Senator Downey of a do-nothing record in Washington and of catering to big business and power interests. Downey charged she campaigned on "personal bias and prejudice," and he linked her with "extremists."

Two months before the primaries Downey withdrew from the race, stating that he was not physically up to "waging a personal and militant campaign against the vicious and unethical propaganda" which he accused Mrs. Douglas of using against him. In reply, Mrs. Douglas said she was sorry Downey was ill. At the same time she reminded the voters that the "illness gimmick" was not new to politicians facing defeat—and her fight switched to Downey's successor in the race. He was Manchester Boddy, editor and publisher of the Los Angeles *Daily News,* the only Democratic newspaper in a large California city.

"It is the same old plot with a new leading man," Mrs. Douglas declared, after Boddy filed for the Senate nomination.

As it turned out, the "new leading man" was accompanied by a new campaign assault that showed how easily and directly Democrats could use issues of Communism and subversion. In the weeks that followed, her fellow Democrats painted Mrs. Douglas every insulting hue of red. Few of them bothered to acknowledge, even obliquely, that she was actually a vigorous foe of the Communist party and had fought Henry Wallace's Progressive party in a Congressional district where *that* took considerable courage.

In the keynote of his campaign Boddy stated: "There is indisputable evidence of a state-wide conspiracy on the part of this small subversive clique of red-hots to capture, through stealth and cunning, the nerve centers of our Democratic party—and by so doing to capture the vote of real Democratic citizens."

He warned that the "blueprint of subversive dictatorship" called for control of the Democratic party by the "red-hots" who would make the party "serve their own twisted purposes . . . good California Democrats who know the score . . . have taken up the banner to preserve the American way of life and protect the true liberalism and honest progressivism which has made the Democratic party great."

Thereafter Senator Downey returned to the battlefront to declare in a state-wide radio broadcast that Mrs. Douglas "gave comfort to the Soviet tyranny by voting against aid to Greece and Turkey." The Senator also charged that she "opposed an appropriation to enable Congress to uncover treasonable communistic activities" and that in this she "joined Representative Vito Marcantonio, an admitted friend of the Communist party."[2] Downey also commented that she wept when Henry Wallace failed to get renominated for vice-president in 1944.

Linking Mrs. Douglas with Marcantonio became a part of every attack from the Boddy camp. A former American Legion commander "alerted" veterans to Mrs. Douglas' "consistent policy of voting along with the notorious radical, Vito Marcantonio." The vice-president of the California Democratic Women's League cautioned Democrats to "wake up and see where she is trying to lead us."

And so it went—in newspaper ads, speeches, billboards, and even in a general letter to California's clubwomen. Ostensibly, the main purpose of the widely distributed letter was "to point out that Helen Gahagan Douglas is neither truly representative of her sex

[2] In the election campaign Senator Downey ignored White House requests that he endorse Mrs. Douglas as a sign of party loyalty. Like several other well-known California Democrats, he favored Nixon.

nor of her party," but a central paragraph told of how she was being "led by the notorious New York radical, Vito Marcantonio" in opposing appropriations to fight Communism and voting "against the Truman administration."

Meanwhile Nixon, with only token opposition for the Republican nomination, stumped the state. He shook hands, addressed street-corner audiences, and set up his public-address system to invite questions in practically every town and village. His favorite speaking topic was the Hiss case, but in the major speech of his primary campaign, delivered in San Francisco, Nixon proposed that President Truman establish a foreign policy advisory board that would serve both the President and Congress, ensuring "a consistent-realistic foreign policy" and inspiring wholehearted bipartisanship.[3] Among Republicans Nixon suggested should be invited to a White House conference preceding the creation of the board were Hoover, Senator Vandenberg, Senator Taft, Governor Dewey, Governor Warren, John Foster Dulles, Harold Stassen, and General Eisenhower, then president of Columbia University.

Occasionally Democrats would come up for breath from their melee and take a swing at Nixon. He was often tempted to respond, especially when Mrs. Douglas stated, offhanded: "I have utter scorn for such pipsqueaks as Nixon and McCarthy." Near the end Nixon almost abandoned his policy of ignoring the opposition. He thought of getting in a lick or two about Mrs. Douglas' votes against the Greek-Turkish Aid bill (the Truman Doctrine) in 1947 and appropriations to keep the House Un-American Activities Committee going. But he was persuaded to tuck away his ammunition for later use, says Chotiner, because "quite frankly, we wanted her to be the Democratic nominee on the basis that it would be easier to defeat her than a conservative Democrat. So nothing was ever said pertaining to Helen Gahagan Douglas in the primary."

The only controversy in the first half of Nixon's campaign was over his bid for the Democratic nomination. He had cross-filed in the Democratic primary, just as Mrs. Douglas and Boddy had in the

[3] This is still one of Nixon's pet ideas, and if he became president one of his earliest acts almost certainly would be the setting up of such a board.

(76)

Republican primary. But Boddy and Will Rogers, Jr., his campaign chairman, angrily denounced Nixon literature mailed to thousands of registered Democrats. They charged Nixon misrepresented himself as a Democrat in a leaflet entitled "As One Democrat to Another."

The campaign leaflet told of how he "broke the Hiss-Chambers espionage case" and quoted various endorsements of his record and activities in Congress. It also stated that Congressman Nixon had "voted and stands for—lower taxes and more take-home pay . . . strong national defense for real security . . . California ownership of tidelands [oil rights] . . . protection of small business . . . Taft-Hartley Act with Wood amendments . . . reciprocal trade treaties with adequate protection for American labor, agriculture and industry . . . jobs for unemployed . . . sound national pension system . . . strong United Nations . . . statehood for Hawaii and Alaska . . . civil rights" and many other programs. There was no direct reference to Nixon's party affiliation, but the names of the chairman and secretary of "Democrats for Nixon for United States Senator" were printed, in small type, under a photograph of the candidate's name as it would appear in the Democratic column of voting machines on primary day.

In his attack on this "viciously false circular," Boddy printed a large photostat of Nixon's latest affidavit of registration, showing that he had declared himself to be a Republican.

Nixon won the Republican nomination handily, and also got 22 per cent of Democratic primary votes. Mrs. Douglas won the Democratic nomination by a plurality, since her total was slightly less than half of the votes cast by Democrats. She also got 13 per cent of the Republican primary votes.

The autumn of 1950 was ready made for mean electioneering. Domestically, the postwar reaction had set in. The nation was on the brink of depression. Spectacular Congressional investigations were depicting Washington as a haven of subversion and corruption. In the Democratic party, which controlled both the White House and the Congress, the traditional division between conservatives and liberals had broken out into a rash of grim primary fights

(77)

in which accusations of subversion were bandied about with a looseness once used with the far less odious charges of nepotism or welfare-statism. On top of all else, war erupted in Korea.

Under the circumstances the general election contest for senator from California, or "the final," as it is called there, was a natural for the times. The issue—"Communism"—embraced every nightmare of treachery a voter could conjure up. Seekers after a variety of offices milked it as best they could. Edmund G. (Pat) Brown, Democratic candidate for attorney general, paraded his "anti-Communism" by praising the state legislature's controversial appropriation of $25,000 for an antisabotage program. James Roosevelt, Democratic candidate for governor, went further—he not only approved the appropriation but declared it should have been larger.

Nonetheless, it was clear from the start that the Communist issue was Nixon's, above all others. Mrs. Douglas, his Democratic opponent, tried first to wish it away. She declared that it was not an issue at all, but "a phony cover-up by Republicans for their failure to advance a positive program for true democracy." She strove to dislodge Nixon from his perch, insisting that she had been more effectively anti-Communist than he.

The Nixon-Douglas campaign had some strange roots and alliances. And invariably they worked to Nixon's advantage. There was, for example, the Democratic primary encounter in which Congressman George A. Smathers unseated Senator Claude Pepper, of Florida. Although Nixon and Smathers were "opponents" in the sense that they belonged to different parties, they were close personal friends and, on many issues, they had the same conservative outlook. At the same time Senator Pepper was a liberal Democrat in the fashion of Mrs. Douglas.

After Smathers' primary victory in May, Nixon carefully studied it and adapted what he could to his own campaign. (Thus "Red Pepper," a slogan in Florida, became "Pink Lady," in California.) Relatively, however, the Smathers plan was only a drop in the tidal wave of help Nixon got from Democrats.

"California Democrats for Nixon," headed by George Creel, publicity man for the Woodrow Wilson presidential campaign in

1915, became the vehicle for a series of assaults that compelled Mrs. Douglas to quote President Truman as proof that she *was*, indeed, a Democrat.

Nixon's greatest windfall, of course, was the mass of accusations her fellow Democrats had hurled at Mrs. Douglas in the spring. Chotiner and his associates gathered them all, added an embellishment here and a nuance there, and played it back in the fall campaign.

The campaign was the most hateful California had experienced in many years. Nixon kept on the offensive all the way—beginning with a statement in which his campaign chairman established the line that Mrs. Douglas' record in Congress "discloses the truth about her soft attitude toward Communism" and a speech in which he, personally, announced his decision to risk the penalty of criticizing a woman because "if she had had her way, the Communist conspiracy in the United States would never have been exposed . . . it just so happens that my opponent is a member of a small clique which joins the notorious Communist party-liner, Vito Marcantonio of New York, in voting time after time against measures that are for the security of this country."

The impact of that speech was such that next day Mrs. Douglas sent telegrams to about two dozen of her closest friends saying, "I have run into a frightening crisis. I need your help, your advice, your support. Will you come to dinner at my house Tuesday, September 26, 7 p.m., so that we can talk over this terrible situation and hopefully find a solution."

An analysis of the Nixon and Douglas campaigns shows that the most notable difference was in the adroitness and calmness with which Nixon and his people executed *their* hyperbole and innuendo. When the Nixon camp questioned her fitness to be even a Democrat, for instance, or bemoaned her inability to judge between what was good for America and what was good for Russia, it was like a team of experienced surgeons performing masterful operations for the benefit of humanity. On the other hand, when Mrs. Douglas characterized Nixon and his followers as "a backwash of young men in dark shirts," the inference of Fascism didn't impress anyone who was not already impressed. And while her charge that Nixon was one of the most reactionary men in Congress had a certain ring of accuracy, because, after all, he *was* a Republican, inferences that he was an isolationist and the charge that "on every key vote Nixon stood with party-liner Marcantonio against America in its fight to defeat Communism," simply sounded and read as false as they were.

For whatever reason—perhaps because Mrs. Douglas and her friends were less blasé and more conscience-stricken by improprieties —when compared with the surgeons of the Nixon camp, Mrs. Douglas' operators performed like apprentice butchers. In a strange election-eve boast, Mrs. Douglas' campaign manager said that the Democrats had wanted Nixon to attack Mrs. Douglas.

Lawrence E. Davies, chief of the *New York Times* bureau in San Francisco, put it this way on October 31, 1950:

As outlined by Harold Tipton, Mrs. Douglas' campaign manager, her strategy was planned at the outset to "needle" Mr. Nixon into showing his hand. Two sentences, one charging that her rival had "voted with Representative Marcantonio against aid to Korea," the other declaring Mr. Nixon had voted with Mr. Marcantonio to cut European aid in half, were thrown into Mrs. Douglas' opening speech in late July.

"They fell for it," Mr. Tipton said. "Nixon was right back with a defense. By September 1 he flooded the state with phony voting records. But our theory was that he couldn't keep up the red smear indefinitely."

Douglas strategists hope that the Nixon campaign will boomerang.

As is well known, it didn't. The Douglas campaign's repeated linkage of Nixon and Marcantonio may have been forgotten, because it was overshadowed by the shrewder manner in which Nixon later tied the much-aligned New York Congressman to Mrs. Douglas. Nixon did not rest his case with just two, three or five Marcantonio votes, as did Mrs. Douglas. Nixon's charges went before the voters as a carefully researched leaflet, filled with dates, reference data and lawyerlike analogies that were just confusing enough to convince laymen of their authenticity. At the top the document was labeled "Douglas-Marcantonio Voting Record." An opening, explanatory statement implied that almost everyone in California was anxious to know the truth about "the voting records of Congresswoman Helen Douglas and the notorious party-liner, Congressman Vito Marcantonio of New York." Then came the revelation: they had voted the same way 354 times. This was followed by a statement that "while it should not be expected that a member of the House of Representatives should always vote in opposition to Marcantonio, it is significant to note, not only the greater number of times which Mrs. Douglas voted in agreement with him, but also the issues on which almost without exception they always saw eye-to-eye, to wit: Un-American Activities and Internal Security."[4]

The first order was for 50,000 copies of the leaflet. Chotiner says he was never able to figure whether its immediate popularity was due to the content or the suggestive hue of the paper he had selected, which was bright pink. Anyway, within a week he ordered another 500,000, and they are known to this day—in pride or in shame—as "the pink sheets."

One of the hitherto not revealed political milestones of that campaign is the strategy by which an endorsement, of sorts, was wormed out of Governor Warren. As all his Republican colleagues quickly learned, Warren was a lone-wolf campaigner whose rare public support of another candidate was always based on the help that individual could give Warren, and not on party affiliation. Warren appointed William Knowland to the Senate to fill a vacancy in 1945. The next year, when Knowland ran for a full term, Warren agreed to endorse him only at the last minute. His reluctance had been based on a desire not to alienate supporters of Will

[4] Marcantonio represented a slum district in New York where the constituents judged him principally by what he did for them in a personal way, like cutting through red tape to get them on the relief rolls. He managed that well enough to feel secure in his office. In the California election Mrs. Douglas was first tied to Marcantonio by her Democratic primary opponent. When he read about it in Washington, Marcantonio went to a friend of Nixon's and said, chuckling, "Tell Nicky to get on this thing because it is a good idea." Marcantonio disliked Mrs. Douglas intensely and normally used an obscene five-letter word when referring to her in private conversations.

Rogers, Jr., Knowland's Democratic opponent. In the 1950 election Warren, seeking a third term, headed the Republican ticket on which Nixon was the candidate for senator. Nixon and Warren had no particular use for each other since Warren indirectly had aided Nixon's Democratic opponent for Congress in 1946 while refusing to acknowledge Nixon. In the Senate campaign the Nixon forces felt a Warren endorsement important because of rumors that the immensely popular Governor actually wanted to see Nixon defeated. Any hope of convincing Warren to come through was complicated by the fact that the Democratic candidates had not expressed any support for each other. Nixon strategists thereupon evolved a plan to anger Warren into saying something.

An earnest young Republican, subsequently elected to Congress, was assigned to follow Mrs. Douglas and ask her during question periods and at press conferences whether she thought James Roosevelt should be elected governor. She ignored the questioner until the Friday before election, when she replied: "I hope and pray he will be the next governor, and he will be, if the Democrats vote the Democratic ticket."

The word was swiftly conveyed to Chotiner. He, in turn, passed it to a friendly newspaperman traveling with Warren. When the Governor was asked for his reaction, he replied that he would have to think about it. Twenty-four hours later he issued the following statement: "I have no intention of being coy about this situation. As always, I have kept my campaign independent from other campaigns. The newspaper reports from San Diego that Mrs. Douglas has said she hopes and prays Mr. Roosevelt will be the next Governor does not change my position. In view of her statement, however, I might ask her how she expects I will vote when I mark my ballot for United States Senator next Tuesday."

Nixon's campaign manager thereupon declared: "Every voter in California who reads his statement will realize that Earl Warren intends to mark his ballot for Dick Nixon on election day."

Whether he actually did is a secret Warren has yet to divulge. Meanwhile the fact that he has become chief justice and Nixon vice-president has not appreciably altered their relationship. "We are not unfriendly," Nixon says. "We are two individuals going our own ways."

On election day, and also the day before, the Nixon organization offered "prizes galore" to individuals who answered with the words "Vote for Nixon" if the candidate's headquarters telephoned. As part of the game Nixon assistants placed telephone calls at random throughout the state, inspiring thousands of people to plug Nixon's candidacy whenever their telephones rang.

Nixon was elected by a 680,000 vote margin. This so delighted and surprised him that he went from one victory party to another most of the night and played "Happy Days Are Here Again" wherever there was a piano.

7

REPUBLICAN successes in the 1950 Congressional elections had the impact of a cold shower on the groggy party. It had lapsed into shock two years before when Harry Truman won the elections and unceremoniously crushed GOP expectations just as the power-starved faithful in many cities were beginning their victory celebrations. Now, with the 1950 results, things were looking up. The party had gained five seats in the Senate and twenty-eight in the House, and its center of gravity in Congress, Senator Robert A. Taft, had vanquished the political forces of organized labor which combined across the nation to defeat him for re-election in Ohio.

Furthermore, the articulate young Congressman whom party professionals viewed as "a real comer" because of the skill in which he "got Alger Hiss" had accomplished something in California to hearten Republicans and concern Democrats nationally. Representative Nixon had demonstrated in winning his election for Senator that a "model Republican" could defeat a "model Democrat" in an industrial state where Democrats outregistered Republicans by a million votes.

Former President Herbert Hoover wrote Nixon: "Your victory was the greatest good that can come to our country." Herbert Brownell, Jr., manager of the two Dewey campaigns for president and later a chief strategist of the Eisenhower campaign, declared that Nixon's "brilliant campaign" in California laid the groundwork for Republican success nationally in 1952. Freshman Senator Nixon quickly became his party's most sought-after speaker and soon blossomed into a Republican meld of Paul Revere and Billy Sunday. Across the land he trumpeted Republican gospel and warned the countryside to stop the Democratic hordes or face disaster. The Republican party had to win the next election, or die, he declared.

On top of his Senate duties Nixon managed to squeeze up to a dozen speaking engagements a month in the year and a half from the convening of the Eighty-first Congress to the twenty-fifth Republican National Convention. The two most significant speeches were at a party fund-raising dinner in New York City, May 8, 1952, and before the National Young Republican Convention in Boston, June 28, 1951. His New York appearance stood out because of what happened rather than what he said, for Governor Dewey informed Nixon after the dinner that he should be the candidate for vice-president on the Eisenhower ticket. The Boston speech a year earlier was important for its content. In it Nixon wrapped up a battle plan and a Republican program for the pending struggle with the Democrats. He entitled the address "The Challenge of 1952" and proposed that the party wage "the kind of a fighting, rocking, socking campaign that will bring home to the people the merits of our candidate and our program." The Democratic administration (Truman was then president) had failed on many fronts, said Nixon. No diplomatic gaffe in history had been worse, for instance, "than the failure of our State Department to get the wholehearted support of our allies in Korea"; therefore, "the American people have had enough of the whining, whimpering, groveling attitude of our diplomatic representatives who talk of America's weaknesses and of America's fears rather than of America's strength and of America's courage." Nixon also chided the Democrats for "piously" talking economy while asking Congress for funds "so that administration officials can ride to work and to their social engagements in chauffeured government limousines." But "the most vulnerable point" against the Democrats was "the failure of this administration to develop an effective program to meet the activities of the fifth column in the United States." "Communists infiltrated the very highest councils of this administration," he charged, yet "our top administration officials have refused time and time again to recog-

(85)

nize the existence of the fifth column in this country and to take effective action to clean subversives out of the administrative branch of our government."

In his discussion of "subversives in government" Nixon spoke in some detail about the Hiss case. "When the case went to the courts," he stated, "two judges of the Supreme Court; the Governor of Illinois, Mr. Stevenson; Philip Jessup, the architect of our Far Eastern policy; and a host of other administration officials testified as character witnesses for Alger Hiss."[1]

In the speech which was to become a model for Republican campaigners, Nixon not only attacked the Democratic opposition ("We have a duty to criticize and to point up the mistakes of the past"), but he also advised fellow partisans that they "should not stop with destructive criticism. We should go a step further and offer our own constructive program to meet the great problems of our times."

He admitted that "the Republican party has some faults" and suggested that they be recognized and corrected. "But one thing can be said to our credit which cannot be said for the party in power," he added, "that is, that we have never had the support of the Communists in the past. We have never asked for that support. We do not have it now, and we shall never ask for it or accept it in the future. And for that reason a Republican administration, we can be sure, will conduct a thoroughgoing housecleaning of Communists and fellow travelers in the administrative branch of the government because we have no fear of finding any Communist skeletons in our political closets."

Nixon said a Republican housecleaning program would have to be "fair, sane, intelligent, and effective" because "indiscriminate

[1] This clear implication that everyone helping Hiss was in the Truman administration registered more effectively with Nixon's audience than the fact, well known to students of government, that Supreme Court justices and governors of states are independent of any president's administration. Incidentally, this speech was delivered at least six months before anyone seriously mentioned Stevenson in terms of the Democratic nomination for president. At the time the Democratic Governor of Illinois was practically unknown outside his state, and his name was misspelled—"Stephenson"—in a widely distributed reprint of the Nixon address that was inserted in the *Congressional Record*.

name-calling and professional Red-baiting can hurt our cause more than it can help it."

In essence, Nixon's program was as follows: "A program which is designed to meet the threat which is presented to our security by the internationalist Communist conspiracy: keep the United States militarily strong. Keep the economy of this nation strong and sound and productive and free. And develop a fair and effective program of internal security. And, above all, mount a mighty ideological offensive which will prove to peoples everywhere that the hope of the world does not lie in turning toward dictatorship of any type, but that it lies in developing a strong, a free, and an intelligent democracy."

Just a month before his Boston speech Nixon made a pilgrimage to General Eisenhower at Supreme Headquarters of the Allied Command in Europe. In reality it was sort of a sideline pilgrimage, since the main purpose of Nixon's European trip was to attend a four-day conference of the World Health Organization in Geneva. He stopped briefly in Paris on the way home, and after a half hour with Eisenhower the Senator offered two observations. One was that building an integrated defense force for the North Atlantic Allies was a tough proposition and Eisenhower "is doing a fine job under very difficult circumstances." The other was that Eisenhower might be available for the presidential nomination in 1952, but the Senator was not altogether clear yet about the General's political identity.

(The young Senator from California was developing confidence. Shortly after his return from Europe, for instance, he was invited to a secret session in New Jersey at which Harold Stassen's closest political friends were asked to discuss Stassen's future with Stassen. Most said they believed Eisenhower would be the Republican party's best bet, so Stassen declared he would run again and promised to pull out if Eisenhower became a candidate.)

Nixon's speechmaking invitations piled up faster and faster in the wake of his address to the Young Republicans in Boston. In the next five months audiences in eleven states heard Nixon tear into the Democrats. Before completing his first year as senator,

(87)

participating at a press conference in Los Angeles on November 16, 1951, Nixon stated:

1. Taft and Eisenhower were the "front runners" for the Republican nomination, with Governor Warren "the strongest dark horse."

2. Warren would beat Truman "or any other Democratic nominee presently considered."

3. Truman would run again. (He added, later, "You can bet it will be Truman or someone he names.")

4. Eisenhower would be "hard to beat," but he "hurt" himself because he still had not indicated his party affiliation. ("The General has been playing it a little too coy and people are beginning to lose some of their enthusiasm.")

5. Eisenhower would not be drafted. ("He will have to make a major move before the first major primary.")[2]

6. The first major primary would make or break Taft. ("The feeling is that he is respectable, that he would be good for the country if he should become president, but there is doubt as to whether he would be a vote getter.")

As a member of the California delegation Nixon was pledged to vote for Governor Warren at the convention—and he did, although he favored Eisenhower. In preconvention maneuvers all presidential aspirants sought his backing, especially since at least a third of the seventy California delegates would vote as he did if Warren released them. Stassen, who produced polls and surveys to "prove" he would benefit from an Eisenhower-Taft deadlock, proposed a Stassen-Nixon ticket. Taft personally solicited Nixon, then assigned their mutual friend, Tom Shroyer, an architect of the Taft-Hartley Law, to bring Nixon into the Taft camp. "I thought

[2] Nixon said considerably more about the General in subsequent months. On February 13, 1952, he observed in San Francisco that it would be "very difficult for Eisenhower to give Taft a real fight" unless he returns to the United States and issues a clear statement of candidacy. After the New Hampshire primary dissipated everyone's doubts about the General's active candidacy, Nixon stated on April 16: "General Eisenhower owes it to his party to state his views before the nominations are made. At present the race looks to me like a tossup between Eisenhower and Taft. It can end in a deadlock. In that case, Warren or General MacArthur might get the nomination."

he was quite sympathetic in our first conferences during the latter part of 1951 and early 1952," Shroyer said. "Nixon liked Taft, but he did seem to have a few doubts about Taft's chances to win." A principal figure in the organization promoting Eisenhower's candidacy recalled: "It was clear to us by April that Nixon was friendly to our group. His hands were tied [by the legal commitment to vote for Warren], but it came to a point where a relationship was established ... where one of us would see him on occasion on the Senate floor and sound him out, get his advice on various things, never going too deep, still going deeper than we could with someone who was completely on the outside."

As the Eisenhower-Taft battle lines tightened in the late spring of 1952, the usual array of "inside reports" by some "political experts" got wilder. None was more absurd than the yarn that Governor Dewey was not seriously supporting Eisenhower but really aimed to maneuver a third nomination for himself. Actually Dewey was not only working vigorously to get Eisenhower the nomination, but he and Brownell also had decided that Senator Nixon would be the best running mate.

"Nixon seemed an almost ideal candidate for vice-president," Brownell recalled. "He was young, geographically right, had experience both in the House and the Senate with a good voting record, and was an excellent speaker.

"The original conception of the *team* had worked out very well," Brownell added. "It was to have the President, who was experienced on the world scene, running with a young, aggressive fellow, who knew the domestic issues and agreed with the President's policies. The President could be presented to the country as one who would stand up against the Communists in the international sphere, and Nixon would lead the fight in the discussion of the domestic issues."

When Brownell mentioned this to Nixon at a Gridiron Club dinner in Washington, the latter said he was flattered but didn't expect to be nominated.

Dewey broached the subject to Nixon after a $100-a-plate New York State Republican dinner on May 8. "I had heard a lot of very fine things about him," Dewey told me. "I checked with a lot of people who worked with him in both the House and the Senate. Everybody whose opinion I respected said he was an absolute star, a man of enormous capacity. They liked and admired him. So I pretty much made up my mind that this was the fellow." Before that decision, however, Dewey wanted to see Nixon in action before a large New York audience. So Nixon was invited to the party dinner. "He made a very fine speech, from notes, not a prepared text," Dewey recalls. "He demonstrated he does not speak from what someone else writes and also has a very fine understanding of the world situation."

Afterwards the Governor asked Nixon to his suite on the twenty-fourth floor of the Roosevelt Hotel for a private chat. "The two of us sat around for about an hour or an hour and a half before he took his train," Dewey said. "That was the occasion on which I discussed with him briefly the possibility of him becoming the Vice-President."

Nixon says he "couldn't believe Governor Dewey was serious."[3]

The nominating convention was still two months off. Eisenhower was to return from Paris in three weeks to take an active role in his campaign for the nomination.

Governor Warren's slate of delegates, including Nixon, won the California primary on June 3. In public statements and in hundreds of letters to people who were urging him to support either Eisenhower or Taft, Nixon emphasized that he would switch from Warren only with the Governor's permission. When it appeared more and more certain that just twenty or thirty votes could make the difference between victory and failure, some Eisenhower leaders tried to pressure Nixon into splitting the California delegation, whether Warren approved or not. At one point Paul G. Hoffman, a leader of the liberal, independent Republicans for Eisenhower,

[3] It was Nixon's first long session with Dewey. Since then Nixon often has looked to him for counsel. "I like to bat ideas around with Dewey. I know you are always going to get a completely honest answer from him. Most people will only tell you what they think you want to hear. You can always count on Dewey to tell you the truth regardless of how much it hurts. He never tries to butter you up."

(90)

tried to convert Knowland, who was so doggedly for Warren that he ignored offers of the Vice-Presidency from the Taft camp and decreed that no California delegate would so much as even talk about an alternate to Warren for the Presidency. Although he was not happy about it, Dewey recalls that he considered Nixon's refusal to "participate in any movement to break the California delegation . . . a very fine attitude." Dewey said, "Nixon maintained his aloofness with perfection." Some Warren devotees charged Nixon with a "double-cross," however, for sending 23,000 questionnaires asking California voters who they thought would be the strongest possible Republican nominee. The answers confirmed Nixon's own belief. Most said Eisenhower. Nixon regards the double-cross allegation as "silly." He said he told Warren and Knowland, "I was an Eisenhower man from the beginning," yet he stuck by his commitment to Warren even when he knew beyond question that it would be best for California to start the inevitable bandwagon for Eisenhower by giving him the mere nineteen votes he needed for nomination on the first ballot. (Stassen grabbed the opportunity and provided the nineteen from his tiny bundle of twenty-four votes in the Minnesota delegation. California didn't switch.)

On June 7 twenty-one Republican congressmen petitioned National Chairman Guy George Gabrielson to select Nixon as keynote speaker for the convention because he was "one of the most outstanding orators in the Republican party, and he can press the Republican cause very effectively." Some months earlier Gabrielson had figured in a conflict-of-interest matter uncovered by the Senate Investigating Committee, and Nixon had demanded his resignation as national Republican leader. The chairman received the Congressional group's proposal with thanks, and selected General Douglas MacArthur to deliver the opening address that, by tradition, was to set the tone of the convention and the campaign and inspire patriots throughout the land to become fervent crusaders for the Republican cause.

There already are two or three conflicting legends about the maneuvers that swirled around Nixon during the period immediately before he was nominated in 1952—and his reactions. People

(91)

most intimately associated with it—including principal movers and shakers—reconstructed what actually happened as follows:

Nixon arrived in Chicago on July 1 as a member of the platform-writing resolutions committee. Like other committees of the convention with serious conflicts to resolve, the resolutions group began to meet a full week before the convention, itself, was to open. Nevertheless, Nixon's early presence on the scene added spice to rumors cropping up in political columns that he would be Eisenhower's running mate because he was regarded as an ideal "bridge" between the seriously divided Eisenhower and Taft wings of the party. (A couple of "experts" predicted Nixon would be Taft's running mate for the same reason.) The Californian scoffed at the speculation, publicly and privately.

On July 3 Nixon issued a statement condemning the Taft-dominated Republican National Committee for seeming to settle the pending fight over contested delegations from three Southern states by granting temporary recognition to the Georgia group committed to Taft with the right to vote on its own status as the permanent delegation. At the time Eisenhower was equating the Taft organization tactics with cattle rustling and horse stealing. Nixon charged that questions of honesty and lawbreaking were involved, and the National Committee's action could "ruin" the Republican party.

On July 4 Nixon flew to Denver to board a special train bringing the California delegation to Chicago. All the delegates were registered Republicans, of course. But personal loyalties had come to mean more in California politics over the years than devotion to party, and as a practical matter the Chicago-bound Californians were really either "Warren men," "Knowland men," or "Nixon men," bound together by an election law that seemed to require them to vote for Warren until he freed them to do otherwise. As the streamlined train sped east, Nixon gave his own followers a rundown on the latest preconvention developments. In essence, he reported that the Eisenhower drive was picking up and said it looked as though the General could win on the first ballot. As expected, bits and pieces of the Nixon report filtered through the non-Nixon sections of the train. Warren men became furious. They complained that the junior Senator had breached senior Senator Knowland's edict that California delegates would refuse even to consider an alternate to Warren. Several Warrenites "confided" to some newspaper correspondents that Nixon tried to entice California votes away from Warren in return for second place on the Eisenhower ticket.[4]

The convention opened on July 7 with a floor squabble between Eisenhower and Taft leaders over sixty-eight Southern delegates that were temporarily seated by the National Committee. The Eisenhower group offered a solution with a snappy title—"Fair Play Amendment"—which appealed to one of the least controversial of American emotions and neatly complemented the moral plane on which Eisenhower orators said they would pitch their arguments. The issue over a few Southern delegates thus was boosted into a struggle between good and evil. The Eisenhower team had launched what the General was later to proclaim his "Great Crusade," and as the nation's voters watched on television, the exasperated Taft team argued in vain that *theirs* was really the honest-to-goodness "Fair Play" position. By voting time Nixon, Knowland, and Warren were united on the issue, and California cast its seventy votes for morality and fair play. As is well known, the vote was more a test of strength between Taft and Eisenhower than anything else, and the Eisenhower side won with the help of men, like Warren and Stassen, who probably would have preferred to sit out that particular test. Nonetheless, it was an Eisenhower victory and, although the nominees were not selected until July 11, Taft was through by noon July 7—and so were the hopes of a Taft-Eisenhower deadlock nurtured by dark horses Warren and Stassen.

Eisenhower leaders were careful not to divert attention from their main goal until it was fully achieved. They avoided public discussion of side issues during the four convention days and nights

---

[4] Before the convention was over a couple of angry Warren enthusiasts laid the groundwork for the "Nixon Fund" sensation that was to dominate the headlines and air waves in mid-September and threaten to ruin Nixon and defeat Eisenhower.

before balloting was to begin for the presidential nomination. But published reports that the inner circle had agreed already on the General's running mate had to be denied to ensure the continued support of some contenders for the Vice-Presidency who controlled substantial blocs of convention votes. Thus Senator Henry Cabot Lodge, chairman of the Eisenhower organization, laughed off a column in which John S. Knight, editor and publisher of the Chicago *Daily News*, predicted two days before the balloting that Eisenhower and Nixon would win. Top-rung political figures know that Knight has ready access to the best possible news sources and is an exceedingly careful reporter. Therefore, his article created a great stir at the convention, and Lodge found himself compelled to state that there had been no discussion of a vice-presidential candidate. Nixon's stock reply to questioners remained: "That's news to me."[5]

Murray Chotiner, who was with Nixon much of the time in Chicago, said he doubts that the Senator thought he would be picked. Chotiner was managing Senator Knowland's campaign for re-election in 1952, but it was over by convention time because Knowland won both Republican and Democratic nominations in the June primaries. "Herb Brownell had some conversations with me at the convention," Chotiner told me. "He wanted my opinion as to Knowland and Nixon. He wanted to know who would be the better campaigner, who would add more strength to the ticket. I gave him my candid opinion, which was that Nixon had a shade as a campaigner and also appealed more to independents and young people. It was just a shade in favor of Nixon. Brownell asked how Nixon's nomination would react on Warren. I said I didn't know but that there had not been any warmth between the two. He asked me what Knowland's reaction would be. Nixon had said before the convention that, if it were a choice between him and Knowland, it should go to Knowland. When I told Helen Knowland [the

---

[5] One of Lodge's principal aides said to me long afterwards: "I saw Dick the very first night of the convention itself and told him things were shaping up his way, that he was going to get it [the vice-presidential nomination]. I whispered it to him. He shrugged. I think he did not believe me."

Senator's wife] what Dick had said—that Bill would make a wonderful candidate, that he was entitled to it—Helen said, 'You tell Dick not to think of saying anything of it, to go right ahead, and if it is awfully close not to think for a moment how Bill would feel about it.' I reported that to Brownell, and he said, 'Well, if Bill Knowland's wife feels that way about it, why that must be it.' "

The night before the convention was to vote for nominees, Nixon reviewed his situation at great length with his wife. He had begun to feel that there was substance to all the talk and he might be offered second place. Mrs. Nixon stuck by her doubts.

At 4:00 A.M. Nixon telephoned Chotiner's hotel room. "What are you doing?" he asked. "Sleeping," replied Chotiner. "Do you want to come down?" Nixon asked.

Chotiner said: "I went down to his room, where he was sitting talking with Pat. He said, 'What do you think? If this thing is offered to me, do you think I should take it?' I said, 'Yes, I do.' He said, 'Why?'

"I could tell that Pat had been talking against it. I said, 'Dick, you're a junior senator from California and you will always be a junior senator from California. Bill Knowland is young and he's healthy, and unless something should happen to him, you will always be second man in California. The junior Senator from California doesn't amount to anything. There comes a time when you have to go up or out. Suppose you are a candidate [for vice-president] and we lose? You're still the junior Senator and haven't lost anything. If you win, and are elected vice-president, and at the end of four years you become all washed up, you could open a law office in Whittier and have all the business in town. Any man who quits political life as vice-president as young as you are in years certainly hasn't lost a thing.'

"I urged him very strongly to take it," Chotiner added. "But he was still debating it at five A.M. when I left to go back to bed."

When the balloting for the presidential nomination began on July 11, the confident Eisenhower leaders labored mightily to hold their delegates while the desperate Taftites worked feverishly to pry some loose. By 1:50 P.M. all the palpitating was over and done with. The convention recessed until 4:00 P.M. to give the party's new standard-bearer time to pass the word about whom he wanted for a running mate.

As major domo of the experienced political group running the Eisenhower operation, Brownell submitted Nixon's name to the General. Eisenhower agreed Nixon would be a good choice, Brownell told me, but was "surprised" to learn "that the presidential candidate could choose the Vice-President as a matter of long-standing custom." After some other possible candidates were discussed, "it was clear that Nixon was the one to be chosen." Nevertheless, Eisenhower said he would leave it to Brownell "to get the collective judgment of the leaders of the party," and they were to understand that "Nixon would be very acceptable."

Brownell summoned about two dozen representative Eisenhower leaders to a meeting at the Conrad Hilton Hotel, across the street from the Blackstone where Eisenhower was staying. At the same time proponents of various candidates for the nomination were invited to present their cases.

Paul G. Hoffman, former foreign aid director and a chief organizer of independent Republicans and Democrats for Eisenhower, recalls, "The first person to be discussed was Taft." Several other names also were brought up "and knocked down," he said, "then Nixon's was offered." Everyone in the room had an opportunity to state his opinion. Hoffman's was: "Nixon fills all the requirements."

Dewey, the first powerful Republican figure to propose both Eisenhower and Nixon nominations, had this earnest recollection of the committee session: "There were a lot of people with a lot of views. I waited until they had gotten down through the list. I didn't say much about it, until finally they had gotten from the East all the way across to the West. Then I named Nixon as the logical nominee."

The committee thereupon voted unanimously for Nixon, and Brownell picked up two different telephones to give the news simultaneously to Eisenhower and Nixon.

Nixon had lent his car to a newspaperman, Earl Behrens, of

the San Francisco *Chronicle*. No taxis were in sight. On a plea from Chotiner, a parking lot guard produced both an automobile and a motorcycle escort.

"Dick was calm and pensive," Chotiner recalled. "As we were speeding to the General's headquarters, he said, 'Murray, when we get up there, will you call the folks at home? They're probably watching TV. Tell them it looks as if I'm going to be nominated for vice-president.' I said, 'Sure.'

"We went up in the elevator at the Blackstone. I've never seen so many newspapermen in my life. The elevator doors opened, and the flash bulbs started popping. Nixon said, 'Boy! They already know it.' Dick went on in the General's suite, and I called Whittier and got his sister-in-law. She said, 'Oh, we know all about it already. It's been on television.' It seemed to me that Dick had been in the position of being the last to learn about it."

Eisenhower introduced Nixon to Mrs. Eisenhower, and the men sat down to talk. Then Nixon left to get ready for his appearance before the convention. There were many telephone calls to make. One of the first was to his senior colleague. Knowland said when he answered the telephone, "I was told by someone whose name I don't recollect . . . that Dick would like to talk with me. Dick came to the phone and he asked whether I would be prepared to place his name in nomination. I had already at that time been informed he was the choice as the nominee for vice-president. I forget whether it was Brownell or someone else who informed me."

At the convention hall most of the morning's excitement and anger had subsided, and the delegates milled around, swapped rumors, and ignored the speeches scheduled at the last minute to kill time. Finally, serious business was resumed at about 5:30. Mrs. Clare Boothe Luce announced she would not propose Senator Margaret Chase Smith for the nomination, as planned, because Mrs. Smith "does not wish to create on this floor any division of loyalties which have not already existed." Then Knowland presented the name of Nixon—the man whose "bulldog determination" enabled "the government to hunt out and unravel the Alger Hiss case". . . a campaigner "who puts forth more of his heart into a campaign [than anyone else Knowland has known]". . . and "a young man who gives to the Republican ticket an appeal to the young men and young women of this nation."

There were four seconding speeches, then Governor John S. Fine, of Pennsylvania, moved that Nixon be nominated by acclamation —and he was. Within an hour Nixon had delivered an acceptance speech which opened with the question: "Haven't we got a wonderful candidate for President of the United States?" and Eisenhower had proclaimed his "Great Crusade for freedom in America and freedom in the world" in an address of acceptance which began with words of congratulations to "this convention on your selection of the nominee for the Vice-Presidency."

The television audience that evening included Nixon's two daughters. According to friends, their reactions were mixed. Patricia, six, reportedly said: "I want everybody to vote for my daddy." Julie, four, is said to have wailed: "I want Mommy."

At the outset Eisenhower informed his running mate that he viewed the Vice-Presidency as an important, meaningful office and believed the Vice-President should be an active participant with full knowledge of all that went on in an administration and not a "figurehead." Nixon agreed entirely and started immediately to become the hardest-campaigning vice-presidential candidate in American politics. During his first day as the nominee he held a press conference (the platform was too ambiguous on civil rights and labor, he said, and the weaknesses would be remedied in campaign speeches); he met with Congressional campaign leaders to devise a co-ordinated drive for the Presidency and control of Congress; he told the Republican National Committee the main campaign issues were "the Truman record" and "Communism at home and abroad" and stated that "any Democratic candidate can be defeated on those issues"; and he joined General Eisenhower at the first of several precampaign strategy sessions in which the respective campaign roles of Eisenhower and Nixon were worked out, with Eisenhower to emphasize the positive and Nixon to lead the offensive against the opposition. Democrats called this a "high road-low road" strategy.

Two weeks after the Republican convention the Democratic National Convention nominated Adlai E. Stevenson for president and Senator John Sparkman of Alabama for vice-president. Earlier Stevenson had compared Nixon unfavorably with the septuagenarian Democratic Vice-President, Alben Barkley, and remarked that "the Republican party makes even its young men seem old; the Democratic party makes even its old men seem young." Now, Nixon described Stevenson as "a 'me-too' candidate in reverse." Furthermore, he said the Democratic nominee was "Jack Kroll's candidate; Jake Arvey's candidate; and—this is his greatest handicap—he's Harry Truman's candidate." (Kroll was director of the CIO-Political Action Committee; Arvey was Democratic boss of Illinois.)

On July 28 practically the whole of Whittier turned out for a Nixon home-coming celebration in the Whittier College stadium. Governor Warren, the chief welcomer, declared, "All the people of California are rejoicing at your success, Dick." A week later the Governor told a meeting of the California Republican Central Committee in Sacramento that Nixon's nomination "is like a breath of fresh air to this country, and I believe the people will respond to it."

Nothing remained for Chotiner to do as Knowland's campaign manager since the senior California Senator was re-elected by virtue of winning both parties' primaries in June. So Chotiner became manager of Nixon's campaign. According to the master plan developed at Eisenhower-Nixon strategy sessions, Nixon was to begin on September 17 with a whistle-stop tour of the West Coast. Nixon wanted first to test his "basic speech" and rub the rough edges from his relatively inexperienced campaign organization, so he introduced something new to politics—the trial run. He scheduled a four-day barnstorming tour of then-safely-Republican Maine, much as Broadway shows try out in New Haven before opening on Broadway. "It paid off," said a Nixon strategist. "It was good for the candidate, the campaign manager, the trip men, the advance men, the publicity men, radio and TV men, and everybody

(99)

else in the campaign." Among things the candidate learned was to be more cautious in complying with requests of photographers. At a lobster plant in Rockport the Nixons were asked to pose picking up lobsters. Mrs. Nixon hesitated. Nixon said there was nothing to it, that the big ones are fat and lazy and move slowly. Then he picked up the biggest one he could find—and its claws flashed open and went for his throat. Mrs. Nixon screamed. The lobster clutched at the candidate's lapel. Photoflash bulbs exploded. And then everyone laughed as Nixon finally freed himself.

Shortly before the all-out campaign began a Gallup Poll reported that only 45 per cent of the voters could name the Republican candidate for vice-president. Just 32 per cent could name the Democratic candidate and only one in four knew the identity of both. This was not unusual for vice-presidential nominees—or even vice-presidents. But Nixon's name managed to move swiftly from the relatively unknown to the well known.

Within a week of embarking on his first major whistle-stop tour Nixon became the most talked-about, most controversial, and, as it developed, the most politically fortunate vice-presidential candidate in history—thanks to a nationwide uproar over an $18,000 "fund" maintained for Nixon by his political friends in California.

8

In establishing the "Nixon Fund" the Senator's boosters tried to envision any troubles it might cause. "We endeavored to set it up so that any possible criticism of it would be completely disarmed," recalled Dana C. Smith, the Pasadena lawyer who became trustee and manager of contributions and expenditures. The objective was to provide money to enable Nixon to campaign continuously for the Republican party and his own re-election instead of waiting until his newly won Senate seat was at stake in 1956. Nixon approved.

Neither he nor his California admirers divined in 1950 that he would be candidate for vice-president within two years. Even then, the fund might have gone unnoticed if Eisenhower and Nixon hadn't sold their Crusade for Political Purity so well. America had to choose, they averred, between looseness and corruption under the Democrats and angelic honesty under the Republicans.

General Eisenhower was stressing the need to change the moral climate in Washington and the need for unsullied public officials the day the first stories about the Nixon Fund appeared. It was Thursday, September 18. The General, campaigning in Iowa, promised to drive the "crooks and cronies" from power and bring a Republican "Honest Deal" to Washington to replace the Democratic "Fair Deal." "When we are through," he declared, "the experts in shady and shoddy government operations will be on their way back to the shadowy haunts in the subcellars of American politics from which they came."

The issue was further highlighted that day by Adlai Stevenson, who was electioneering in Connecticut, and by Governor James F. Byrnes, of South Carolina. Byrnes, once a power in the Democratic party and still a significant force in its Southern wing, put Dixie's stamp of approval on General Eisenhower. Stevenson would be "under too great an obligation to those responsible for the 'mess in Washington,' " he said. "It will take a man like Eisenhower" to clean it up.

Stevenson made a speech on campaign ethics. Ethics were more important than victory, he said. "Victory can be bought too dearly." Observers assumed this was a jibe at Nixon, who had launched the major assault phase of the Republican campaign the night before with a rally that resembled a religious revival.

"What corruption means to all of us is that every time we pick up our paper, every day, we read about a scandal," said Nixon. "You know, as a matter of fact, this administration is going to go down in history as a scandal-a-day administration because you read about another bribe, you read about another tax fix, you read about another gangster getting favors from the government . . . and are sick and tired of it."

Bernard Brennan and Murray Chotiner, then Nixon's principal political lieutenants, had proposed the year-round campaign in 1950. Creating a special fund was Dana Smith's idea. He was acquainted with arrangements to finance public figures of modest means whose expenses for off-season politicking could not be paid from formal campaign treasuries. He knew how to shake the money tree in their behalf. In 1950 Smith was treasurer of Nixon's campaign and during the uproar in 1952 he was chairman of Volunteers for Eisenhower in Southern California. "I do not know of any instance in which . . . Senator Nixon . . . ever did anything for any contributor to his political expenses, whether or not strictly campaign funds, which he would not have done for any responsible constituent," Smith stated.

Senator Nixon's gross salary was $12,500. He was also provided $2,500, tax-free, for general expenses, a maximum of $2,000 for telephone, telegraph and stationery bills, $70,000 for a staff, and one round-trip home per session. Furthermore, he earned a bit more for lectures and after-dinner speeches, but it all could hardly finance his operations. In his freshman year as a senator he crossed the continent three times on speaking tours, went halfway across— and back—thirteen more times, made three visits to the South, and ten up and down the East Coast. His bill for Christmas cards alone was $4,237.54.

"After the very difficult 1950 campaign," said Nixon, "the people who had been active—my finance committee as well as others—sat down with me and said: 'We want you to start campaigning right now for 1956, and we think that the way to do it is to have available the funds to make speeches, make trips to California and so forth.' We discussed the practical possibilities. They asked me, 'What can you do?' Of course, as you are aware, most congressmen and senators have a campaign fund unless they are independently wealthy. I didn't ask them for any money. The idea of the year-around campaign was theirs. They said: 'We want you to keep in touch with all your [campaign workers].' They knew that when I was in the House I had sent out Christmas cards [to all who helped in the House campaigns], for example. I said, 'Do you realize that we had over 25,000 people as workers in the Senate campaign?' So it was worked out. [What was created] was simply a campaign fund."

Smith agreed to become its manager. A special trust account was opened in Smith's name at a Pasadena bank. Audits were scheduled. And an estimated budget of $16,000 a year was agreed to. An orthodox public appeal for money was felt to be too complicated and unnecessary, so it was decided to solicit the more generous backers of Nixon's campaigns for Congress and the Senate.

Donations were solicited by telephone, personal contact and mail. "A group of us here, after the dust of battle had settled and we found that Dick was safely elected, began to realize that electing him was only part of what we really wanted to accomplish," Smith wrote potential contributors. "We not only wanted a good man in the Senate from this state, but we wanted him to continue to sell effectively to the people of California the economic and political systems which we all believe in. It was immediately apparent to us that this would take money and that Dick himself was not in a position financially to provide it. We have therefore set up a pool, to which a considerable number of us here are contributing on an annual basis, to meet expenditures which seemed necessary to accomplish this object. . . . We have limited contributions to a minimum of $100 a year and a maximum of $500 . . . so that it can never be charged that anyone is contributing so much as to think that he is entitled to special favors."

The type of activities the fund would support were listed as transportation and hotel expenses, air-mail and long-distance telephone charges, preparation and dissemination of Nixon's speeches, questionnaires, newsletters and the like, the Senator's Christmas cards to campaign workers and contributors, radio, television, advertising, and general publicity.

Smith assured those he solicited that "nobody is drawing any salary or other compensation out of this, so you can count on it that the money will be effectively used where it will do all of us, including Dick, the most good." Furthermore, he wrote, "We have only included in our group [of contributors] people who have supported Dick from the start, so that it does not provide any way for people who are 'second guessers' to make any claim on the Senator's particular interest."

Many responded more liberally with praise than with cash, so the base was broadened. The privilege of contributing was extended to late-comers on the Nixon band-wagon, and Smith asked the United Republican Finance Committee of Los Angeles County, the regular party organization's treasury unit, to take over the Nixon fund—contributor lists, bankbooks, bills and all. However, the committee said it couldn't because its powers were too limited.

On June 28, 29, and 30, 1951, Smith, Chotiner and Brennan went on a barnstorming operation to urge state-wide support. They addressed Republican groups from San Francisco to San Diego. Everywhere the party faithful acclaimed the program. But the response was disappointing. In September Smith again solicited individuals by mail. The fund was solvent mostly because Nixon was spending less than anticipated.

By primary day in June, 1952, Nixon's associates had explained the fund to about five hundred possible donors, who, in turn, told another five hundred or more throughout California.[1] Yet checks had come from fewer than one hundred, and they added up to a total far below expectations. So Nixon decided that the regular party fund-raising organization had to assume the responsibility if it wanted any more co-operation from him. Nixon wrote Smith on June 9, 1952:

> I think the time has now come for us to have a showdown with Republican Finance on obtaining assistance for our program. I believe that we should make our requests modest.

He suggested $10,000 a year from the southern California organization and $5,000 from the northern.

> I think that this request can be justified on several grounds. The most important one is that the purpose of all these off-year expenditures is, in the final analysis, to assure the election. Another good argument is that this type of expenditure is taken care of customarily by Republican Finance in other states like New York and Pennsylvania.
> I feel very strongly on this matter, and frankly, I intend to condition my future co-operation with Republican Finance on whether they support our program. After all, I am the only man who appeared at the various Republican Finance dinners who has received no benefit whatever from them. This, of course, was due to the fact that I did not happen to be running this year. As you are aware, appearing at such a dinner is not politically advantageous and by reason of having to accept such engagements it became necessary for me to turn down some open meetings which would have been much better from a political standpoint for me to accept.

Nixon added that he felt "tremendously indebted to our special group for what they have done to make our programs possible in the past, but I don't feel that they should continue to bear this burden indefinitely."

In a confidential reply dated June 11, 1952, Smith complained

[1] Paul G. Hoffman said, "There was general knowledge of the fund's existence. I would have contributed if I had been asked to, but was in Washington at the time the initial fund was raised."

to Nixon that the Republican leaders in San Francisco had been promising a $5,000 contribution for eight months, but "it is apparently more convenient for them to forget about it." Despite these and other collection troubles, Smith suggested that the fund goal be raised to "a minimum of $20,000 rather than $15,000 because we know that it is very desirable to step up your activities after this year, as your own re-election year begins to come closer and you would not have to soft-pedal your activities on account of a Knowland campaign coming up." (Senator Knowland had, in fact, been re-elected by virtue of winning both the Democratic and Republican nominations in the primaries a week before Smith wrote this letter.)

"As things stand now, I still have not paid the last $1,000 of that printing bill at the Capital City Engraving Company and have on hand $879.24," Smith continued. "I do not like to cut this fund down any lower than that to make a further payment on the Capital bill. I do not see much additional money coming in, short of another general appeal to the previous contributors, which I had hoped to avoid. Bernie [Brennan] said he had a promise of an additional $500 a couple of weeks ago, but it has not shown up. If that comes in promptly, I could clean up the Capital bill and still have a little in the bank to take care of your convention expenses and so forth. After the convention I might have a little more time to scare up enough more money here and there to see us through the summer, even if Northern California continues not to come through."

Stray whispers about the fund were started at the Republican National Convention in July by a couple of California delegates who made a project of confiding to strangers that Nixon was despised by fellow Californians, that he "double-crossed" Governor Warren, and that he was being "kept" by a band of favor-seeking millionaires. Variations of the story soon reached some news correspondents, of course. But the 1952 Republican Convention was a scandalmonger's paradise and the Nixon story was lost, like a nursery rhyme in a sea of garish murder mysteries. In fierce battle between Eisenhower and Taft partisans no reputation of importance was spared, and gossipers among the Republican faithful became as suspect as the dirt they peddled.

One version of the Nixon story, as heard by Peter Edson, Washington political columnist for Newspaper Enterprise Association, appeared to merit checking, however. It was that Nixon got a "supplementary salary" of $20,000 a year from a hundred California businessmen, each of whom chipped in $200. Edson asked several California political correspondents and editors, including James Bassett, of the Los Angeles *Mirror*, who later became Nixon's campaign press secretary. None put any credence in the story. Two months later—on September 14—Edson appeared with Nixon on the television program "Meet the Press" and afterward he asked the Senator about the alleged supplementary salary.

"Without a moment's hesitation, he told me that the rumor as I had it was all wrong," Edson wrote subsequently. "But there was a story there and it would be all right for me to use it. He didn't attempt to duck the question in any way." The Senator suggested that Edson telephone Dana Smith in Pasadena for details, because Smith ran the fund and knew much more about it than Nixon did, himself. Edson called the next day, and Smith discussed the general background and specific aspects of the fund. He also suggested that other states adopt the plan to keep senators who had no independent incomes from having to bow to outside "pressure."

Later that day Smith reviewed the fund operation again, this time with Leo Katcher, of the New York *Post*; Richard Donovan, of *Reporter* magazine; and Ernest Breasher, of the Los Angeles *Daily News*. These reporters were digging into Nixon's background for biographical material that went beyond the mostly favorable sketches previously published. Smith told them substantially what he had told Edson.

Meanwhile, Nixon left Washington for California, with a stop in Denver to review with General Eisenhower final plans for the campaign offensive which was to begin at 8:30 P.M. on September 17. After the chat with Edson, Nixon turned his mind to other matters. Senator and Mrs. Nixon arrived in California at nightfall, September 16. A representative of the Los Angeles *Daily News* mentioned to Bassett, Nixon's press secretary, that his paper had a story for release on Thursday about a Nixon fund. Bassett told

Nixon, who said it probably was Edson's story and therefore an accurate one because Edson was to get the complete picture from Dana Smith.

Richard Nixon is about as superstitious as the average successful politician. He is respectful of the mysterious power called "luck." Thus his first stumping tour of the presidential campaign began at Pomona, a community in Los Angeles County where he had started his surprisingly successful campaigns for Congress and Senate. The send-off rally on Wednesday night brought 15,000 well-wishers to the railroad heading. A flag-waving delegation from Whittier was led by Nixon's aging parents. Governor Warren officiated. The Senator's whistle-stop route was up central California through Oregon and Washington, the same route Governor Stevenson had followed the week before. Nixon promised to "nail down those lies" told by the Democratic candidate. He paraded the basic Republican assault weapons, labeled "Korea, Communism, Corruption, and Costs." And he declared that "no administration with the greedy, gouging, grumbling history of the Truman regime" could accomplish the great things for America which General Eisenhower proposed.

As the rally wound up, the eleven-car campaign train started slowly to pull out of Pomona, with Nixon, on the back platform, imploring one and all: "If you believe as I believe, come along on this great Crusade . . ." The tracks stood out under angled floodlights, creating a vision of the path to glory. Hundreds of magnetized listeners found themselves following behind the crawling train with Nixon's outstretched arms seemingly their goal. If it were possible, thousands of television viewers would have joined the trek which ended when the train rounded a curve a hundred yards from the starting point, and the trackside lights were turned off.

It had been a good meeting and all aboard the Nixon Special were gay in anticipation of the campaign ahead. Most of the staff had been through it before. The only newcomers to the entourage were William P. Rogers, who later was appointed attorney general by President Eisenhower, and Miss Rose Mary Woods, the Senator's executive secretary, who became head of the vice-presidential staff. Neither had experienced a political campaign before. Rogers came along as a sort of assistant-without-portfolio on the campaign train after Nixon "assured me that nothing ever happens to a candidate for vice-president."

A messenger from Republican headquarters in Los Angeles met the train at a water stop before midnight. He brought word that a "fund" story to be printed in newspapers the next day could cause trouble. Nixon summoned a few advisers to his private car at 1:00 A.M. The fund was reviewed in considerable detail. Rogers, who hadn't heard of it before, gave as his judgment that no impropriety was involved; therefore, "the facts" would neutralize possible criticism. Chotiner, who was reputed to possess an extra, supernatural sense that spotted things of political importance before they even germinated, was not disturbed either. "Hell, there's nothing to this thing; it's ridiculous," he said.

Because of a four-hour time lag between the east and west coasts, the Nixon fund story was already stirring political tempers in New York and Washington on Thursday, September 18, before Nixon had begun the first full day of his journey. The New York *Post* was on the streets at ten o'clock, its front page dominated by the words: "Secret Nixon Fund!" The story was on the second page under a two-line banner headline that said: "Secret Rich Men's Trust Fund Keeps Nixon in Style Far Beyond His Salary." Peter Edson's column was printed later that morning and afternoon in other newspapers. It was written as a straight news story, and lacked the speculative flamboyance that made the New York *Post* article seem more sensational. The United Press and the Associated Press relayed the substance of both reports to other daily newspapers.

Word reached the Nixon train at Bakersfield. Nothing had appeared yet in California newspapers, however, and the large, early-morning trainside audience was friendly. When the Senator concluded his speech with the *big* question, "Who can clean up the mess in Washington?" the crowd responded, "Ike can!"

The press contingent started to grow at Tulare, the second stop.

Nixon refused to comment about the fund, however, and at Fresno, the third stop, reporters were barred from Nixon's private car.

Tension on the train mounted with the rumors, which grew and multiplied as the morning wore on. In the early afternoon at Merced —the fifth stop—Nixon issued a brief statement outlining the "facts" of the fund and declaring: "I might have put my wife on the federal payroll as did the Democratic nominee for vice-president . . . nor have I been accepting law fees on the side while serving as a member of Congress. I prefer to play completely square with the taxpayers."[2]

Meanwhile, in Washington, panic groups clanged at Republican and Democratic National Headquarters. The Democrats, surprised and delighted by a windfall of incalculable value, rushed to the offensive. National Chairman Stephen Mitchell demanded—via a mimeographed statement, press interviews, and radio and television appearances—that Eisenhower throw Nixon off the ticket at once or eat his fulsome observations on "public morals."

The Republicans, fearing the consequences of a possible scandal and at the same time hoping to mousetrap the excited Democrats, launched an offensive and defensive simultaneously. Robert Humphreys, public relations director and senior staff member then at headquarters, issued a statement in the name of Senator Karl Mundt labeling the whole thing a "left-wing smear" and a "filthy" maneuver by a pro-Stevenson newspaper. He also called the Eisenhower train in the Midwest for permission (which Chairman Arthur Summerfield readily gave) to commit the national party organization to a policy of "down the line support for Dick." Late in the afternoon Humphreys accepted a call from Republican Headquarters in Chicago. "We've been trying for days to interest someone in a Stevenson fund we have uncovered," said a voice. "It is worse than the Nixon fund we just read about." Humphreys replied, in effect, fine, but let's worry about Nixon now and deal with Stevenson later.

[2] Senator Sparkman, the Democratic candidate for vice-president, campaigning some three thousand miles away in Florida, snapped that there was "nothing sub rosa" about the job his wife had in his office. "She has given excellent service," he declared.

General Eisenhower's eighteen-car campaign train—the "Look Ahead, Neighbor" Special—was passing among the voters of Iowa and Nebraska. In reply to questions in the morning, Press Secretary James Hagerty said, "We never comment on a New York *Post* story." In the late afternoon he said the General would have nothing to say. The General's staff was saying plenty, however, in the privacy of compartments and washrooms beyond earshot of the candidate, at one end of the train, and the reporters, at the other. All day they held conferences, analyzed reports and rumors, and weighed the problems of switching vice-presidential candidates in mid-campaign.

At strategy meetings the month before Governor Sherman Adams, chief of the Eisenhower staff, and Chotiner, the Nixon manager, formulated a new, foolproof liaison plan to keep the two campaign teams in intimate and constant touch during the final period of electioneering when a mistake by one of the candidates might be compounded unwittingly into a disaster by the other. The Adams-Chotiner plan set up direct communications between the respective echelons of the two teams. Thus Eisenhower would deal with Nixon, and vice versa; Chotiner would talk with Adams or Senator Fred A. Seaton; Hagerty and Bassett would discuss press matters, man to man, and so forth. As sometimes happens with even the best-laid plans, however, this one failed in the emergency of September 18 because Eisenhower simply didn't call Nixon and Nixon didn't call Eisenhower.

Newspapers picked up in the evening along the route of the Nixon Special in California reported that Midwestern audiences were reacting favorably to Eisenhower's charges that the Truman administration's legacies to the nation were "a problem of morality in government," "crazy federal spending," and "deficits that cheapen our money." A hoped-for statement of the General's unqualified support and faith had not materialized. Nothing had been heard from that direction, in fact, except questions—and, of course, rumors. The Nixon party might have viewed the General's silence more charitably if it had been privy to a decision of the Eisenhower strategists. The decision was to break the news about the fund to

(111)

the General *after* his principal speeches so as not to risk upsetting him.

A large and friendly crowd awaited Nixon at Sacramento, the ninth and last stop that Thursday. But he sensed a strangeness in the reception committee of politicians. Instead of elbowing and maneuvering to be first in line, some seemed to hesitate when the time came to pose for pictures with the Senator. As his campaign special continued up the valley that night a gloomy and angry vice-presidential candidate sought the solitude of his compartment; and Pat Nixon, blinking back the tears she seldom tolerated, wondered if any political office was worth the sacrifice of a good name.

A half continent away that night *one* important individual on the Eisenhower train had reached a firm conclusion. Republican Chairman Summerfield had before him a report on the procedure for changing a candidate. In the mass of unnoticed resolutions adopted routinely during the rush to adjourn the National Convention was one that left the responsibility entirely to the National Committee. If Nixon withdrew, the Republican organization probably would split irretrievably in a fight over a successor. Summerfield redoubled his conviction that Nixon should stay.

Two newspaper articles set the mood on the Nixon train for Friday, September 19. One was an official announcement that the California franchise tax board would investigate the Nixon fund. The other was a "notice" issued by the Democratic National Committee to editors and correspondents citing criminal law on "bribery and graft . . . by members of Congress." The expense fund stories had blossomed overnight into implications of tax cheating, bribery and graft.

At Democratic Headquarters in Sacramento early that morning the northern California campaign manager for Stevenson suggested that Young Democrats could strike a blow for the cause and enjoy themselves at the same time by heckling Nixon about the fund. Glen Wilson, a party field man, snapped up the idea, loaded his car with loud-voiced youngsters, and streaked off for Marysville, Nixon's first stop. The Republican candidate had concluded his talk and the train was pulling away slowly when the hecklers ar-

(112)

rived. They bounded from the car, and one of them shouted, "Tell 'em about the $16,000!"

Nixon wheeled around and yelled, "Hold the train! Hold the train!" It stopped; the crowd pressed forward; the grim-faced Nixon paused to control his anger, pointed to the questioner, recognizable in a spotted tie, and answered:

"You folks know the work that I did investigating Communists in the United States. Ever since I have done that work, the Communists, the Left-Wingers, have been fighting me with every smear that they have been able to. Even when I received the nomination for the Vice-Presidency, I want you folks to know—and I'm going to reveal it today for the first time—I was warned that if I continued to attack the Communists and crooks in this government they would continue to smear me, and, believe me, you can expect that they will continue to do so. They started it yesterday—you saw it in the morning papers. They tried to say that I had taken the money, $16,000.

"What they didn't point out is this: that what I was doing was saving you money, rather than charging the expenses of my office, which were in excess of the amounts which were allowed by the taxpayers and allowed under the law, rather than taking that money.

"Rather than using the money, the taxpayers' moneys for those purposes, what did I do? What I did was to have those expenses paid by the people back home who were interested in seeing that the information concerning what was going on in Washington was spread among the people of their state. [Long applause]

"I'll tell you what some of them do. They put their wives on the payroll, taking your money and using it for that purpose. And Pat Nixon has worked in my office night, after night, after night, and I can say this, and I say it proudly, she has never been on the government payroll since I have been in Washington, D.C. [Applause]

"Point two: What else would you do? Do you want me to go on and do what some of these people are doing? Take fat legal fees on the side? During the time I've been in Washington—and I'm proud of this—I've never taken a legal fee, although as a lawyer I could legally but not ethically have done so. And I'm never going to in

(113)

the future, because I think that's a violation of a trust which my office has . . ."

The crowd cheered, the heckler scowled. Nixon waved and smiled, sternly.

Eisenhower ended his silence on the fund in Kansas City that morning. He predicted "the facts will show that Nixon would not compromise with what is right." The General's comment was relayed immediately to the Nixon train—and spirits were lifted a little, at least until the train reached Chico, where a telephone call was waiting. It was Senator Seaton, with Eisenhower's first message for his running mate since the fund uproar had started. Seaton told Chotiner, then Nixon, that the General was anxious to get to the bottom of this thing. Chotiner said that was mighty fine, but what more does the General require than the Senator's word? Seaton implied that the General might answer that himself in a direct telephone conversation which might be arranged in the next day or so.

The talk with Seaton delayed Nixon's Chico speech thirty-four minutes. But the crowd waited, and listened attentively, as Nixon beat the hecklers to the fund question by asking it himself. The answer was much like the one he gave in Marysville, and he followed it up with the safest promise a politician ever made on an American election stump: that a Republican administration would fire Dean Acheson as secretary of state. The crowd roared approval, and the Nixon Special proceeded north.

The fund issue was becoming a national sensation. Commentators analyzed, and speculated; radio and television programs were interrupted for late bulletins; the Democrats, sensing an opportunity to nullify the corruption issue, which they considered phony anyway, jibed sarcastically at Eisenhower's "Crusade"; Adlai Stevenson announced he would reserve judgment until the Republicans explained how Nixon had used the money; Democratic Chairman Mitchell wondered when the General would "cast away" his erring running mate. Among Republicans, Senator Taft flatly approved the Nixon action and scoffed at talk of changing candidates, and

Oregon's Governor McKay demonstrated his backing by boarding the Nixon train with flags flying, a band playing, and practically all the state's Republican hierarchy in tow. But most other Republicans of consequence either crossed their fingers and hoped for the best, in silence, or sent Eisenhower and his staff assessments of the situation that showed Nixon had to be dumped or the ticket would lose. At an Eisenhower whistle stop in Missouri a telephone call from General Lucius D. Clay, in New York, created a stir because the candidate halted his campaign speech abruptly to take it. Clay was an intimate of Eisenhower's and a key figure in Citizens for Eisenhower, a movement which rather looked down on regular Republican organization people as *politicians*. Although the nature of that September 19 telephone call was never disclosed, it was commonly believed—and frequently reported, in print—that Clay advised Eisenhower to get a new vice-presidential candidate. Long afterwards, in 1958, Clay told me that was not so. "I personally did not take a position on that particular thing," he said. "All I asked [Eisenhower] to do was please not to commit himself or make any statements until Herbert Brownell had been able to reach him at his stop that night and they could talk it over. I have complete confidence in the sagacity and the intelligence of Herb. He did get there that night and they talked it all over—and out of that came the decisions which led to the radio talk" (Nixon's nationally broadcast explanation the following Tuesday).

The most important telephone call made *from* the Eisenhower train on September 19 was to Paul Hoffman. Sherman Adams made it at Eisenhower's direction. Although he still may not know it, Adams reached Hoffman in the Pasadena Hospital, recovering from a head injury caused by a stray golf ball. "He asked me to begin an immediate investigation of the Nixon Fund, to find out if it was clean," Hoffman recollected. From his hospital bed Hoffman retained Gibson, Dunn and Crutcher, a Los Angeles law firm, and the Price, Waterhouse accounting organization. Fifty lawyers and accountants—the cream of both firms—went to work at once and stayed at it over the weekend.

Adams also had telephoned Senator Knowland in Hawaii—as

did Brownell—to urge that he join the Eisenhower train as quickly as possible. Knowland was scheduled to do so in about a week, but Adams and Brownell told him he was needed immediately in the mounting crisis. Knowland was not aware until after he arrived that there had been guarded talk among Eisenhower strategists about having him on tap as a substitute should Nixon be dropped. The moment Knowland boarded the Look Ahead, Neighbor Special, however, he became a vigorous backstop for Chairman Summerfield, until then the only unqualified pro-Nixon voice around Eisenhower.

During the afternoon of September 19 Eisenhower issued a statement. He had "long admired and applauded Senator Nixon's American faith and his determination to drive Communist sympathizers from offices of public trust." Nixon was "an honest man," the General added, and would prove this by placing "all the facts before the people, fairly and squarely."

In California Dana Smith made public the fund donor list of seventy-six names and a report on the income—it totaled $18,250—and disbursements—about the same amount. This bore out what Nixon had been saying, but the impact of a properly timed release was lost because Smith gave it out before getting a prearranged signal from Chotiner. Smith's explanation was that two reporters told him they were in a hurry to meet deadlines—and in late, low circulation editions, no less.

Meanwhile editorials calling for Nixon's replacement began to appear in some newspapers that supported the Republican ticket. The New York *Herald Tribune,* Eisenhower's favorite paper and also a Nixon favorite, called the fund "ill-advised" and suggested that the California Senator make a formal offer of withdrawal from the ticket, which Eisenhower could accept or reject as he saw fit. This was flashed to Chotiner at Medford, Oregon. It was the hardest blow yet, and Nixon's lieutenants decided to keep the news from him, at least overnight. Nevertheless, he heard about it from a Washington correspondent whose newspaper wanted a story on Nixon's reaction. Nixon shook his head; he had nothing to say. Pickets were at his last stop with taunting signs. He pretended to ignore them. He made his campaign speech and forced a smile as the town's organization of cave men initiated him into their order with a long ritual.

Saturday, September 20, was memorable mostly for General Eisenhower's off-the-record observation that Nixon would have to prove himself clean as a hound's tooth. That was one of the late-afternoon incidents.

In the morning there was a near riot at Nixon's rally in Eugene, Oregon. The signs carried by pickets read: "Shh! Anyone who mentions $16,000 is a Communist" and "No Mink Coats for Nixon, just cold cash." While Nixon spoke there was a scuffle and exchange of insults between the pickets and people behind them who complained that the signs hid their view of the candidate. Nixon ignored it until his speech was concluded. Then, pointing to the "Mink Coat" sign, he said, angrily, "That's absolutely right—there are no mink coats for the Nixons. I'm proud to say my wife, Pat, wears a good old Republican cloth coat." The campaign train pulled away, a fight started, and the "Mink Coat" sign was torn to shreds. No one was injured, to speak of, but there was one arrest—a "citizen's arrest" by Charles O. Porter, a Democrat elected to Congress from the district four years later. Porter charged his "prisoner" with disorderly conduct, but nothing came of it beyond newspaper notices. "I was head of the local ADA [Americans for Democratic Action] Chapter at the time and on the Democratic party executive committee," Porter recalls. "We were sitting there talking at our breakfast strategy meeting and my law partner and I got the idea that since Nixon was coming to town we ought to picket him to point up what the newspapers were saying about the fund. So we thought up a couple of good things to put on signs and got young Democrats at the University of Oregon to carry them." An elephant—the symbol of the GOP—and about one thousand people were at the rally, and the elephant keeper hit one of the sign-bearers "with the elephant pick or something," said Porter. "I was surprised at the vituperation that this boy was taking. They were calling him a homosexual and such stuff. Just people coming up there and insulting him. At one point I held up the signs for him for a

(117)

moment, but I did not picket Nixon myself. Not that it was below my dignity, but that just isn't the way the work was assigned. When Nixon pulled out, the crowd surged over with fists flying. I was mad because we had a right to be there and express our opinion. I was mad and disappointed that people should treat this boy like that for expressing an opinion. People kept calling 'Dirty Communist!' This is what Nixon had done. It had repercussions for me. I even got accused of being an atheist. It broke up my law partnership." Porter said the partnership was subsequently resumed, however.

In the rash of public statements that day former President Hoover said, "If everyone in the city of Washington possessed the high level of courage, probity and patriotism of Senator Nixon, this would be a far better nation"; the CIO charged that Nixon had been bought by the real estate interests who "knew a good investment when they saw one"; and Senator George D. Aiken, the liberal Republican from Vermont, said, "I know that no senator can maintain a family in Washington and stay in the Senate on his present salary unless he has some outside financial help." Democratic Chairman Mitchell called Nixon "a Holy Joe that's been talking pretty big—now let him put up some facts."

On his campaign train late that afternoon General Eisenhower sent word to the press car that he would like to join the reporters in a glass of beer. That meant he would like to talk informally, and off the record—to give the press his views, as background information, with the understanding that what he said would not be quoted or attributed directly to him. The first question asked was "Do you consider the Nixon thing a closed incident?" Eisenhower frowned, and said, "By no means." He learned of the Nixon fund on Friday, a day after newspapers printed the original stories, he explained, and was greatly disturbed. He hadn't known Nixon very long and still didn't know him well, but the Senator seemed to exemplify the kind of honesty, vigor and straightforward aggressiveness that he admired and wanted to see more of in young leaders. Furthermore, he couldn't believe Nixon would do anything crooked or unethical, but Nixon would have to prove it—and convince "fair-minded" people. Then Eisenhower said, "Of what avail is it for us to carry on this Crusade against this business of what has been going on in Washington if we ourselves aren't as clean as a hound's tooth?"

The resulting news articles attributed the "hound's tooth" quotation to "highest authorities," informed sources, and the like.

When Nixon was told about the Eisenhower session, he forced a disbelieving smile and muttered something to himself. Mrs. Nixon, who had held back for three days her resentment, wondered to a friend, "Why should we keep taking this?"

In reminiscences, some of the campaign assistants have speculated that Eisenhower would not have gotten a single vote from the Nixon staff if the ballot had been cast that night, in Portland, Oregon.

When the Nixons returned from church on Sunday, September 21, there was a telegram from Harold Stassen:

After a thoughtful review of the entire situation, Dick, I have regretfully reached a conclusion which I feel that I should frankly tell you. I consider it to be imperative for the success of the Republican campaign to clean out Washington, and for your own long-term future that you now send General Eisenhower a message of this nature:

"I deeply regret the embarrassment which has been caused to you and to your campaign by the Dana Smith funds which had assisted in my expenses these past two years. I assure you that I have not personally profited one cent from these funds, and my relationship to the committee has been honorable in every way. It is obvious to me, however, that the entrenched opposition will now use this situation to blunt the drive of your superb campaign to clean out the mess in Washington and will handicap the effort to bring in your urgently needed leadership for future peace for America.

"Above all else your campaign must succeed for the good of America. My situation must not become a diversion for them to draw across your path. I, therefore, herewith extend to you my offer to withdraw as your running mate and assure you and the people of my continued devoted efforts to serve our country in the ranks and to defend America against Communist infiltration and subversion."

I do not know, Dick, what the General would then do. If he decides to accept your offer, Earl Warren should be named to step in. I am certain that for the success of the Eisenhower campaign he must have the opportunity to make a clear-cut decision. Otherwise, it will divert

(119)

and drag from here on for him, for you, and above all, for the essential movement for good government in Washington.

In the long run it will also strengthen you and aid your career, whatever may be the immediate decision or results. With my best wishes— HAROLD E. STASSEN.

The Nixon party spent the weekend at the Benson Hotel, in Portland. Stassen's was one of several hundred telegrams Nixon got on Sunday. Most were from friends in California and Congressional colleagues urging him not to quit the ticket. But generally the messages throughout the day contributed to Nixon's weary despondency. Rogers, who manned the telephones, said, "We had calls from everybody, all offering advice. There were only a few of us that day who were reasonably sure it would work out all right." Governor Dewey agreed Nixon should bare his soul on national television as quickly as possible, then reported that seven of the nine people at his dinner table believed Nixon should resign from the ticket. Another major figure in the Eisenhower movement, calling from Washington, confidentially urged Rogers to abandon Nixon immediately or risk his own future. It was obvious that Eisenhower felt the Dana Smith reports and Nixon's statements on the fund were not enough. The various "inner circles"—Nixon's, Eisenhower's, and the National Committee's—talked about a radio-television report. A Westinghouse Company offer to sponsor it caused Chotiner to remind the Eisenhower train: "If Dick is off the ticket, all the printing you'll have to do over again will cost you a lot more money than a television program."

At six o'clock Nixon spoke at a dinner of the Temple Beth Israel Men's Club. "For all we knew, it was going to be the last speech of the campaign for him," Chotiner said. It was a low point for the Senator. "Dick was ready to chuck the whole thing, and frankly it took the toughest arguments of some us us to hold him in check," said another Nixon intimate. Before leaving the hotel for the Beth Israel speech, Nixon saw a survey that showed the newspapers to be 2 to 1 against him.[3] When a "Have Faith" message was handed

[3] The New York *Daily News* predicted Nixon would "return this belly punch." The New York *Post* warned that Nixon "will haunt and harass General Eisenhower until election day."

him from his mother, Nixon stepped into a vacant room to hide his tears.

Following the evening speech, Nixon's campaign doctor massaged his neck to ease painfully tense muscles. Then his staff advisers came to the bedroom for a full-dress discussion of what to do. Rogers said Nixon had no alternative but to resign if Eisenhower requested it. Chotiner disagreed. He said the General and a lot of people around him knew very little about politics, and if Nixon was dumped the Republican party was sure to lose the election. Nixon listened in silence. He got up once, during a pause in the discussion, and said, as though to himself, "I will not crawl."

The strategy session was interrupted at 10:05 P.M. by the long-awaited telephone call from Eisenhower, in St. Louis. Nixon sat on a couch and propped his feet on a table. Pleasantries were exchanged. The running mates talked a little about their respective whistle-stop experiences. The Senator told the General that Dewey also thought it would be good to put the fund story before the people on television. "I'm at your disposal," Nixon said. Then he told the General the important thing was for the Republicans to win. "I want you to know if you reach a conclusion either now or any time later that I should get off the ticket, you can be sure that I will immediately respect your judgment and do so," the Senator said. Eisenhower replied, in effect, that he didn't think *he* should be the one to make that decision. At this Nixon stiffened and said sternly, "There comes a time in a man's life when he has to fish or cut bait." (Actually his words were stronger.)

At midnight Adams, Summerfield and Humphreys notified Nixon from the Eisenhower train that radio and television time now could be arranged—because three Republican party organizations had pledged the necessary $75,000. So Nixon broke off his campaign tour and flew to Los Angeles to prepare.

A small group of his original supporters and Young Republicans was at the airport to welcome him. They had banners and made a lot of noise—but the home-coming was quite a contrast to the hero's send-off just five days before.

9

NIXON had been in politics only six years. Just a week before his arrival in Los Angeles on September 22 he was at a peak of his phenomenal career—and still headed upward. And now, as William Rogers put it, "he faced as severe a test as anyone could cope with. It was not just that his integrity was challenged; it was the possible consequences generally. If he got off the ticket, it would have been the first time in the history of our country such a thing happened; by the same token, if the Republicans lost, he would be the scapegoat."

The Senator exiled himself in the Ambassador Hotel to await the climax of "the worst experience of my life." Mrs. Nixon went to the home of Mrs. Helene Drown, a friend who had been her companion on the campaign train.

A national hookup of 64 NBC television stations, 194 CBS radio stations and practically the entire 560-station Mutual Broadcasting System radio network was contracted for by Batten, Barton, Durstine and Osborn, the Republican party's advertising agency. But getting the "perfect" time for Nixon's speech was a problem. Ted Rogers, the Senator's friend and television adviser (and no relative of William Rogers), wanted a ready-made audience. The spot after the "I Love Lucy" program on Monday night was available, but Nixon couldn't be ready in time to fill it. So they got the half hour immediately following the Milton Berle show on Tuesday night. No event in history involving a vice-presidential candidate got such attention—before and after. For four days Nixon was talked and written about much more than the

(122)

candidates for president. In the forty-eight hours that preceded his speech rumors about him were "bulletin" material for the nation's news media. Radio programs were interrupted for "reports" that he had collapsed. They were interrupted again for his doctor's statement that he was "in perfect health." Eisenhower's deferred judgment was announced—and printed a dozen different ways. There were flat predictions that Nixon would stay on the ticket. There were also predictions that he would get off. The Los Angeles *Daily News* said, "Anything short of an enthusiastic burst of public support . . . will be interpreted in favor of what [Eisenhower and his strategists] have already decided—that corruption cannot remain a campaign issue as long as one of their candidates is tainted with the slightest suspicion. Thus, Nixon will probably be asked to resign . . ."

On Monday afternoon the lawyers and accountants hired by Paul Hoffman sent their 18-page, single-spaced reports to Sherman Adams. The study was based on Dana Smith's files and, in effect, found everything to be legal and in line with what Smith had made public a few days before, except for about $11,000 deposited in the fund account after Nixon's nomination, and Smith said it would be accounted for as campaign contributions.

Monday was also the day of the "Stevenson Fund" disclosure. An official of a mimeograph machine company doing business with the state of Illinois charged that Governor Stevenson "personally promoted" contributions from private businessmen. Stevenson immediately confirmed it, said it "has never been any secret," explained that the money supplemented the state salaries of members of his administration who left better-paying jobs in private business to serve Illinois. Stevenson insisted that none of the money went to him or any other elected official, and there was "no question of improper influence, because there was no connection between the contributors and the beneficiaries."

Nevertheless, the word "fund" had been battered into something that looked and sounded sinister, and the fact that he had a "fund" made Stevenson a target for the pointed questions, implied charges and innuendo to which Nixon had been subjected because of his "fund." It also gave Nixon an opportunity to suggest in a manner that could hardly be misunderstood that both Stevenson and his running mate, Sparkman, had better bare their financial souls, as Nixon was doing.

Normally, Nixon would work a full week, at least, on a major speech. There was less than two days for him to prepare the most important one of his life. He started on the airplane flight from Portland to Los Angeles. "I was pretty tired by that time," he recalls. "I tried to sleep, but after dozing a little while I woke up. I began to think about the broadcast, what could I say—how could I put this thing in a way people would understand. I pulled out some United Airlines postcards from the souvenir packet at the seat and made notes. It was not an outline of the broadcast, but of general ideas. The way I do it whenever I write a speech. I have a general idea of the theme I am going to hit, then I just let the thoughts flow into my mind and I write them down. That was when the idea came to me to mention the girls' dog, Checkers, the cloth coat, and Lincoln's reference to the common people."

Nixon worked at it intensively for almost twenty-four hours before the telecast. Late the first night he rushed from his room looking for someone to double-check the Lincoln quotation. In the hall he bumped into Pat Hillings, a member of the campaign inner circle, who didn't remember it. Nixon called his Whittier College history professor, Dr. Smith, who, in turn, called the English professor, Dr. Upton. The quotation was "The Lord must have loved the common people because he made so many of them." Nixon's reference to Checkers was inspired by Franklin Roosevelt's masterful use of his dog Fala in a 1944 campaign speech that made the Republicans a national laughing stock. Nixon tried his ideas on Bill Rogers and Chotiner. He credits Dewey with the proposal that caused more than a million Americans to wire, write and telephone after the speech. "Dewey suggested that I ask listeners to wire me indicating whether I should stay on the ticket or get off."

Shortly before Nixon was to leave for the studio, Sherman Adams telephoned Chotiner to find out, for Eisenhower, what Nixon would say. When Chotiner replied he didn't really know, Adams

(124)

said, "Oh, come now, Murray, you must know . . . he has a script, doesn't he?"

"No," replied Chotiner.

"What about the press?" asked Adams.

"We've set up television sets in the hotel for them, and we have shorthand reporters to take it down, page by page," answered Chotiner.

"Look, we have to know what is going to be said," Adams insisted.

"Sherm," Chotiner replied, "if you want to know what's going to be said, you do what I'm going to do. You sit in front of the television and listen."

Eisenhower was campaigning in Ohio on Tuesday, September 23. His telegrams and messages were running three to one against Nixon. All day the General repeated to callers that he would not make up his mind until after the broadcast. Chairman Summerfield was at his office in Washington. Just after lunch he called Robert Humphreys over and said, "We have got to get to Cleveland immediately." He had just gotten word that one of Eisenhower's personal friends had boarded the campaign train with what seemed to be an impressive argument for replacing Nixon. Summerfield and Humphreys took the first plane. The General was to address a rally in the city auditorium that night. He planned to watch the Nixon telecast first, however, and arrangements were made to pipe it into the auditorium for the rally audience.

About an hour before the Eisenhower party was to leave for the auditorium, General Jerry Persons, an Eisenhower assistant, summoned Humphreys to the General's room. Eisenhower was reclining on the bed, his head propped up by pillows and the headboard. Adams stood on one side, Persons on the other. "One of the rumors we've gotten is a very difficult one," said Persons. "It is that when Nixon bought his house in the Spring Valley section of Washington, Mrs. Nixon paid $10,000 in cash for the decorations, the interior decorating." Did Humphreys have any information on that? Humphreys said the report had to be untrue. He had been at the Nixon home just a week or two before and seen the only "decorations" being hung. They were living-room draperies which had just arrived with a circular couch from the Nixons' house in Whittier.

"The General listened intently, said practically nothing, and seemed to be satisfied with the answer," Humphrey recalls.

Before leaving for the auditorium the Eisenhower staff gathered for another inconclusive discussion of Nixon's fate. At the auditorium, the General and his party climbed three flights of stairs to the manager's office, over the stage. A television set was perched in a corner. Eisenhower and Mrs. Eisenhower sat on a small couch in front of it. Next to the couch, on a chair, was William Robinson, publisher of the New York *Herald Tribune* (and now president of the Coca-Cola Company). Summerfield, Hagerty, and about thirty other campaign assistants stood against the walls.

An intensive rehearsal for the Nixon program was going on, meanwhile, half a continent away at NBC's El Capitan Theater in Hollywood. Nixon, himself, refused to rehearse—or even talk with the program director. So Ted Rogers hired a stand-in, a salesman Nixon's size, who had Nixon's coloring, and was dressed as Nixon would be. The cameramen, electricians, control-room operators, directors—everyone having to do with the program, except the star, rehearsed all day Tuesday, September 23. Rogers put the stand-in through the movements Nixon might make, and instructed the cameramen to keep the lens directly on Nixon regardless of what he did. Just before going on the air he (Ted Rogers) told them to focus on Mrs. Nixon when the Senator talked about her. Draperies were hung over the glass "client's booth" to keep Nixon from being distracted by the "audience"—Chotiner, Bassett, and Ted Rogers.

About one hour before broadcast time a telephone call came from "Mr. Chapman" in New York. That was the code name Governor Dewey used during the campaign to avoid attention. Congressman Hillings said Nixon was not available. Then, according to Hillings:

"He said, 'Don't give me that business. I've got to talk to him. It's absolutely essential.'

"I said, 'My orders are, Governor, he's not to talk to anybody.'

"He said, 'You get him right now. I'm not going to get off this phone until you do it.'

"So I went out and told Chotiner. And Chotiner said, 'I think I know what it is.'

"Chotiner, who was particularly anxious to keep disturbing news from Nixon until after the telecast, took the phone and said, 'I'm awfully sorry. He's out someplace and I can't reach him.'

"He said, 'Well, I'll hold the phone.'

"I said, 'I haven't the slightest idea when he'll be back.'

"He said, 'I don't care how long it is, I'll hold this phone'—and if you know Mr. Chapman," Chotiner winked, "you know he's the kind of guy who will hold that phone."

Finally Chotiner got Nixon, who was across the hall. Dewey's message was that he had polled the campaign leaders and found that most felt Nixon should resign.

"Dewey didn't say that was his own feeling," recalls Nixon. "He said 'I am reporting that the group feels you should. I regret this very much.' " Although Dewey didn't say so flatly, and Nixon didn't ask, it was implied that Eisenhower agreed with the majority.

"Dick looked like someone had smashed him," said Hillings.

That is exactly how Nixon felt. "The call was really a block-buster," he told me. "I asked all the staff to leave me completely alone until time to leave for the broadcast so that I could decide what to do. I didn't describe the details of the call, but they knew who it was from and I told them I might require a complete change in approach. That is why my closest advisers told the literal truth— hard as that is to believe—when they said they actually did not know when the broadcast began what I was going to say.

"I sat alone for at least thirty minutes, debating as to what I ought to do. I had a tremendous respect for Dewey as a man and for his superb political judgment. The question I had to decide was whether I was justified in putting my judgment above his as well as possibly the General himself by not announcing my resigna-

(127)

tion from the ticket, which was the course of action the Dewey message seemed to imply so clearly."

Nixon added that "it was Chotiner who really saved the day as far as I was concerned. He was truly a tower of strength. He came into the room as I was shaving about ten minutes before departure time, and said, "Dick, a campaign manager must never be seen or heard. But if you're kicked off this ticket, I'm going to call the biggest damn press conference that has ever been held. I'm going to break a rule. I'm going to have television present. I'm going to break every rule in the book, and I'm going to tell everybody who called you, what was said, names and everything."

Nixon looked at him surprised, Chotiner recalls, and asked, "Would you really do that?"

"I said, 'Sure.' 'Why?' he asked. And I told him, 'Hell, we'd be through with politics anyway. It wouldn't make any difference.'"

"Some way Chotiner's cold, realistic logic broke the tension," said Nixon, "and, while I didn't make a final decision at that point as to what to do, I was able to think clearly and decisively on the ride to the studio. By the time I got there I had made my decision not to follow the course of action which had been suggested by the General's advisers, but to submit the case to the country and let the people decide."

By broadcast time the speech was scrawled, in note form, on a lawyer's yellow note pad. His own mind was clear on what to tell the country except for the item of quitting or staying. His inclination was to leave it to the National Committee and hope for the best. "Even riding over to the broadcast I still hadn't decided for sure how I would conclude it," Nixon told me.

In reminiscing six years later, Nixon said, "You have to expect in a campaign that your integrity, your loyalty, your honesty, your intellectual honesty may all be questioned. That's fair game. You have got to be able to take it. But what was involved was even more important than that. In questioning my integrity and trying to prove it was bad, they questioned the integrity of the Republican party, the judgment of General Eisenhower in selecting me and approving me as a candidate, and the whole 'mess in Washington' issue. I realized that if I failed I would be off the ticket, of course. I also believed there would be a great risk that the ticket would lose, and that I would carry that responsibility for the balance of my life."

The program opened with a picture of Senator Nixon's calling card. Then the camera switched to the Senator, seated behind a desk.

My fellow Americans, I come before you tonight as a candidate for the Vice-Presidency . . . and as a man whose honesty and integrity has been questioned. . . .

. . . I am sure that you have read the charge and you've heard it that I, Senator Nixon, took $18,000 from a group of my supporters. Now, was that wrong? And let me say that it was wrong—I'm saying, incidentally, that it was wrong and not just illegal. Because it isn't a question of whether it was legal or illegal, that isn't enough. The question is, was it morally wrong?

I say that it was morally wrong if any of that $18,000 went to Senator Nixon for my personal use. I say that it was morally wrong if it was secretly given and secretly handled. And I say that it was morally wrong if any of the contributors got special favors for the contributions that they made.

And now to answer those questions let me say this:

Not one cent of the $18,000 or any other money of that type ever went to me for my personal use. Every penny of it was used to pay for political expenses that I did not think should be charged to the taxpayers of the United States. . . .

. . . Let me point out, and I want to make this particularly clear, that no contributor to this fund, no contributor to any of my campaigns, has ever received any consideration that he would not have received as an ordinary constituent.

. . . Now what I am going to do—and incidentally this is unprecedented in the history of American politics—I am going at this time to give to this television and radio audience a complete financial history; everything I've earned; everything I've spent; everything I owe. And I want you to know the facts. I'll have to start early.

I was born in 1913. . . .

. . . Well, that's about it. That's what we have and that's what we

(129)

owe. It isn't very much but Pat and I have the satisfaction that every dime that we've got is honestly ours. I should say this—that Pat doesn't have a mink coat. But she does have a respectable Republican cloth coat. And I always tell her that she'd look good in anything.

One other thing I probably should tell you, because if I don't they'll probably be saying this about me too, we did get something—a gift—after the election. A man down in Texas heard Pat on the radio mention the fact that our two youngsters would like to have a dog. And, believe it or not, the day before we left on this campaign trip we got a message from Union Station in Baltimore saying they had a package for us. We went down to get it. You know what it was?

It was a little cocker spaniel dog in a crate that he sent all the way from Texas. Black and white spotted. And our little girl—Tricia, the six-year-old—named it Checkers. And you know the kids love that dog and I just want to say this right now, that regardless of what they say about it, we're going to keep it. . . .

. . . You have read in the papers about other funds. Now, Mr. Stevenson, apparently, had a couple. One of them in which a group of business people paid and helped to supplement the salaries of state employees. Here is where the money went directly into their pockets.

And I think that what Mr. Stevenson should do should be to come before the American people as I have, give the names of the people that have contributed to that fund; give the names of the people who put this money into their pockets at the same time that they were receiving money from their state government, and see what favors, if any, they gave out for that.

I'm going to tell you this: I remember in the dark days of the Hiss case some of the same columnists, some of the same radio commentators who are attacking me now and misrepresenting my position were violently opposing me at the time I was after Alger Hiss. . . .

And now, finally, I know that you wonder whether or not I am going to stay on the Republican ticket or resign.

Let me say this: I don't believe that I ought to quit, because I am not a quitter. And, incidentally, Pat is not a quitter. After all, her name is Patricia Ryan, and she was born St. Patrick's Day—and you know the Irish never quit.

But the decision, my friends, is not mine. I would do nothing that would harm the possibilities of Dwight Eisenhower to become President of the United States; and for that reason I am submitting to the Republican National Committee tonight, through this television broadcast, the decision which it is theirs to make.

Let them decide whether my position on the ticket will help or hurt; and I am going to ask you to help them decide. Wire and write the Republican National Committee whether you think I should stay or whether I should get off; and whatever their decision is, I will abide by it.

Just let me say this last word: Regardless of what happens, I am going to continue this fight. I am going to campaign up and down America until we drive the crooks and Communists and those that defend them out of Washington.

And remember, folks, Eisenhower is a great man, believe me. He is a great man . . .

Mrs. Nixon sat at one side, her eyes glued to her husband. ". . . I am submitting the decision to the Republican National Committee . . . ." Ted Rogers slipped into the studio and signaled vigorously "your time is almost up!" Nixon looked at him, but didn't see. He kept coming, and talking to the camera. ". . . Wire and write the National Committee on whether you think I should stay or whether I should get off, and whatever their decision is, I will abide . . ." He was off the air, but still talking. "I'm terribly sorry I ran over," Nixon said to Rogers. "I loused it up, and I'm sorry." He thanked the technicians. Then he gathered the notes from the desk, stacked them neatly—and threw them to the floor. "Dick, you did a terrific job," beamed Chotiner, patting his back. "No, it was a flop . . . I couldn't get off in time," he replied. When he reached the dressing room, Nixon turned away from his friends—and let loose the tears he had been holding back.

A crowd outside cheered as he and Mrs. Nixon got into their car. There was great excitement at the hotel. Someone shouted, "The telephones are going crazy; everybody's in your corner!" Nixon accepted a call from Darryl Zanuck: "The most tremendous performance I've ever seen." Nixon began to come to life.

In Cleveland the Eisenhower group had watched, seemingly without drawing breath. Mrs. Eisenhower and several of the men clutched handkerchiefs and dabbed their eyes. The General had a small notebook in his hand. He jabbed at it with a pencil, his eyes never leaving the television screen. When the program ended, he said to Summerfield, "Well, Arthur, you surely got your $75,000 worth." Downstairs 13,000 people screamed and shouted, "We want Dick!" Eisenhower wired Nixon. "Your presentation was magnificent." Then the General explained that before he would "complete the formulation of a decision I feel the need of talking to you and would be most appreciative if you could fly to see me at once. Tomorrow night I shall be at Wheeling, West Virginia."

Shortly thereafter, when he appeared before the Armory crowd, the General's praise grew more lavish. As a "warrior," he had never seen "courage" to surpass that shown by Nixon, he said, and in a showdown fight he preferred "one courageous, honest man" at his side to "a whole boxcar full of pussyfooters."

The General didn't get around to telling the crowd what it wanted most to hear, however. "I am not ducking any responsibility," he declared, "I am not going to be swayed by my idea of what will get the most votes. . . . I am going to say: Do I myself believe this man is the kind of man America would like to have for its vice-president?"

The crowd shouted, "We like Dick!"

Telephone and telegraph lines were clogged across the land. Despite Nixon's plea that messages go to the National Committee, they were sent to everything that sounded Republican—from the Eisenhower train to local political clubs—and the sentiment seemed almost unanimous: "Keep Nixon."[1]

Reports of the reaction raised Nixon's spirits. He felt the ordeal was over and everything had turned out fine. "After this, nothing could seem tough," he confided to Bassett. The song "Happy Days Are Here Again" rang out in the hotel. Then a reporter brought to the Nixon suite an incomplete news bulletin about Eisenhower's

[1] All the messages were never totaled. Party headquarters in Washington, alone, got 300,000 letters, cards, telegrams and petitions, signed altogether by a million people. They have been given to Whittier College, where Dr. Robert W. O'Brien, head of the sociology department, and Mrs. Elizabeth Jensen Jones, an associate, are studying them for clues to sociological motivations. Underclassmen have dubbed the huge collection, "The Dead Sea Scrolls."

telegram. The telegram itself hadn't come, and the bulletin stressed Eisenhower's desire for a further face-to-face explanation from his running mate. Nixon read and reread it. His smile disappeared. He dictated to Miss Woods a telegram to National Chairman Summerfield resigning as candidate for vice-president pending the selection of a successor. Chotiner followed Miss Woods out of the room and tore the telegram to shreds. The secretary said she wasn't going to send it anyway.[2]

An hour later Nixon got the full text of Eisenhower's telegram proposing a conference in Wheeling, West Virginia, the next night. In reply, the Senator wired that he intended to resume at once his campaign tour which would end Saturday, September 27. "Will be in Washington Sunday and will be delighted to confer with you at your convenience any time thereafter," Nixon added. This unusual show of independence delighted the Nixon staff and shocked more people than it pleased in the Eisenhower entourage.

At about 10:30 P.M., as the Nixon group was preparing to leave the hotel, Summerfield telephoned to urge that Nixon come to Wheeling, as requested. He was told that Nixon was going to Missoula, Montana, to campaign the next morning. Nixon would meet Eisenhower only after the General's mind was made up, one way or the other. "Dick is not going to be placed in the position of a little boy coming somewhere to beg for forgiveness," Chotiner said.

More calls followed from the Eisenhower train, and finally the General himself sought to reach Nixon. By then the Senator's party was en route to Missoula.

Dozens of messages forwarded from Los Angeles were at the hotel when Nixon arrived at four in the morning. A news report quoted Dewey as calling the Nixon telecast, "A superb statement by a man of shining integrity and great purpose in the service of his country." A telegram from the Republican National Committee

---

[2] As it developed, this insubordination didn't displease Nixon. He recalls: "We were all on edge and quite high strung at the time. The whole experience had been an ordeal. And, obviously, we thought of [Eisenhower's message] in the context of the Dewey call."

reported that 107 of its 138 members had been reached in a quick poll and all voted "enthusiastically" to keep Nixon on the ticket. There was also a telegram from Harold Stassen: "Congratulations on a superb presentation, Dick, and best wishes always to you and to Pat. Sincerely."

Awaiting Chotiner was a telephone call from Summerfield, relaying Eisenhower's assurance that everything would be all right. So Nixon slept a couple of hours, campaigned briefly in Montana, then headed for the emotional reunion with his chief. The plane landed at Wheeling in the late dusk. Chotiner rushed off to find out where Nixon was to go. At the same time a lone figure in the waiting crowd darted up the ladder into the plane and asked, "Where's the boss of this outfit?" Frank Kuest, a correspondent, pointed forward and said, "Up there, General." Eisenhower went up to his running mate as he stood helping Mrs. Nixon with her coat.

Nixon remembers he was "flabbergasted" to see him there. "What are you doing here, General? You didn't have to come here to meet us," he said. Eisenhower put his arm around Nixon and said, "I certainly did, Dick. You're my boy." Nixon turned his head to the window and tried to keep back the tears. Mrs. Nixon patted her husband and said, "Shall we go?" Eisenhower and Nixon posed for pictures, shaking hands. Then Nixon spotted his senior colleague, Senator Knowland. "It was quite a tense and emotional situation," Knowland recalls. "I said, 'Everything's going to be all right, Dick,' and he came over and said, 'Good old Bill.' " The picture of Nixon weeping on Knowland's shoulder was one of the most poignant of the campaign.

The running mates rode together at the head of a large caravan to the Wheeling Stadium, where Eisenhower declared that Nixon had "completely vindicated himself." Nixon said, "This is probably the greatest moment of my life."

The next day—exactly one week after the uproar—all was peaceful, happy and harmonious in Republican ranks. "The Order of the Hound's Tooth" was founded, with Nixon as president and all in his entourage during the "fund" week as charter members. The membership card, designed by the candidate, featured a portrait of Checkers.

That summed up the new, high-riding attitude of the Nixon group. His staff was even more optimistic than the candidate. A week after the fund speech, for instance, Chotiner threatened a showdown with the Eisenhower staff over a half hour of Nixon's reserved television time which was suddenly pre-empted for the General. Nixon had already prepared a major speech on the Hiss case. His campaign manager promised to "get" the necessary network television facilities—and did, too—but he never told Nixon how. Chotiner used a unique form of persuasion. When national party headquarters insisted it couldn't afford to replace the pre-empted telecast, Chotiner said he would ask the *public* to put Nixon on another network at the same time as the General, with the dual speeches being billed as a contest for the biggest audience. Party officials in Washington laughed nervously and were audibly relieved when the problem was presented to the "money people" in the Citizens for Eisenhower organization. They solved it, at the urging of Herbert Brownell.

Nixon had transformed himself into a campaign asset. Within twenty-four hours the entire Republican hierarchy was singing hosannas, including the leaders who felt the program's emotional pitch to be revolting. His success sent the Republican campaign soaring, establishing him as a national figure and the best-known largest-crowd-drawing vice-presidential candidate in history. Letters to the Republican National Committee included enough small donations to pay for the television and radio time. Dana Smith got $3,200 in sums of $1 to $5 and sent it to the campaign treasury. Checkers became a national hero—or to others a symbol of Madison Avenue sentimentality.

Newspaper support swung back heavily in Nixon's favor. "The air is cleared," said the *Herald Tribune*. The New York *Journal-American* called the speech "an eloquent and manly explanation." The Denver *Post* said, "Senator Nixon talked his way into the hearts of millions . . . by speaking plainly and honestly about the dilemma of a poor man and the rich sweepstakes of politics."

(135)

The favorable reaction was hardly unanimous. *Variety*, the newspaper of show business, considered the telecast "a slick production . . . parlaying all the schmaltz and human interest of the 'Just Plain Bill'–'Our Gal Sunday' genre of weepers." Walter Lippmann was disturbed, "for this thing in which I found myself participating was, with all the magnification of modern electronics, simply mob law . . . the appeal to the people should have come after, not before, the case had been judged by Eisenhower." And a year later the term "The New Nixon" appeared in print for the first time in an editorial saying Nixon wasn't as bad as his fund speech would indicate. "This mawkish ooze ill became a man who might become the President of the United States," said the Montgomery (Ala.) *Advertiser.* "We have found ourselves dissolving our previous conception . . . the New Nixon rejoices us."

In retrospect, the affair was bad for Nixon. The people who remember it most vividly thought it was horrible. The Democrats and Nixon's Republican enemies have kept the embers aglow. Much of the "I don't like Nixon, but don't know why" talk stems from the incident. But if it weren't for the immediate impact of that speech Nixon probably would have been done for and Eisenhower might have lost.

No participant in the fund episode—Democratic or Republican —came out of it clean as a hound's tooth. One of the hoariest of American hypocrisies is our attitude toward political financing. Few candidates in closely contested areas—whether running for mayor, governor, congressman or president—let themselves be hindered by codes regulating political contributions and expenditures. It becomes shameful only if you are caught in circumstances that could cost votes. The Eisenhower forces, with Nixon as combat commander, compounded the hypocrisy by going to ridiculous extremes in the "purity" barrages they fired at the Democratic administration's scandals. There was so much sanctimony and rationalization in the 1952 campaign that even the most notorious political rogues, of both parties, took to reaching for halos. Yet when the seemingly questionable "funds" became an issue—Nixon's and Stevenson's— the strong judgments, Republican and Democratic, were based on their immediate effect on the election. "Morals," "ethics," and even simple fairness to Nixon and Stevenson, as individuals, didn't figure.

Mrs. Nixon never regained her taste for politics after that. She dislikes to think back on the experience. Nixon treats the day of his television speech as an anniversary. "After it, very few, if any, difficult situations could seem insurmountable if anything personal is involved," he said. "Nothing could match it. Nothing could top it because not so much could again depend on one incident.

"I know," Nixon says, "there are congressmen and senators who continue to accept fees from their law firms after they come to Washington. And there is always the question as to when it is proper to take speech honorariums, entertainment and personal gifts. I have always been pretty strait-laced about such items. I avoid accepting entertainment from people who might have business with the government, and from other than personal friends, unless I am able to reciprocate. And all the time I've been in Washington I have refused to ride in a private airplane unless the ride was furnished in connection with a speaking engagement which I had accepted. We have turned down literally hundreds of social engagements, weekend invitations, and so forth in the time we've been here. It isn't that I question the personal honesty of those who may not be as careful as I have been in this respect on such matters. But after the experience that Pat and I went through in 1952 over a fund from which we did not receive one cent of personal benefit we realize that it isn't what the facts are but what they appear to be that counts when you are under fire in a political campaign. The best advice I can give to young men entering politics is to take to heart the Caesar's-wife admonition and to follow it to the letter."

10

WHEN he took office as vice-president a week after his fortieth birthday in January, 1953, Nixon symbolized a new generation of Republican politicians. Only John C. Breckinridge, a pre-Civil War Democrat, had been younger than he. None had been more eager to make something of the Vice-Presidency—and of himself. Despite his enterprise, however, the first year was a disappointment. But the second—1954—was far worse. It was, in fact, the worst of Nixon's first twelve years in politics, and he probably would just as soon see it erased from the calendar.

The 1954 Congressional election had its dismaying aspects. People "liked Ike" and his one-year-old administration better than ever, and politicians hadn't yet forgotten the power implicit in the Eisenhower vote. It was plain, therefore, that 1954 was *the* year to build a strong, national Republican party—just as the Democrats had capitalized so effectively on the Roosevelt victory of two decades before. Eisenhower and his high command talked about it at Cabinet meetings. Proposals were made and accepted. Slogans were adopted, money raised, the Citizens for Eisenhower organization revived. But, to Nixon's disappointment, few got around to *doing* much. Furthermore, when the campaign reached the bloodletting stage, Nixon found himself again at the point of assault, without defenders on his flanks and almost no supporting force behind. This time there wasn't even a Senator McCarthy off in the bushes slashing away independently at the Democrats and drawing some of their fire.

Senator McCarthy had gone nonpartisan. The nonaggression

pact Nixon had worked out between him and the Eisenhower administration collapsed early in the winter, and for thirty-six days the country watched on television as the Republican administration and McCarthy grappled for each other's throats. Though neither McCarthy nor the Eisenhower "team" ever quite measured up to the virility of their public reputations, their performances were disgusting. Eisenhower remained aloof, of course; but his party couldn't. Nixon, who regarded party unity as imperative, would have preferred to give the voters a more inspiring view of "the Republican family."

Party politics and McCarthy didn't cause all Nixon's doldrums that year. A new street in his home town was to be named Nixon Boulevard. A local organization objected. To avert a quarrel the city fathers called it Mar Vista Lane instead. During the winter Nixon's father became gravely ill. When his brother objected to a local union's organizing the butcher in the grocery store, enemies of the Vice-President charged this showed *he* was anti-labor. In the spring Nixon delivered the Commencement Address at Whittier College and the school president had to form a second reception line after the ceremony for those not wanting to shake the Vice-President's hand. Only two students took it. At Duke University, Nixon's other alma mater, a faculty meeting for the first time exercised its prerogative in such matters to veto an honorary degree the trustees had voted for Nixon. (The vote was 61-42 against Nixon. Only 103 of the 606 faculty members attended, none from the Law School.)

All in all, Nixon had ample reason in 1954 to re-examine the merits of politics as a career. In mid-February he and his wife discussed their future from all angles, and the 41-year-old Vice-President agreed to retire from politics after his term ended in 1956. At Mrs. Nixon's request he noted the date and the decision on a piece of paper that he tucked into his wallet.

Adlai Stevenson declared at a Democratic fund-raising dinner in Miami on March 6, 1954, that "a group of political plungers has persuaded the President that McCarthyism is the best Republican formula for political success." Therefore, he added, Eisenhower is personally responsible for the "demagoguery and deceit of Mc-Carthyism." This was broadcast on radio and television networks, and the wall of Republican hopes for unity came tumbling down. Eisenhower quickly directed Republican National Chairman Leonard W. Hall to demand equal time on the networks, before McCarthy got it, which Hall did. Then the President chose Nixon to reply for the administration and the party. This ended what remained of the Vice-President's influence with the Wisconsin Senator and caused Nixon and Stevenson to square off again as the principal national campaigners of the respective parties, taking up where they had left off in 1952—with Stevenson soon calling Nixon "McCarthy with a white collar" and Nixon branding Stevenson a snob.

Nixon first met McCarthy in 1947 at a "cheese party" for newly elected Republican congressmen. Wisconsin backers of Harold Stassen for president were the hosts. For the next three years there was no particular contact between the two men. Nixon says he "began to know [McCarthy] well in the campaign of 1950." McCarthy had entered the anti-Communist arena with a speech at Wheeling, West Virginia, on February 9 in which he reportedly said: "While I cannot take the time to name all the men in the State Department who have been named as active members of the Communist party and members of a spy ring, I have here in my hand a list of two hundred and five, a list of names that were made known to the Secretary of State as being members of the Communist party and who, nevertheless, are still working and shaping policy in the State Department."

When the uproar began over that charge, McCarthy asked Nixon to help him prove it. "At the time," Nixon recalled, "I told him, 'Now, the important thing—when it comes to this field—is one rule I would urge you to follow: always understate, never overstate your case.' I told him this in the very first conversation. He said he was going to Los Angeles. That is the reason he called me. He said he was going to have a press conference there and was sort of on a spot. I said, 'As far as your statement in Wheeling is concerned, I haven't read it, but you will be in an untenable position if you claim that there were umpteen, or however many, card-carrying Communists in the State Department, because you cannot prove that. On the other hand, if you were to say that there were so many people whose records disclosed Communist-front affiliations and associations, this you can prove. You've got to state it in the context of what is provable and not the other way.' But he did not listen and from then on that case was out the window."

Nixon was running for senator that fall. When McCarthy came to California he called Chotiner, Nixon's campaign manager, and asked "What can I do for Dick?" Chotiner said he explained that Nixon didn't want outside help. "Some archconservative group had invited Joe to speak," Chotiner said. "We were sore because it could destroy our campaign strategy, which was to run our own campaign without anybody from the outside. I told this to Joe, and he said, 'You don't have to tell me again. I won't do a thing to harm Dick.' "

Meanwhile, after a Senate committee was instructed to investigate McCarthy's charges, Nixon lent his files to the Senator for whatever clues they might offer. Late in the summer Nixon charged the inquiry was "rapidly degenerating into a political squabble" and urged, as he had done a month after the McCarthy speech in Wheeling, that McCarthy's allegations were grave enough to merit "vigorous" investigation by an "impartial, nonpolitical commission" of eminent jurists.[1]

Nixon's other contact with McCarthy that year was on December 12 at a party at the Sulgrave Club. Many congressmen and Washington personalities were there, including McCarthy and Drew Pearson, whose fifty-third birthday was the next day. The Senator and the columnist, who had been saying and writing uncomplimentary things about each other, soon were arguing. Subsequently, the angry discussion adjourned to the washroom. A few minutes later Nixon, on going for his hat and coat, found Mc-

[1] Two years later Nixon told the Wisconsin Republican convention which endorsed McCarthy for a second term that a "fair investigation" of McCarthy's charges "will never be made until the Republican party comes into power."

Carthy and Pearson grappling. Nixon says that as he went over to part them, McCarthy slapped Pearson on the face and said, "That one is for you, Dick." Nixon, who was no friend of Pearson's, pushed between the combatants saying, "Let a Quaker stop this fight." Then he grabbed McCarthy's arm and said, "Come on, Joe, it's time for you to go home." McCarthy snapped, "No, not until he goes first. I am not going to turn my back on that s.o.b." Pearson left and, since McCarthy had forgotten where he had parked his car, Nixon searched the area with him for a half hour, and found it.[2]

There was a flurry of criticism in January, 1951, when McCarthy, as senior Republican on the Senate Government Operations Committee, made room for Nixon on its investigating subcommittee by ousting Senator Margaret Chase Smith. Mrs. Smith had incurred McCarthy's displeasure some months before by issuing a "Declaration of Conscience" urging the Republican party not to "ride to political victory on the Four Horsemen of Calumny—Fear, Ignorance, Bigotry and Smear."

On becoming a senator Nixon had requested assignment to the Labor Committee. "Senator Butler, of Nebraska, the chairman of the Committee on Committees, asked if I would like the Committee on Government Operations also," he recalled. "I told him that I would be delighted. So I went on it. After that I had nothing to do with the appointment of subcommittees. That was McCarthy's appointment [as a matter of seniority]. He named me to the Subcommittee on Investigations presumably because I had had experience in investigations. But the first I knew of any conflict with Margaret Smith was when I read in the paper that she had been shunted aside by McCarthy. Under the circumstances, of course, I wasn't going to argue with McCarthy about what he should do about his committee. As you know, a new member takes whatever assignment he can get."

The full flavor is lost if one judges incidents of the McCarthy

[2] Pearson said McCarthy used below-the-belt tactics. A close friend of McCarthy's recalled: "Joe said he had heard from an Indian that if you kneed a guy hard enough, blood would come out of his eyes. He said he would have found out if that was true if Dick hadn't come in when he did."

era in the context of modern times. In the dawn of Senator Mc-
Carthy's impact—the late 1940's—case histories on Communists-
in-government were lying around Washington easily available to
politicians who could juggle hot potatoes without fumbling. In
this period the Wisconsin Senator was toying with other matters
such as housing and agriculture. In 1950 anti-Communism already had become a political asset. As McCarthy was rolling
up his sleeves, the Red attack in Korea made it the principal C
in the formula of that magic potion Republicans used so effectively:
K_1C_3, representing one part each of Korea, Communism, Corruption and Costs.

For various reasons McCarthy quickly became the foremost
name in headlines about the anti-Communist fight, and he managed to symbolize either a holy, unswerving crusade against Communist subversives or hate, character assassination, and selfish
political opportunism. Those who viewed him as the hero of the
"crusade" outnumbered the others, however, and the McCarthy
era became a historic fact with the Senate election in Maryland.
In that unusually strong Democratic state, the Wisconsin Senator
fought out his assertions about Communists in the State Department with the chairman of the Senate committee that investigated
those charges. The chairman, Senator Millard Tydings, a senior
Democrat who had been powerful enough to withstand President
Roosevelt's purge, was beaten. Almost overnight frightened Democrats elsewhere began to vie with gleeful Republicans for Senator
McCarthy's approving smile—or, at least, his nonopposition. In
Congress Democratic leaders rationalized their apparent insensi-
tivity even to McCarthy's "twenty years of treason" accusation by
assuring each other again and again that "Joe is a Republican
problem." By and large, the strictly "Eisenhower Republicans" disapproved of McCarthy—but not enough to turn down his two-
fisted support of the General in the 1952 campaign. Many encouraged it (discreetly, of course). After all, McCarthy was said to
carry great weight with some traditionally Democratic nationality
and religious blocs. Furthermore, they told each other, a Republican
administration would solve the McCarthy problem simply because

(143)

the Senator wouldn't dare accuse members of his own family of softness on Communism. Nixon made that point in a different way. Without agreeing or disagreeing publicly on the McCarthy issue, Nixon said, "The way to get rid of so-called 'McCarthyism' is to elect a new administration which will deal with this problem [Communism in government] honestly, as has not been done up to this point."

The Californian spoke no ill of his Wisconsin colleague. He endorsed McCarthy for re-election, as he did all Republican candidates, and sometimes spoke well of him. McCarthy, in turn, asserted, "The Communists know Nixon's election will be a body blow to the Communist conspiracy." During the acrimonious exchanges over the Nixon fund McCarthy charged: "The left-wing crowd hates Nixon because of his conviction of Alger Hiss, the man for whom Adlai Stevenson testified."

As the one most responsible for the first effective anti-Communist investigation, Nixon was not particularly awed, from a personal standpoint, by McCarthy's power. But he was anxious that the party benefit however it could from the Senator's influence with bloc-voting Democrats and extreme Republicans. Nixon also felt that an affront to McCarthy could split the Republican party. From the start Nixon was sympathetic to McCarthy's zeal in fighting Communists. He saw such vigor and enthusiasm as a decided long-term asset, if sensibly channeled. The Vice-President told me he never shared the belief of some in the Eisenhower administration that "Communism to McCarthy was a racket." Nixon felt that the Senator "believed what he was doing very deeply."

With Eisenhower's election, preserving party harmony became a near obsession with Nixon. A split over McCarthy would damage the administration and the President's prestige; he felt it would also stunt the party's growth when its prospects of development were better than they had been in decades, and give the Democrats the 1954 Congressional election. Nixon insisted that most of the columnists and commentators urging an Eisenhower-McCarthy showdown were not friendly to either, and an open fight with Eisenhower would serve only to increase McCarthy's stature and

(144)

lower the President's. At Cabinet meetings and in private conversations the Vice-President suggested that each matter McCarthy might bring up should be treated on its individual merits, and the administration should co-operate when McCarthy proved to be right. In addition, he cautioned fellow members of the Eisenhower team to remember their campaign promises regarding a cleanout of security risks in government.

A few nights after Eisenhower's election McCarthy was invited to Bill Rogers' home. Nixon and Jerry Persons, of Eisenhower's staff, also were there, and it was a fine, friendly evening. McCarthy agreed that perhaps he had been a little extreme in some things he had said and maybe even a bit irresponsible at times. He explained also that he believed seriously in what he was doing. Nixon and the others applauded and said they did not want him to take his eye off a single Communist. In the interest of promoting the anti-Communist cause, they urged that he co-operate with fellow Republicans in the White House.

This aura of peace and good will lasted for almost a month after the Republican administration was inaugurated. Then McCarthy made it known he didn't like Eisenhower's appointment of Charles E. Bohlen as ambassador to Russia and James Conant as high commissioner of Germany. He tried to block their confirmation despite Nixon's assurances that they were patriotic Americans. In May the Senator branched out into the international sphere. Angered by the administration's failure to stop our allies from trading with Communist countries, McCarthy issued critical statements, then summoned a group of Greek ship operators and had them sign a "treaty" by which they promised to stop sending their ships to Communist China.

After a public hearing on this subject at which Harold Stassen, then chief of the administration's Mutual Security Agency, denounced McCarthy for "undermining" the Eisenhower foreign policy, Nixon stepped in to mediate. He believed the public approved McCarthy's private boycott against Red China and that it wasn't really a bad thing anyway. He was certain, too, that it was not the issue on which the administration should have a showdown with the Senator. So he arranged a sort of summit conference between Secretary of State Dulles and McCarthy, at which Dulles issued a statement praising the Senator for acting in "the national interest" and McCarthy issued one pledging to touch base with the State Department before negotiating international agreements in the future. It looked like quite a victory for the Senator. But after he got to thinking about it and discussing it with advisers, McCarthy decided he hadn't *really* done as well in the Dulles negotiations as it appeared. His uneasy feeling was fortified by testimony that Europe's trade with Red China was increasing and two British-owned ships had carried Communist troops. Thereupon the headlines proclaimed a new crisis—this one involving Eisenhower himself.

At the suggestion of Democratic Senators Stuart Symington and John L. McClellan, McCarthy sent a letter to the President formally requesting a clear-cut statement of the administration's policy on Western trade with Communist countries. This produced a dilemma for Eisenhower. The President's reply had either to be a strong statement that would cause trouble between the United States and its allies or a noncommittal, evasive one that would seem to nullify campaign pledges of anti-Communist action. For two days the letter was unclaimed. Technically, it didn't exist as far as the White House was concerned. Then Nixon telephoned McCarthy. He asked if the Senator really wanted to go through with this tremendous bonanza for the Democratic opposition. McCarthy agreed to pull back, and he asked Nixon to intercept the letter before it reached Eisenhower's desk.

A month later Nixon, Rogers and Persons were hosts at a private dinner for McCarthy. It was an amiable affair. The talk centered around the fine accomplishments that could follow if McCarthy joined the team as a constructive associate of the President. McCarthy agreed. And although Nixon soon was energetically heading off additional crises—including an assault on Eisenhower's supersensitive Central Intelligence Agency and a much-discussed investigation of Communist influences in the Protestant clergy— the Vice-President continued to have hopes, long-range hopes, that is. They were based more on wishful thinking than substance, for the odds against the harmony Nixon sought were tremendous. Aside from McCarthy's own quirks, some of his advisers were calling the Nixon peace project a sellout and, on the other side, important Republican forces were declaring that there was no alternative but for Eisenhower to slap down the Wisconsin Senator. The Denver *Post,* an enthusiastic Eisenhower supporter, typified that view editorially on June 29, 1954: "Mr. Nixon is an ambitious young man. He is supposed to be a smart politician. He seems to believe that for the sake of harmony Republicans should swallow their conscientious scruples against McCarthy-type smears and McCarthy-type attacks on civil rights. Mr. Eisenhower is not a politician. But he has been forthright in his opposition to all that McCarthyism means. We believe that he has made more votes for the GOP by his attitude toward the Wisconsin Senator than Mr. Nixon can ever make with his amoral talk about the necessity for appeasing Joe."

McCarthy's quarrel with the Army, which finally led to the showdown, had already begun when he visited Nixon and Rogers, then deputy attorney general, who were spending a few days at Key Biscayne, an island near Miami. McCarthy arrived December 30, 1953, for what became the most amicable of all his moderation sessions with the Vice-President. Nixon's advice was: "Don't pull your punches at all on Communists in government. It doesn't make any difference if they are in this administration or in previous ones, if they are there, they should be out. On the other hand, remember that this is your administration. That the people in this administration, including Bob Stevens [the Army Secretary], are just as dedicated as you are to cleaning out people who are subversive. Give them a chance to do the job. Go to these people, discuss the matters with them and give them a chance to do the job."

While still in Florida McCarthy announced at a press conference that his investigating committees would broaden their inquiries to include tax cases compromised "at ridiculously low figures" during the Truman administration. The following week, when newspapers indirectly quoted Nixon as saying McCarthy had agreed to place more emphasis on fields of inquiry other than Communism, the Senator blew up. "It's a lie," he said.

Meanwhile the Senator's feud with the Army was gaining momentum. He charged the Army promoted a dentist, Dr. Irving Peress, from captain to major and honorably discharged him although it had information that he was a Communist. McCarthy demanded to know why the dentist was treated so well and implied that subversion in the military establishment was responsible. A major blowup came in mid-February when Secretary Stevens refused to permit Brigadier General Ralph W. Zwicker, commandant of Camp Kilmer, New Jersey, where Peress was stationed, to testify again before the McCarthy Committee. The General had done so once, but McCarthy considered his testimony unsatisfactory and told him such conduct made him "unfit to wear the uniform." A week later, on February 24, Stevens, McCarthy and three other Republican members of the investigating committee had a two-hour luncheon in the Capitol. The celebrated food was chicken and the talk was compromise. From it came a written "memorandum of understanding" which, in effect, was the Army's capitulation.

In reflecting on the period Nixon told me: "Frankly, we tried to mediate with McCarthy until we were blue in the face. At the famous so-called Chicken Luncheon which was held in my room [the Army problem] was supposed to be worked out that way. McCarthy and Stevens agreed to work this thing out without carrying it to the ultimate extreme of open warfare. Our efforts failed with the result which anybody could have anticipated—a suicidal bloodletting for both the administration and McCarthy."

Frantic peace efforts followed. The principals—Eisenhower and McCarthy—were not brought together. But Nixon, Rogers, Chairman Hall, Senator Knowland, who was party leader in the Senate, and practically every other prominent non-anti-McCarthy Republican participated at one time or another. Washington was the general locale. Much of the action took place in the Woodner Hotel, where both McCarthy and Hall had apartments. The peacemakers went about their project assiduously. So did the "warmongers"—

that is, Democrats, anti-McCarthy but legitimate Republicans who whispered in Eisenhower's ear, and the anti-Eisenhower intimates of McCarthy who whispered in his.

It was in this atmosphere that Adlai Stevenson hit exposed nerves in Washington with a broadcast charging that the Republican party was "divided against itself, half McCarthy, half Eisenhower." Under other circumstances Nixon would have been delighted to answer Stevenson, as spokesman for the administration. But he made it clear to Hall and others that he wanted no part of this answer for fear of compromising his position as mediator. Furthermore, his good-will tour of Asia had received favorable reaction and lifted his prestige generally. He believed that from a personal standpoint, no matter how well he did in replying to Stevenson, he was bound to lose more than he could gain. Nonetheless, when Hall, Sherman Adams, Hagerty and James Bassett, the Republican press director, met with Eisenhower to discuss the reply, all agreed Nixon was the ideal man to handle it. The President then and there telephoned his Vice-President to convey the assignment. Nixon exiled himself to a hotel suite to prepare. He confided to a friend later that it was one of the toughest writing jobs he ever undertook. On the day of the speech Nixon discussed it for forty-five minutes with Eisenhower, who then took off for a weekend at his retreat in the Maryland hill country which Roosevelt called "Shangri-la" and Eisenhower renamed "Camp David."

Nixon spoke from Washington's CBS studio and told the audience he chose that sedate setting because the issue was too important for handling the way Stevenson did, "with a rip-roaring political tirade." The speech covered several subjects, as had Stevenson's, but the highlight was McCarthy and Communism—and Nixon both praised and chastised the Senator, by indirection.

"Men who have in the past done effective work exposing Communism in this country have, by reckless talk and questionable methods, made themselves the issue, rather than the cause they believe in so deeply," he said. "When they have done this they not only have diverted attention from the danger of Communism but have diverted that attention to themselves. Also, they have allowed those whose primary objective is to defeat the Eisenhower administration to divert attention from its great program to these individuals who followed those methods."

Without mentioning his name the Vice-President also asked the question often posed by McCarthy—why worry about being fair when you are shooting rats?—and answered it this way: "I agree they [Communists] are a bunch of rats. But just remember this, when you go out to shoot rats, you have to shoot straight because when you shoot wildly it not only means that the rats may get away more easily—but you make it easier on the rats. Also, you might hit someone else who is trying to shoot rats, too."

(There was a delayed-action sentence in the Vice-President's talk that has been quoted in practically every criticism of *his* methods since then. It was: "Incidentally, in mentioning Secretary Dulles, isn't it wonderful, finally, to have a Secretary of State who isn't taken in by the Communists, who stands up to them?")

The televised Army-McCarthy hearings began the following month, to Nixon's chagrin and disgust. "I prefer professionals to amateur actors," he said when asked what he thought of the show. He always had opposed televising committee hearings because "there is inevitably too much of a tendency for both the witnesses and the committee members to play to the cameras rather than the facts." He wouldn't watch a moment of it and advised others that they, too, should make better use of their time.

From then on there was occasional contact between Nixon and McCarthy, but no serious effort at conciliation or friendship, and McCarthy proceeded to lump the Eisenhower period with that of Roosevelt and Truman in his "years of treason" attacks.[3] When censure charges were brought against McCarthy later, Nixon appointed to the bipartisan investigating committee senators recommended by their respective party leaders. An erroneous report at the time (which still crops up in columns and magazine articles) had it that Nixon struck the word "censure" from the title of the Senate resolution. Actually, he couldn't have done that if he

[3] There never had been a full measure of trust. From the beginning Nixon was careful to have someone with him whenever he saw McCarthy. Frequently it was Rogers, whom McCarthy regarded highly and invited to be his lawyer before the Tydings Committee.

wanted to. The Senate voted to change the word "censure" in the resolution to "condemned," and as Senator Arthur V. Watkins, the committee chairman, explained to me, "The amendment to the title was accepted by the Senate without question because it did not change the meaning of the resolution or the action which the Senate had taken." Nixon's only involvement was to praise the Watkins Committee.

One of McCarthy's closest personal friends told me the Senator "had a conviction that Nixon could have helped him and not only didn't but was active in the opposition to him." In October, 1955, when a news service asked Republican senators their choices for the presidential nomination, McCarthy placed Nixon last on a list of six names. After Stassen started his movement to prevent Nixon's renomination the following year, McCarthy issued a long statement which appeared to support Nixon but was devoted mostly to attacking "the left wing of the Republican party," notably Eisenhower, its "leader," and such other figures as Stassen, Sherman Adams, Dr. Milton Eisenhower, Dewey, and Paul Hoffman.

In reflecting on his experiences with McCarthy, Nixon said: "My feeling is that the McCarthy thing was a tragedy. I think he was really a casualty in the great struggle of our times, as Hiss was a casualty on the other side. Both deeply believed in the cause they represented. The reason McCarthy became a casualty was because in dealing with this conspiracy it takes not only almost infinite skill, but also patience, judgment, coolness . . . it takes all this plus dedication and courage and hard work. He had the last three qualities in abundance. But in the other respects he was erratic. To an extent he destroyed himself, but he was also destroyed because of the very character of the force he was fighting. This does not imply that all those who were against McCarthy were Communists. On the contrary, many people just as honest as he was opposed him because they felt his methods hurt the cause to which they were dedicated. It is important to remember that when fighting Communists in the United States, domestic Communism, it isn't enough to be right on the merits. You have got to bend over backwards to be fair in tactics because those who oppose you are smart enough never to attack you frontally. They always direct their fire at how you do it, rather than what you do. The reason I succeeded in the Hiss case when McCarthy failed in some others is because I was right on the facts and I did not give the opposition any target to shoot at on the tactics."

When the time neared, in 1954, for getting out to stir up the voters, Nixon confided to a few intimates the only consolation was that it would be his last campaign. To at least one friend, he added, "I'm tired, bone tired. My heart's not in it." Although some Democrats complained that their people knuckled under too much to Eisenhower, the Republican viewpoint was that the Democrats had been hammering at the administration without letup on Dixon-Yates, the 1954 recession, farm problems, seeming differences on points of foreign policy between Eisenhower, Dulles and Nixon, and other issues. "They have a 'murderers row' to come out at the drop of a hat and issue statements and fight for their party," Nixon said at the time. "We have practically nobody to stand up and fight back." He was weary of being the lightning rod for Republican leadership. It was evident he would have to take on again the job of Republican hatchetman ("Every campaign has one out front slugging," he admitted) and the prospect wasn't a pleasant one.

Nixon wanted to campaign personally for all who requested his help. That meant practically every Republican candidate in the country. The schedule he mapped out for himself—unmatched in the history of nonpresidential campaigns—called for forty-eight days of electioneering in thirty-one states, beginning September 15. On September 14 Democrats swept the Republican stronghold of Maine. At the airport the next morning an associate noted that Nixon looked "tired, flaccid and with none of his old crusading zeal." He was not amused, either, when Chairman Hall grinned at him and boomed, "What's the matter, Dick? You look as if you'd been the candidate for governor of Maine."

At the first stop, the Ohio Republican State Convention at Columbus, Nixon declared, "The election of a Democratic Eighty-fourth Congress in November will mean the beginning of the end of the Republican party. It is that simple."

A major effort was required simply to convince voters that an "Eisenhower Congress" meant a "Republican Congress." While the national Democratic strategy was to blast at the administration, many of the party's candidates—in some areas, most of them— were implying or flatly saying they would support the popular Eisenhower in Congress more effectively than their "right-wing Republican" opponents. Republicans, meanwhile, adopted a heated-up version of their 1952 strategy. The emphasis, as enunciated by Nixon, was that a Democratic Congress would impair the Eisenhower administration's policy of hardness on Communists and return the country to the days of Truman administration softness. Nixon dealt with the issue almost everywhere, even in New Jersey, where Clifford P. Case, the Republican candidate for senator, was himself a victim of softness-on-Communism accusations.[4]

Eisenhower was a more interested participant in the campaign than his relatively limited speaking schedule and the news stories of that period would indicate. From the outset Nixon cautioned the White House against optimism. In his first telephone conference from the field on September 19 the Vice-President, in Minneapolis, told Brownell, Summerfield and Persons, in their Washington offices: "Don't give the President the idea that things are in good shape. They're not!" In fact, he predicted the loss of fifty House seats if the Republicans didn't move quickly in several fields. Before Eisenhower left on September 22 for his first campaign speech, he wrote Nixon.

"This afternoon I am starting off on my trip to the Northwest and to California," he said, in part. "I shall make four talks, two of them formal. I don't dread this so much as I do the motorcade; sometimes I fear that I am getting a little old for this sort of thing. I expect to see Pat at the Los Angeles meeting. That will at least be one bright spot."

[4] No candidate got more vigorous support from Nixon than the liberal, frankly anti-McCarthy Senator Case. The Vice-President insisted to Republican doubters that Case proved himself to be a bona fide, anti-Communist Republican by helping to draft the Mundt-Nixon Communist Registration Bill in the late 1940's. Case was elected by only 3,200 votes. Without Nixon's help he would have lost.

A week later, on September 29, Eisenhower wrote from his vacation headquarters in Denver:

Dear Dick: Good reports have been reaching me from all parts of the country as the result of your intensive—and I am sure exhaustive—speaking tour. Now that I have just read the excerpts of the talk that Rose Woods [Nixon's executive secretary] has sent us, I understand more than ever why the comments I have had have been so enthusiastic. Please don't think that I am not unaware that I have done little to lighten your load. On the contrary, I am, in point of fact, constantly suggesting other places for you to visit. You will have to consider these burdens that I impose upon you as penalty for being such an excellent and persuasive speaker.

One thing that has come of this is that you are constantly becoming better and more favorably known to the American public. This is all to the good.

I am looking forward to your visit to Denver (but not, in all honesty, to our television stint). I hope we will be able to have a golf game while you are here. Don't bother to bring your clubs unless they are already on your plane, but I would suggest that you pack your shoes. Incidentally, John McClure tells me that you distinguished yourself recently both at golf and at the presentation of the Eisenhower Trophy. ... With warm regards ... As ever, DWIGHT EISENHOWER.

A week or so later, in Denver, the President expressed to a private get-together of party and Congressional leaders his appreciation of the Vice-President's campaigning, and he admonished the others to fight as hard. "I was feeling low because I didn't think we were getting enough help in the campaign and were carrying it pretty much alone," Nixon recalls. The President's words encouraged him. As a matter of fact, Eisenhower's continuous encouragement spurred Nixon on at other times too, although his only public indication that he approved Nixon's drive came as the campaign reached election eve. In a letter of October 27, released that day to the press, Eisenhower complimented Nixon and said that "no man could have done more effective work" toward returning a Republican Congress.

Others also had been exhorting the Vice-President. Congressman Charles Halleck, now Republican leader of the House of Representatives, said, "You've got to give 'em hell, Dick! Sam Rayburn's just been to town [Indianapolis]. He was murdering us!" In New York, Governor Dewey advised Nixon to "hit harder . . . people like a fighter." Harold Stassen sent a note October 11: "I wish to commend you on the splendid and hard-hitting contribution you are making to this campaign." On October 20 he sent a memorandum, stamped "Confidential," proposing that the "issue" be shifted in the final week to Eisenhower's "rollback" of international Communist power. Stassen suggested a publicity offensive that might include such eye-catchers as a visit to Washington by the Guatemalan President who had ousted his country's Communist-dominated regime, an announcement that Dr. Milton Eisenhower, the President's brother, would go to Indo-China "for a good-will survey of the non-Communist forces and to plan further the re-building of their economy," an announcement that President Eisenhower intended to visit Europe in the future "for personal conferences on the progress of our partners for peace." A confidential survey made for the Republicans by the Batten, Barton, Durstine and Osborn agency showed foreign policy to be the number one concern of the voters; Communism in the United States was a close second.

Meanwhile the campaign was developing a lead of invective uncommon to off-year elections. Nixon's barnstorming put Democrats on the defensive. In speech after speech he declared that "thousands of Communists, fellow travelers and security risks have been thrown out" of government jobs by the Republican administration. He warned that the Democratic "left wing" would take over if that party won the Congress. He listed five Democratic candidates for senator in the West as "left-wingers" (two of them won, three lost). And he asserted the Communist party was fighting Republicans "desperately and openly" because "the candidates running on the Democratic ticket in the key states are almost without exception members of the Democratic party's left-wing clique which has been so blind to the Communist conspiracy and has tolerated it in the United States." In the climactic last week of the campaign the Vice-President invited Democrats and independents to "put their party in their pocket and vote for an Eisenhower Congress [because] we recognize the Communist menace and this administration is determined to crush that menace."

The Democrats spent much energy swinging back. Their charges centered on the words "smear" and "gutter campaign," but some added a local touch. A Colorado Democrat insisted, for instance, that Nixon opposed him for the "deceitful purpose" of weakening Colorado's fight against Nixon's native California over certain water rights. Democratic responses to Nixon's claim of mass Communist and security risk discharges ranged from countercharges of "Fascist type attack" to a "numbers game." Their demand that the Republicans name the Communists and actual subversives they fired was denied. After much prodding from Nixon the Civil Service Commission reported three weeks before the election that 6,926 federal workers had been dismissed or had resigned under the security risk program, and 1,743 of them had data in their files indicating "in varying degrees" either "subversive activities, subversive associations or membership in subversive organizations." The others were considered either sex perverts, alcoholics or undesirable for other reasons.[5]

While "Communism" was the battle cry, the sacred word of the Republican campaign was "Eisenhower," and Democrats foolish enough to use it irreverently found themselves tangling with Nixon. Adlai Stevenson, who described the Vice-President's campaign as "an ill-will tour," was a frequent tangler.

Nixon worked as tirelessly for fellow Republicans as he had ever done for himself. He drove harder, in fact, than many of the candidates, and as the campaign ended it was clear to Nixon's friends that he was dissatisfied with much that had happened—or, more accurately, had *not* happened. He felt that too many in the administration had done nothing or next to nothing. Chotiner, who managed the Vice-President's activities, recalls that with a few exceptions "Dick was about the only man [in the top echelon] willing to stick his neck out and campaign for Republicans though he knew that if the party won, they would say it was because of the

[5] Fifteen months later the Civil Service chairman told a Senate committee that a subsequent survey showed that 41.2 per cent of the dismissed or resigned security risks actually had been hired *after* Eisenhower had taken over the executive department from the Democrats.

administration, and if it lost, they would say it was his fault. He felt the people didn't stand by him who should have." He was disappointed also in the caliber of many Republican candidates and the party's organization generally. "We're in tough shape," he confided to a friend while en route to Denver for the final, election-eve address. "This administration is giving the country the best government it has ever had—but the problem is to sell it."

Chotiner recalls that on the flight back to Washington the next day Nixon handed him seven pages of notes and said: "Here is my last campaign speech. You may like to keep it as a souvenir. I'm through with politics." Then, as if to show that he was serious, Nixon discussed the relative merits of opening his own law office or joining an established firm.

The Democrats regained control of Congress by picking up twenty seats in the House and two in the Senate. This net gain was smaller than had been normal for the "out" party in an off-year election. Nixon interpreted that outcome as a Democratic victory technically but a dead heat in reality. McCarthy said it was "a bad defeat" for the Republicans and blamed the administration's "jungle warfare against those of us who were trying to expose and dig out Communists." Stevenson called it a demonstration of the people's disenchantment with the Republicans and their "resort to abuse, slander and distortion."

Nixon's campaign solidified his position as Hero of organization Republicans and Villain of organization Democrats. In ensuing months the Democrats promoted *their* picture of him with considerably more enterprise than the Republicans did theirs.

When I asked Nixon long afterwards why he changed his mind about leaving politics, he said it was "circumstances" more than any particular event. "Pat felt very, very strongly about it," he explained. "Ever since the fund thing she hasn't been keen on this business." Then he added:

"Once you get into this great stream of history you can't get out. You can drown. Or you can be pulled ashore by the tide. But it is awfully hard to get out when you are in the middle of the stream—if it is intended that you stay there."

11

$\text{I}_{\text{N THE}}$ seemingly serene Republican year of
1956 Eisenhower decided to seek re-election, and he offered Nixon
a Cabinet post instead of a second term. Nixon planned to quit
public life in disgust, then resolved to run again, whereupon
Harold Stassen tried to shove him out. The Stassen venture would
have been an even more fascinating show if the public had been
treated to the whole Stassen-Nixon story, past and present, instead
of brief and often inaccurate glimpses of the byplay.

Nixon's friends now sputter at the mention of the man's name.
But the Vice-President still has "a rather friendly feeling for
Stassen." They met during World War II. Stassen was already
being talked about as a Republican sure to be President someday
when his plane put down on Bougainville, a South Pacific island,
in 1943, and was met by a lieutenant (junior grade) named Richard
M. Nixon. He never forgot the splendid impression left on him
by Stassen's handshake.

After the war Nixon decided to try for a political career—on
the Stassen bandwagon, if possible. On May 20, 1946, he wrote:

Dear Mr. Stassen: As you will note from the enclosure, I am the
Republican candidate for Congress in the Twelfth District [of Cali-
fornia] to oppose Mr. Jerry Voorhis.

I have been very interested in following your campaign to liberalize
the Republican party because I feel strongly that the party must adopt
a constructive, progressive program in order to merit the support of the
voters.

As you may recall, I met you on Bougainville in February of 1943.

I was the Officer-in-charge of the SCAT detachment there, and you arrived on one of our planes on an inspection tour.[1]
I am planning to attend the Pasadena Junior Chamber of Commerce dinner on May 28 at which you are to speak. Although I realize that your time will be at a premium, I would greatly appreciate the opportunity to talk with you briefly, if possible, at some time during your stay in California. . . .

They met and talked, and Stassen consented to being photographed with Candidate Nixon. The great man also agreed to send along an endorsement at the proper time, and Nixon quickly did what he could to make every voter in his district aware of it. In an election-eve editorial the Los Angeles *Times* declared Nixon "is a friend of Governor Stassen, and his political philosophy is along the lines advocated by Stassen. He is no reactionary in his thinking, but he is distinctly not a leftist or a parlor pink."

The year 1946 demanded a major decision of Harold E. Stassen. He had an opportunity to be elected senator. But he chose, instead, to begin running for president. He had supported sixty Republicans for House and Senate seats that year. Forty-one of them were elected, forming a core of lively Stassenites in Congress. One of them, a senator from Wisconsin named Joseph R. McCarthy, subsequently led the Stassen primary campaign in Wisconsin—the crucial one which Stassen thought would lead to his nomination for president in 1948.

In California, where the established organization Republicans were associated with Governor Warren, the young Stassenites were shunted aside. Congressman Nixon therefore attended the 1948 Republican Convention as a spectator, and introduced a friend or two to his friend Harold. But he had no responsibilities that interfered with his fascinated absorption of all the goings-on. Before the convention he had done a little something for Harold at the behest of their mutual friend, Congressman George MacKinnon, of Minnesota. Stassen and Governor Dewey had staked their prospects

[1] Stassen denies that meeting, as he does any "close" association with Nixon. "I don't have any recollection of that at all," Stassen told me repeatedly when I asked him during a long interview about various phases of his relationship with Nixon before Nixon was nominated for vice-president in 1952.

(159)

for the nomination—and, it was generally believed, the Presidency itself—on a debate in Portland, Oregon. The issue was whether to outlaw the Communist party. Stassen was for it; Dewey against. Although Nixon was unknown outside his district, the Mundt-Nixon Bill to control Communists was well known. As its co-author, Nixon helped to prepare a telegram favorable to Stassen's argument. It was a concise, compelling statement, and Stassen backers believed their man would have won the debate if he had read it as a highlight of his rebuttal. The debate was broadcast nationally over three networks and nine hundred radio stations and left little doubt as to who would be nominated. Dewey won the debate and nomination.

A year later the Volunteers for Stassen organization in California was the first group to endorse Nixon for senator. On October 16, 1950, Stassen wrote his friend: "I trust the people will respond with a resounding victory for you." Nixon won, and Stassen began to warm up for another try at the Presidency. In 1951 Senator Nixon was among forty-five men invited to a private conference to help Stassen decide his future.[2] The conferees met June 23 and June 24 at the Clarksboro, New Jersey, estate of Amos J. Peaslee. Practically everyone there felt General Eisenhower was the strongest possible Republican candidate, but a few believed the General would not run. All figured that Eisenhower-inclined voters would thus support Stassen, so Stassen made a formal announcement of his candidacy for the Republican nomination on December 27, 1951. Privately he had promised his major supporters to withdraw if Eisenhower became a candidate. ("I have an agreement in my safe that states that Harold would get out of the primaries if Ike got in," his national campaign manager, Bernard M. Shanley, told me.) On January 6, 1952, Senator Henry Cabot Lodge proclaimed Eisenhower a candidate, and the next day the General gave Lodge and his coworkers a bright green light to go ahead with an Eisenhower nominating campaign. Three days later, on January 10,

[2] Governor Sherman Adams, of New Hampshire, couldn't attend, but asked to be posted so Bernard M. Shanley, Stassen's campaign manager, went to Concord, N. H., after the conference to brief Adams on the decisions, including Stassen's pledge to withdraw as a candidate if Eisenhower got into the race.

Stassen's chief campaign aide wrote Nixon: "The following is very confidential, but you should know that the slate of delegates to be entered in Wisconsin has been almost completed." The letter also noted that "a very expertly done" poll—"limited to a Stassen-Taft contest because it seems to us that this is the realistic situation"— showed "that Harold leads Taft at almost a 60-40 basis."

The first primary of the campaign was that of New Hampshire, March 1. The result was: Eisenhower, 46,661; Taft, 35,838; Stassen, 6,574. Two weeks later Stassen's was the only major name on the ballot in the Minnesota primary. An attempt to add Eisenhower's name was voided because of legal technicalities. Nevertheless, Eisenhower got almost as many votes by the troublesome write-in process as were given to Stassen, who ostensibly was the only candidate.

Earlier Stassen had visited Eisenhower in Paris. On returning he infuriated Lodge and others on the Eisenhower committee by implying that he *knew* the score: it was that Eisenhower would *not* run. Stassen also confided to friends that his own prospects were better than ever, and at a conference in Nixon's suite in the Senate Office Building he offered the California Senator the vice-presidential spot on his ticket if he would line up Stassen support in the California delegation. An intimate to whom Nixon unburdened the story within minutes after Stassen left the office told me, "Nixon couldn't have been more surprised at the brazenness of that offer. . . . He shrugged it off on the grounds that he felt Eisenhower was going to run." The California delegation, of which Nixon was a member, was committed to Warren.

The nineteen Minnesota votes pledged to Stassen at the 1952 Republican Convention switched in time to ensure Eisenhower's nomination on the first ballot. Stassen then became a contender for the vice-presidential nomination. Friends say he swallowed hard, but kept smiling, when it went to the boyish Californian whose ambition so recently had been merely to bask in Stassen's political sunshine. Outwardly Stassen's attitude toward Nixon never changed. Even his telegram advising Nixon to resign from the ticket during the 1952 campaign uproar over the Nixon fund was friendly in tone. After President-elect Eisenhower picked Stassen as Mutual Security Administrator, Nixon wired congratulations: "I am sure your designation will meet with the unaminous approval of the country." Stassen replied: "I am looking forward with anticipation to working with you . . . and welcome your advice and counsel in the problems which lie ahead." There were other friendly exchanges during the administration's first term.[3] But Nixon was not altogether surprised by Stassen's subsequent drive to oust him. "I think his opposition to me was more a case of personal ambition in this instance," Nixon told me. "Stassen has been a very able public servant, and could still be used, perhaps. . . . He can present a case better than anybody I've ever seen. I would think that he would have made a remarkable president in certain times."

Although Stassen became the symbol of Republicans opposed to Nixon's renomination in 1956, his was not the first move. A quiet effort in behalf of Governor Christian A. Herter, of Massachusetts, was started early in 1955 by Arthur J. Goldsmith and others following a conference at Harvard. This endeavor was pro-Herter and not necessarily anti-Nixon. Herter was informed. He approved tacitly, but did not participate. Like those favoring other potential candidates, his supporters were uncertain whether their aim for Herter was the Presidency or the Vice-Presidency, since Eisenhower had been indicating long before his heart attack that he might not run again. Goldsmith, a wealthy New York businessman known to right-wing Republicans as "the mystery man of the Waldorf Towers," because that's where he lives, contributes lavishly to liberal causes and candidates. He also has been a major supporter of Stassen. But Stassen was not part of the original Herter movement, of which Senator Jacob K. Javits, then attorney general of New York, was among the prime movers.

Dewey made it clear that his prestige and power in the Republican party would again be behind Nixon for vice-president. But

[3] Stassen kept it up until his departure from the administration in the second term. He even sent the Vice-President copies of memorandums to the President, including one of September 24, 1957, advising Eisenhower to go to Little Rock to take personal command of the school desegregation fight.

there was still plenty of opposition. Most of it was hidden—or masked by protests of friendship—since Nixon, after all, could still possibly succeed to the Presidency before the Eisenhower first term expired in January.

Eisenhower announced on February 29 that he would be a candidate again. But he refused to discuss what would happen to Nixon. Nixon immediately issued a statement praising the President and his decision to run. In a note of thanks Eisenhower said, "I do want you to know that this expression—characteristic as it is of everything you do—touches me deeply." At his next weekly press conference Eisenhower revealed he had asked Nixon to "chart out his own course."

That, broadly, is what he had told the Vice-President, in private. And it caused Nixon and those close to him many anxious (and some embittered) days during the six months until the Eisenhower-Nixon ticket was renominated on August 22. Weeks before the President had charted his own course he was getting advice on what Nixon's should be. It came inadvertently via the pollsters, columnists and political writers he read in newspapers and directly from Eisenhower friends and associates, some of whom bespoke Nixon's interests. Eisenhower's affection for his understudy had increased greatly because he felt Nixon had shown mature judgment and limitless tact in the delicate period after the Eisenhower heart attack. Thus no one dared attack Nixon frontally in Eisenhower's presence. Even Stassen, who ultimately brought his anti-Nixon position into the open, prefaced his observations with "Dick is a fine fellow, and is doing a grand job, but . . ." The "buts" varied. Some contended it would be "healthier" for the party and would keep the convention from looking like a dictated affair if the vice-presidential nomination was kept open; others said Nixon's future would be brighter if he headed a major department as a Cabinet member in the second term; still others believed Nixon was considered too partisan and would hurt the ticket, particularly in a year when the Vice-Presidency would be emphasized because of Eisenhower's health.

The Cabinet and "open convention" ideas appealed to Eisenhower. In a long, intimate conversation at the White House he reminded Nixon that no vice-president had been elected president, directly, in more than a hundred years. He pointed out that, on the other hand, men like Herbert Hoover had done well enough as Cabinet members for the Presidency to become their natural next step. He asked Nixon to consider whether a Cabinet position would broaden his experience as an administrator and suggested an immensely challenging spot—Secretary of Defense. He further indicated that Nixon might have almost any other except the State Department, which was reserved for Dulles.

The President was "being friendly" and was anxious that "I consider all the facts before I made up my mind," Nixon says, in retrospect. Dulles, who had the confidence of both Eisenhower and Nixon, told me that Eisenhower "did not want to seem arbitrary. He wanted to leave [the vice-presidential selection] to the convention. He wanted the convention to be free. This did not mean that he did not want Nixon. He did. But he did not want to appear to be dictating. This is the President's nature. This was a delicate situation." Dulles recalls also that it was "a very difficult time for Nixon." Other friends of the Vice-President agree wholeheartedly. One of them who suffered through the whole emotional ordeal with Nixon told me Eisenhower's reluctance to come out flatly and ask Nixon to be his running mate was "one of the greatest hurts of his [Nixon's] whole career."

"I think it might have been naïve on Eisenhower's part, but I don't think it was innocent on the part of whoever advised him," added the friend. "It was definitely an effort to ditch Nixon. I think the President was naïve and sincerely felt that Nixon had a better political future from a Cabinet post. But Nixon had a much shrewder judgment and reached the conclusion very early in the whole episode that either he had to go all the way and win through or get out and be finished." Another close Nixon associate told me, "While Dick was being kicked around like that, I went to the White House one day and asked Adams, 'What's going on around here?' Adams said, 'Well, Dick's a fine young fellow, but maybe it would be better if he took a Cabinet job.' That was the line, you see."

After Eisenhower's "chart your own course" statement at his March 7 press conference, Nixon figured it probably would be best for him to leave public life and accept the presidency of a large California business enterprise or a partnership in a New York law firm that guaranteed him an annual income in excess of $100,000. Both positions had been offered him on an "any time you want to come" basis. He did not seriously consider entering the Eisenhower Cabinet. ("I would have been like Henry Wallace if I had taken a Cabinet job," he told me.) On a Wednesday he told two or three friends he would call a press conference the next day to make an announcement of retirement from public life. Vic Johnston, executive director of the Republican Senate Campaign Committee, chanced to hear it from Nixon when they almost bumped into each other in the Capitol. Johnston rushed downtown to tell National Chairman Hall and then to the White House to alert Major General Wilton B. Persons, the President's deputy for legislative affairs, who succeeded Adams as chief of staff. Hall and Persons dashed to the Capitol. They cornered Nixon and persuaded him to put off his decision for a while. Their arguments, and those of several other major supporters who rushed to the Capitol like firemen answering a general alarm, were that his friends would regard him as a "quitter" if he let them down. They also insisted his departure would split the Republican party and would be interpreted generally as a suggestion of doubt about Eisenhower's chances of surviving a second term. Nixon agreed to defer his decision. Meanwhile Senator Styles Bridges passed the word that Nixon should be shown how highly he is regarded by Republicans. And that week he was given 22,202 write-in votes for vice-president in the New Hampshire primary. (In May, this demonstration of popularity was repeated in the Oregon primary, where 30,000 voters "wrote in" Nixon's name on their ballots.) Previously, only an occasional vote was ever cast for vice-president in primaries, usually by accident.

Nixon told me the New Hampshire primary and the Republican

leadership's violent reaction later that year to the Stassen ouster efforts convinced him that he should seek re-election.

"If Stassen hadn't intervened himself in this, there would have been a much better chance that I would have gotten off, even after the New Hampshire primary," he added. "That primary was convincing mostly in that it changed the attitude of the opinionated, those who were saying and writing that I would be a drag on the ticket. They couldn't write that any more after New Hampshire. But the major factor was the mail, the telephone calls and the scores of political leaders around the country who came to me and said, 'Stay on or we are through. We've had it.' The New Hampshire primary convinced me from the positive standpoint; the letter writers and political leaders convinced me from the negative standpoint. You see, if Stassen hadn't been in it, the negative factor would not have been there. If I had decided on my own to get out, without appearing to be pressured by Stassen, then the so-called Taft people and the other Republican organization leaders wouldn't have been mad. They would have said, 'This is what Nixon wants to do; it is up to him,' but they were not going to have Stassen push me off. That's why Stassen made it inevitable that I stay on. The reaction in party circles to Stassen's activities convinced me that my getting off would be a liability to the ticket. So I decided to stay on if the President wished me to, and I knew that I had to make a necessary fight."

Incidentally, Nixon says that he has seen no concrete evidence that Adams or anyone else on the White House staff helped Stassen and the others who sought his displacement. He was—and still is —flooded with reports of "intrigues" against him by the "palace guard." "I've seen so much of that in my relatively brief experience in public life that I discredit virtually all of it," he said. "I have found that ninety per cent of it is gossip, and the rest is planted or caused by a misunderstanding."

Rumors and "reports" of this kind reached a peak during the troubled half year before the Republican 1956 Convention. To keep current with the denials would have required a staff several times the size of the Vice-President's. Nixon was happy to take personal cognizance of many disavowals, however. When Drew Pearson reported in his newspaper column that Dr. Milton S. Eisenhower was behind the Stassen drive, for instance, the President's brother wrote Nixon on August 6, 1956, in part:

I . . . I want to say to you, with directness and finality, that it has never occurred to me that anyone but you should be considered for the vice-presidential nomination. My support is of little consequence, but I am for you one hundred per cent.

It happens I think Harold Stassen's action was unforgivable, harmful and childish. I was particularly resentful of the fact that he took his action at the very time that the President was receiving magnificent publicity on the work for inter-American unity and then at the last moment Stassen buried the good under the bad.

With high regard and friendship, I am . . . Sincerely . . . MILTON.

After lunch on April 26 Nixon went to the White House to tell the President he had charted his course—that he would be pleased to run again. "I guess I was the first to know after the President," said James C. Hagerty, the White House press secretary. "The President rang for me. I went into his office. The Vice-President was sitting there. The President and Dick had big grins on their faces. The President said, 'Jim, Dick just told me he would be happy to be on the ticket, and he has made up his mind that he would like to run again with me.' Adams came in, and we later saw Persons. We told them. The President said to me, 'What do you think we ought to do on the announcement?' I didn't have to think long about that. 'Why not let Dick go out and say it?' I replied. The President said, 'Jim, you go with him, and after he finishes his announcement, you say [to the press] I was delighted to hear this news from the Vice-President.' " Thereupon Nixon went into Hagerty's office to conduct his first press conference in the White House.

Peaslee, a principal Stassen backer in previous campaigns, and a friend of Nixon's, wrote: "Dorothy and I are completely delighted! It is a great day for the party and the country." Sidney J. Weinberg, the financier and money raiser for the Citizens for Eisenhower organization, wired: "It will be good to work for the same team we won with in '52." Weeks before, Weinberg had denied emphatically to Nixon the published speculation that he opposed the Vice-President's renomination, and at the peak of the Stassen drive in August he told Eisenhower, "I am for Dick Nixon one hundred per cent." Eisenhower reportedly replied, "So am I." The friendly reaction to Nixon's candidacy was hardly unanimous, however, despite the signs of Eisenhower's approval. The opposition's great hope and encouragement was Eisenhower's continued refusal to say flatly that he wanted Nixon, period. Jacob K. Javits, Republican candidate for senator in New York where Nixon was said to be especially unpopular, stated the Vice-President had done "a remarkable job as a presidential assistant in his travels overseas, but he has been bitterly partisan in some areas which I think are subject to criticism." At the annual Governors' Conference, in June, all the Republican governors signed a petition pledging support for Eisenhower. But Nixon's name was omitted because he was "controversial." The Democrats also began to stir. National Chairman Butler charged that Nixon's "whole political career has been built on an un-American and divisive campaign technique" and demanded that Eisenhower "assume responsibility for the kind of campaign Nixon will probably pursue on behalf of the President in the coming months." In Nixon's home state, Edmund G. ("Pat") Brown, then campaign manager for Adlai Stevenson, declared: "The people of California don't like Nixon. Give us a good vice-presidential candidate with Stevenson and we will carry California this fall."[4]

Late in May the name of Murray Chotiner, Nixon's campaign manager, came up in a Senate Investigating Committee's investigation of a garment manufacturer accused of stealing government property. Chotiner was his lawyer. Nixon was in no way implicated. But every news story tied Chotiner to him. This delighted those still anxious to bypass Nixon's nomination and caused the Vice-

[4] The Eisenhower-Nixon ticket won California that fall by 607,000 votes. In New York, where Javits feared the effects of Nixon's candidacy, the Eisenhower-Nixon majority was an unprecedented 1,590,000 votes, or double the margin of 1952.

President to sever his political relationship with his ingenious campaign technician.

On June 9 President Eisenhower suffered an ileitis attack which required an immediate abdominal operation. This sharpened the health issue and further revived intense interest in the Republican vice-presidential nomination. Hagerty stated a month later, while the President was convalescing at Gettysburg, that neither Eisenhower nor Nixon had altered his plan to run again. But that didn't impress Harold Stassen, Eisenhower's "secretary of peace."

Stassen himself isn't certain when he actually decided to undertake his 1956 preconvention operation which the public came to know as a "Dump Nixon Movement"—although Christian Herter, ostensibly its intended beneficiary, prefers to call it "a comic opera."

"I had, of course, thought about it for some months," Stassen told me. But he actually did nothing more than discuss the matter with an intimate or two until May 6, when he returned to Washington from a long and fruitless disarmament conference in London.

The anti-Nixon operation that appeared to be making headway when he left was petering out for lack of leadership, an alternate candidate, and effective encouragement from the White House. Interest revived quickly when President Eisenhower became ill early in June. But no Republican of national standing would indicate it publicly, at least not until Eisenhower's own status had been clarified. Even Stassen hesitated for a while to challenge openly the Vice-President, who might succeed to the Presidency any day. During the month after Eisenhower's ileitis operation Nixon went about his business with tact and an outward show of confidence, while Stassen consulted frequently with his ever-diminishing knot of followers and had the popularity of various potential candidates tested, secretly, by a poll taker who had conducted such surveys for him in the past.

"I knew that Len Hall and Dick Nixon were pressing Chris Herter about renominating Nixon," Stassen insisted. "Consequently, it was very late then, and you either took the stand or that moment was forever gone when anybody could take a stand.

. . . It became a matter of either moving or never moving, and I decided, all things considered, that I'd better move."

Things began to stir aggressively on July 10, when Hagerty made it known at the Gettysburg White House that the President's new illness would mean nothing to the political lineup already in the works. In other words, he stated Eisenhower and Nixon were still running. What happened thereafter must be related chronologically to be comprehended.

On July 12 Chairman Hall was summoned to Gettysburg. The President, the chairman, and Hagerty decided Representative Charles E. Halleck, of Indiana, should make the presidential nominating speech at the convention in August. Hall proposed that they also select someone to place Nixon's name before the convention and announce both nominators at once. The three men agreed Herter would be ideal. Eisenhower suggested it be cleared with Nixon and Herter. Hall telephoned the Vice-President in Washington, as Eisenhower and Hagerty sat by, attentive. Nixon hesitated. He wasn't sure a "package announcement" was best, he said, and furthermore he understood Herter might be interested in the nomination himself. Hall put Hagerty on the phone, but Nixon insisted on waiting at least a day. Eisenhower said nothing.

July 13—Nixon and Hall met, and Hall called Herter. Herter said he "probably will be glad to" nominate Nixon, but he wanted time to think it over. Stassen learned about the call that night through a friend of Herter's.

July 14—Herter telephoned Sherman Adams at the White House to confirm Hall's intimation that Eisenhower had participated in selecting Herter as Nixon's nominator. Adams said it was so, but if Herter would prefer to second Eisenhower's nomination, instead, that would be most agreeable to the President. Herter replied that he would think about it. During the day Stassen asked for an appointment with Eisenhower as soon as the President was able to have a talk about an "important political matter."

July 15—Stassen telephoned Herter, first in Boston and then at a conference of New England governors that Herter was attending in Rhode Island. "He told me that he was calling merely to

(170)

inform me that he had been making some independent researches of his own," Herter noted in a personal, diarylike memorandum in which he tried to keep up with "this extraordinary performance" as it developed. "Stassen said he had come to the conclusion that Nixon would be a substantial drag on the President if he were the vice-presidential candidate; and that as a result of the polls he felt that I would be the least drag on the President. He then added that he felt this situation was of such importance that he was asking for an appointment to see the President and had been promised one the following week. I told him that I had been asked to put Dick Nixon's name in nomination, and he requested that I defer decision on this until he had talked with the President, which I agreed to do."

July 20—Stassen was admitted to Eisenhower's office at 9:31 A.M. The President was preparing to leave that day for a meeting of Inter-American Chiefs of State in Panama. It was to be his first strenuous activity since the ileitis operation six weeks before. He wasn't particularly anxious to talk politics. Stassen told him he was looking fine, as usual. Eisenhower said he felt all right. Stassen declared that world peace hinged on Eisenhower's re-election. Eisenhower nodded. Stassen then proceeded to report that he had made an intensive study of the election prospects and his private poll showed that Nixon, being a controversial figure, would detract enough from the ticket to create problems, whereas others—Herter, for instance—would have little or no effect on the outcome. Eisenhower frowned. He mentioned his liking for Nixon, then pointed out he had closed no doors on the vice-presidential nomination because he would not dictate to a convention which hadn't yet even renominated him for president. Stassen thanked Eisenhower, wished him well on the Panama trip, and left at 9:55 A.M. He had been with the President twenty-four minutes. By 10:30 A.M. he had notified Goldsmith and others that Eisenhower had given him a tacit go-ahead. "The President said he is for an open convention," Stassen told them. Eisenhower had said as much publicly, whenever asked, in the weeks before his illness. But the words appeared to assume meaning to associates when repeated by Stassen.

(171)

Stassen's report was justified, perhaps, on the basis of his intensive study of the President's characteristic responses to the proposals of various kinds. Stassen saw these reactions as "situations." He listed them for me as follows: "You have a situation where [Eisenhower] asks you to do something, and if you can at all honorably do it, you try to carry it out. Or there are situations where he asks you not to do it, and if you are a member of the team, you don't do it. Or there are third situations where, in effect, he doesn't express a view either one way or another, and then you have to make your own decision and move under those circumstances."

In this case it was "situation" number three. Stassen made his "own decision," moved "under those circumstances," and Herter noted in his diary that night: "Stassen called me in Manchester . . . saying that he had talked to the President and that the President appeared very much interested in what he had to say. He said that he advised the President that he was planning to talk to both the Vice-President and Len Hall to give them the benefit of his own conclusions; and that the President had interposed no objections to his doing so."

Herter later appended to his July 20 entry: "This was the last time I had any direct communication with Mr. Stassen until ten minutes before the President's press conference in San Francisco on Wednesday, August 22." (That was the press conference at which Eisenhower announced that Stassen would second the Nixon nomination.)

During the day of July 20—this was a Friday—Stassen called for an appointment with Nixon. Nixon's secretary said the Vice-President was tied up and suggested Monday morning. (Stassen suspected an informant had tipped Nixon as to what was up, and the Vice-President was ducking. The amazing fact is that neither side had much foreknowledge of what the other was doing throughout this bizarre operation.)

July 23—Over the weekend Stassen communed with a few friends and with himself. Since the National Convention was only four weeks off, he decided it was now or never, so this became action day.

(172)

Coincidentally, Nixon told his secretary to put the Stassen appointment off until Tuesday or Wednesday, if possible, because Stassen normally took more time than Nixon had to spare that Monday morning. As Nixon's receptionist was calling Stassen's office, Stassen arrived at Nixon's office. "We've just been talking about you," the receptionist said. "The Vice-President would appreciate it if you would postpone your appointment." Stassen smiled and left. A little later a messenger brought an envelope marked "Personal and Confidential." It was from Stassen to Nixon and looked important, so Rose Mary Woods, the executive secretary, took it to the Capitol where Nixon was having lunch, privately, with Hall and General Persons. The 2½-page letter was typed neatly in light-blue ink on stationery with Stassen's name and home address atop each page in bold black letters. Nixon scanned it hurriedly and gave a nervous chuckle. "Let me read this to you," he said to his guests: " 'I regret that it was not possible for you to see me. . . . I would have preferred to advise you personally of a conclusion I have reluctantly reached after a thorough and thoughtful review of the political situation in these recent weeks, and of which I advised the President on Friday morning. I have concluded that I should do what I can to nominate Governor Chris Herter for vice-president at the coming convention. I sincerely hope that after careful reflection during the coming weeks you will conclude to join in supporting Chris Herter. I have reached this conclusion notwithstanding my long and continuing personal friendly feeling toward you because of these reasons . . .' " The remainder of Stassen's letter became the substance of a public statement he released at a press conference that afternoon.

Hall and Persons agreed that this could be serious. The luncheon ended quickly. Persons returned to the White House, Hall to Republican National Headquarters, where he called his principal assistants—Campaign Director Robert Humphreys and Public Relations Director L. Richard Guylay—to his office. They readily agreed that "the thing had to be closed off fast" to prevent confusion in the party ranks, Hall recalled. "I didn't think Stassen would get anywhere, but he could create doubt in people's minds, and you'd have a lot of candidates. Dan Thornton [former governor of Colorado] and Ted McKeldin [governor of Maryland] were after the vice-presidential nomination anyway. [Senator] Margaret Chase Smith [of Maine] wanted her name to be presented to the convention. Stassen even convinced Goodie Knight [governor of California] that Eisenhower had a list of six names, any one of whom was acceptable."

Hall wasted no time in passing the word, publicly and privately. With confidence (and still with little more than intuition to go on) he stated: "Nothing has changed. The ticket will be Ike and Dick."[5]

At three o'clock Stassen invited the press to his office and announced his undertaking "in loyalty to Eisenhower." His private polls showed Nixon would cut the Eisenhower vote by 6 per cent, he said, while Herter would do practically no harm. He also stated that everyone would be happier, including "important portions of the population abroad," if Nixon was replaced. Stassen said he was "confident President Eisenhower will be pleased to have Chris Herter on the ticket." He also explained, quite carefully, that "the Republican party will realize I did them a favor" because he was giving those hoping to replace Nixon an active movement to join.

Among the things Stassen did not reveal at the press conference —or to this day—is the fact he had told Eisenhower he would talk with Nixon, Hall and other principal party figures before going ahead with his movement. He planned to call a conference of the Vice-President, the national chairman, Attorney General Herbert Brownell, Deputy Attorney General William Rogers, Ambassador Henry Cabot Lodge, and a few others. Stassen believed he might convince them, with his poll, that Nixon's candidacy would be a handicap to Eisenhower. That, in turn, could lead to Nixon's voluntary withdrawal from the race, he figured. When neither Nixon nor Hall would see him, however, Stassen felt he had no alternative but to forget the conference and go ahead with the enterprise.

After his press conference Stassen again sought an immediate appointment with Hall. The chairman was "busy," but suggested lunch the next day. Then Stassen tried to telephone Herter. "For

[5] When Eisenhower saw Hall afterward he laughed and said, "You're holding the reins a little tight, Len."

the first time in my life I was watching a professional golf tournament being played in Massachusetts," Herter recalled. "I was riding around in a little cart following the players when all of a sudden some of the newspaper boys came up with a walkie-talkie and told me what Stassen had done. He hadn't said a word to me about announcing it. He just went ahead and announced it. It was all a little confused, so I said until I knew what the score was I couldn't say anything. I went to the front office and tried to call Washington to find out what was going on. It was then I learned Stassen had tried to reach me by phone, but went ahead and shot anyway." In his diary-memorandum Herter noted: "Stassen did not call me that evening or any time thereafter."

Eisenhower learned of the Stassen announcement in Panama by way of a news service correspondent whose office had cabled for the President's comment. Press Secretary Hagerty, clearly surprised, rushed the message to Eisenhower. Milton Eisenhower and Secretary Dulles were in the room. "You have anything that concerns me?" Dulles asked. "No," said Hagerty. Dulles sighed, obviously relieved that Hagerty's "crisis look" wasn't caused by an international crisis. But the President and his brother were anything but pleased by what Hagerty read to them.[6] Frowning, Eisenhower dictated this statement: "Mr. Stassen did inform the President on Friday of his decision to make such a statement and also to inform the Vice-President of it before issuing it. The President pointed out to Mr. Stassen that, while he had every right as an individual to make any statement he so desired, it was also equally obvious that he would not make such a statement as a member of the President's official family."

Hagerty recalls: "When Stassen injected a United States political story into the last day of the Panama meeting, the President and everyone else was upset and peeved. I don't know anyone down there who thought well of it." (Weeks later, said Hagerty, "Stassen publicly accused me of doing everything possible to block him. I agree; he was right.")

There was no question about it—the Stassen story in Washing-

[6] Stassen insisted afterward that Eisenhower never subsequently indicated displeasure over either the announcement or its timing.

ton took the front-page play from the Eisenhower story in Panama. Some political correspondents interpreted it as "the opening shot in what promises to be a bitter battle for the Vice-Presidency."

July 24—This was a day of frantic stock-taking by top-echelon Republicans. By nightfall practically all who counted had taken sides—with Nixon. Nonetheless, Stassen smiled broadly and confidently, in public, as though his undertaking was a robust child with great promise, instead of a stillborn corpse. Nixon, who had reason to smile, didn't. He told well-wishers rushing to his bandwagon: "Don't underestimate Harold. He's smart and resourceful."

Herter wrote the principal paragraphs in the day's addition to American political lore. Following President Eisenhower's return from Panama early that morning, the Massachusetts Governor called Sherman Adams "to try to find out what the score was from the point of view of the White House." Herter said he explained he "had no interest in nor desire to be the vice-presidential candidate, but as I felt that my only role was trying to be helpful to the President, I hoped I might be able to talk with the President. Sherman Adams requested me not to come down to the White House, but said he would be seeing the President shortly and would call back. He telephoned back in about an hour and said that he had talked with the President and that, in so far as the President was concerned, he had merely been told by Stassen how Stassen felt and how Stassen believed it to be his duty to go ahead with the course which he was pursuing, and that the President had been much surprised at the [Stassen] press conference of the day before."

In his diary-memorandum Herter wrote: Adams said that "The President held me in very high esteem, that if I wished to be vice-presidential candidate, that would be a matter of my own choosing, but that the President had more or less expected that when I was through as governor I might be available to help in the international field, and that he, as president, had already talked the matter over with Dulles. Adams then made it clear that I would have to make my own decision and that if I decided to become a vice-presidential candidate I could not, of course, expect to have the backing of the White House. It would have to be on my own even though I was an entirely acceptable candidate to the President. I told Sherman Adams that prior to Mr. Stassen's press conference I had planned to go to Washington on that very day, Tuesday, July 24, to talk to Len Hall with regard to the nomination of Nixon but that now, as things stood, I thought it best for me to call Hall on the phone and advise him that I would place Nixon in nomination, thereby cutting off any further efforts on anybody's part to make me vice-presidential candidate."

Adams said, "All right, let's consider it settled that way." At noon Herter advised Hall by telephone that he would be "glad to place Nixon in nomination." He also asked Hall for suggestions as to what should be in a formal statement. A few minutes later Nixon telephoned Herter. "He very candidly and sincerely explained to me that he had not himself asked me to put his name in nomination because he knew I had many friends who might want to consider me a candidate and that he felt it would be much less embarrassing to me to refuse to Len Hall than to him directly," Herter said. "Nixon was most cordial and straightforward and I think his explanation as to why he had not called me personally was entirely genuine." At this point Herter appended in his memorandum: "From that day until I had completed my nomination speech for Nixon I discouraged every individual who asked my opinion as to whether he or she should assist Stassen in his efforts just as strongly as I could."

Herter was the only principal participant to consider the matter closed, however. Leonard Hall, who had played a cat-and-mouse game of mutual distrust with Stassen at lunch, wanted Herter to announce at once his intention to nominate Nixon. Herter preferred to wait a day until his son would be available to help with a formal statement. Hall then announced it on his own.

Meanwhile, Stassen held two press conferences. In the first, prior to the news of Herter's action, he solemnly declared he hoped "Vice-President Nixon will think this over in the next weeks and decide to join and support Governor Herter." In the second, after the news from Herter, he said the fact that Hall had asked Herter to make the nomination "is a confirmation of Herter's very strong

(177)

standing in the party" and did not mean any lack of interest by Governor Herter in obtaining the Vice-Presidency. When asked if he had consulted Herter on this, he replied, "I didn't say that I did not consult him."

July 25—Although well aware of its death, all the principals continued to act as though the Stassen movement was still quite alive. Both Stassen and Nixon could hardly have been busier that day. Stassen started at a 7:00 A.M. coast-to-coast television program, the first of several important television shows on which he agreed to appear during the coming weeks. Stassen's day was filled with his declarations of devotion to Eisenhower and Herter. He also made statements promising to drop his enterprise if Eisenhower asked him publicly to do so, and he charged that Chairman Hall was antagonistic toward him. The highlight was a public memorandum in which Stassen urged "all voters" to support his movement by writing letters to newspapers, calling and writing to Republican party officials at all levels, and sending contributions to Eisenhower-Herter Headquarters, 1610 K St., N.W., Washington 6, D.C.

In Boston, Herter formally endorsed Nixon at a press conference. The *New York Times* correspondent wrote: "It was obvious to State House observers that the Governor would have liked to have been considered for the vice-presidential nomination. But with the stoicism of years of diplomatic service, he gave no outward sign, even by so much as a flick of his bushy eyebrows."

Nixon's office was like a political headquarters on election eve. Party leaders from everywhere came or called to affirm their loyalty and offer prescriptions for banishing the Stassen threat. Governor Dewey recommended that Nixon barnstorm the country. Senator Knowland proposed that Stassen quit his post at the White House. Several suggested a showdown with Eisenhower. Nixon listened attentively to all, and decided to operate quietly and prepare for the worst. A meticulous state-by-state check of convention delegates showed he could count, under any circumstances, on 800 of the 1,323 votes that would be cast for the vice-presidential nomination. Both the "Modern" and the "Taft" wing of the party contributed to that safe majority. The Taft devotees, all powerful organization people, were solid in their support even though some were actively unhappy over Nixon's failure to back Senator Taft in 1952 and his down-the-line loyalty to Eisenhower policies since then. Their unanimity stemmed from a detestation of Stassen that had deepened, if anything, since 1948, when the Minnesotan ignored a tradition precious to politicians by challenging Taft in a primary contest in his home state. Many Modern Republicans had doubts about Nixon, but most had more compelling doubts about Stassen.

A cross-country survey of political leaders convinced the New York *Herald Tribune*—"the principal beneficiaries of Harold Stassen's dump Nixon exercise appeared to be Vice-President Nixon and the Democrats. If something was needed to cinch Mr. Nixon's nomination, this is it. The Vice-President couldn't have hoped for a less virile preconvention showdown with his Republican detractors than the one Stassen dished up."

July 26—Stassen announced he was taking another poll, and would withhold further "adverse comment" about Nixon until it was completed.

July 30—Stassen visited Eisenhower for a few minutes at the Gettysburg farm, then announced the President had granted him a four weeks' leave of absence.

On another front that day Americans for Democratic Action, an organization composed mostly of liberal Democrats, issued a 28-page pamphlet severely questioning Nixon's "moral qualities" and stating "the career and character of Richard Nixon pose a somber issue in the 1956 campaign" since Eisenhower could hardly survive another full term.

July 31—Stassen predicted that Nixon's name on the ticket would cost Eisenhower "millions of votes." Nixon received a petition of endorsement signed by practically every Republican in Congress. (Representative Patrick Hillings, a close associate of the Vice-President's, confided that the petition's principal aim was to bolster Nixon's morale. "He is a pessimist, and was running scared," Hillings said.)

August 1—Eisenhower told a press conference that Nixon "is

(179)

perfectly acceptable to me as he was in 1952." The President refused to name any other "acceptable" candidate but said, "I do uphold the right of the delegates to the convention to nominate whom they choose." Stassen greeted that with a statement declaring "the convention is now definitely open. The problem of the vice-presidential nomination can now be considered deliberately and thoughtfully for the next three weeks."

August 3—Stassen announced that his studies showed Nixon's candidacy could cost Eisenhower 3,600,000 votes.

August 4—Governor Knight, of California, joined the Dump Nixon movement publicly—the only prominent Republican other than Stassen to do so. Knight said Nixon's home state would go Democratic if Nixon was on the Republican ticket.

August 9—In a 5,000-word letter Stassen confided to a number of Republican leaders that he had "counseled" Nixon the year before to make "a special effort to overcome his weakness with independent voters, labor, minorities, and progressive-minded Republicans." Nixon continued to be unpopular with that important element of voters, however, Stassen added. He undertook the anti-Nixon movement "with a heavy heart," Stassen continued, knowing "full well the hot flash-back of opposition which I would encounter from some of the top leadership of our Republican organization. . . . I was aware of the political price that I would have to pay . . . but believed that after the first blast of opposition, and the second phase of attacks about my timing, there would come a third phase in which the Republican party and the Vice-President would consider, on the merits, the points I have raised."

August 13—Stassen announced $6,535 had been contributed to his crusade, and it was doing fine.

Meanwhile the Democratic National Convention opened in Chicago, with a keynote speech in which Governor Frank G. Clement, of Tennessee, described Nixon as the Republican party's "Vice-Hatchet Man," who went about his "double-faced campaign . . . slinging slander and spreading half-truths while the top man [Eisenhower] peers down the green fairways of indifference."

August 14—The latest Gallup poll said Nixon had slipped in

popularity since May, but was still ahead of Herter. The polls said 74 per cent of the nation's Republicans favored Nixon, a drop of 9 per cent from May, and 14 per cent favored Herter, an increase for him of 4 per cent. Among independent voters the spread was 54 per cent for Nixon and 22 per cent for Herter, with 24 per cent having no opinion.

August 15—Governor Knight complained in California that "steam-roll pressure" was being applied to force him to stop opposing Nixon. Privately Knight told Chairman Hall he had "inside word" that Eisenhower soon would announce six acceptable alternatives to Nixon, and the list would include Knight, McKeldin, Thornton, Stassen, Lodge, and Arthur Langlie, of Washington. (The source of the "inside word" turned out to be Stassen.)

On the other side of the continent that day Herter sent Nixon a draft of his nominating speech. "Will see you before Thursday in San Francisco, and I hope that all the flurries and alarums would have subsided completely by then," he told the Vice-President in a note.

August 16—With the Republican Convention only four days off, Herter announced categorically that he would forbid his name to be submitted for the vice-presidential nomination, and Stassen sent letters to Nixon and Deputy Attorney General Rogers, each marked "Personal and Confidential."

"Dear Dick: I deeply regret that the situation, as I understand it to be, made it necessary for me to follow the course which I have taken in these recent weeks," Stassen wrote the Vice-President. "I hope the time will come when with perspective you do conclude that the action I took under all the circumstances was the right thing for me to do.

"I also hope that as you continue to review the matter, and if you do become convinced that President Eisenhower would run stronger and win an easier victory, with someone else as the running mate this time, and if you conclude that Chris Herter is the best available candidate, that you will take the initiative and the lead in securing his nomination in San Francisco.

"It is my deep conviction that if you decide to take this step it

(181)

will be best not only for our country and for the President, but best, in the long run, for your future career. . . . Sincerely, Harold."

To Rogers, he wrote: "Dear Bill: If you are willing to look at the results of a nationwide poll, I will make them available to you in such time and manner as you wish. I am also willing to discuss the situation with you personally, if you wish. I assume, of course, that you will do neither, unless the Vice-President is willing that you should do so. . . . Sincerely, Harold."

August 18—Nixon and Stassen arrived in San Francisco for the convention, but not together. Each established a headquarters and began a round of meetings with delegates. Both talked with reporters. Nixon claimed the Eisenhower administration had given Americans "the best three and a half years of our lives." Stassen claimed his latest poll showed Nixon continued to be a serious handicap to the Republican ticket.

Senator Styles Bridges, Nixon's friend from New Hampshire, announced that he, too, had a poll. After Stassen revealed that his latest poll showed an Eisenhower-Nixon ticket getting only 45.7 per cent of the vote, or between 8 and 13 per cent less than an Eisenhower-Herter ticket, Bridges declared his poll showed 54.3 per cent of the voters favoring an Eisenhower-Nixon ticket and 25.7 per cent an Eisenhower-Herter ticket.[7]

August 19—Stassen announced, with an air of confidence and authority, that Eisenhower would make his position known "in an unmistakable manner" within two days.

August 21—Eisenhower arrived in San Francisco. After settling down in the St. Francis Hotel, he summoned Chairman Hall for a report on the Stassen situation. Hall said Stassen had gotten nowhere. Eisenhower anticipated as much, and asked what Hall would suggest to stop the foolishness and unify the party. Hall replied that Stassen should second Nixon's renomination. Eisenhower thought that wasn't a bad idea. He noted that Stassen was coming

[7] To no one's surprise, although Bridges announced his poll with a chuckle as compared with the solemnity of Stassen's announcement of his poll, the Bridges poll proved to be more nearly accurate. The Eisenhower-Nixon ticket got more than 57 per cent of the vote in November, an increase of 2 per cent over 1952.

(182)

to see him the next morning, and he told Hall to talk with Stassen first and tell him about the decision.

August 22—This was the day of the grand finale—but its most dramatic climaxes were witnessed only by the participants.

At nine o'clock Stassen left his room on the ninth floor of the St. Francis Hotel to see Eisenhower, on the sixth. He checked in first, as was required, with Sherman Adams, who occupied an office suite close to Eisenhower's. Hall darted into the Adams rooms behind Stassen. When the two met, Stassen handed the chairman a written ultimatum demanding that nominations for vice-president be postponed until the next day instead of following Eisenhower's renomination that afternoon, as scheduled. Hall took a deep breath to fortify his sense of humor and self-control.

"Are you a delegate?" he asked, as quietly as he could.

"No," replied Stassen.

"Are you an alternate?"

"No."

"Well, who the hell is running this convention, you or the delegates?" Hall thundered.

"All Republicans have responsibilities," Stassen said calmly. His purpose, he added, was to help bring about "an open convention" as proclaimed by Eisenhower. Adams then joined the discussion, and Hall recollects "it went on and on."

Finally Hall and Adams told Stassen firmly he would be permitted to see the President only if he agreed, first, to restrict his conversation in the Eisenhower suite to a suggestion that he be permitted to second Nixon's nomination in the interest of party harmony.

At 10:53 A.M. Stassen agreed and at 10:54 he and Adams walked across the hall to the Eisenhower rooms, Adams leading the way.

Within five minutes Stassen had slipped back to his own room, and Press Secretary Hagerty had announced the President would hold a press conference.

At the press conference a half hour later Eisenhower stated: "Mr. Stassen called to see me a few minutes ago . . . after several days here he had become absolutely convinced the majority of the delegates want Mr. Nixon. And in these circumstances he no longer—and particularly since his own candidate had withdrawn so decisively—he saw no reason for going further with his effort, and he thought, in order to get his own position clear before the convention and the American public, he was going to ask the convention chairman for permission this afternoon to second . . . the nomination of the Vice-President incumbent, Mr. Nixon, for renomination."

The unprecedented presidential press conference was televised nationally. Stassen watched it in his hotel room, then sent Nixon a telegram:

"I have concluded that I would like to second your nomination for vice-president at the convention and join wholeheartedly and cheerfully in support of the nominees of the convention—President Eisenhower and yourself—for November, urging the voters who had felt as I had to join with me in this result. I have so advised the President. Best wishes to you. Harold E. Stassen."

Nixon learned of all this on returning to San Francisco that afternoon from his home in Whittier, California, where he had been visiting his dying father. Nixon scowled and told intimates he would accept Stassen as a seconder only if Stassen did not replace one of the six other seconders and was restricted to a two-minute speech, like the others. Rogers, who had reviewed the speeches prepared by the six original seconders and coached them on their timing, was told by Nixon to make absolutely certain that Stassen got not a split second more than "my friends who have been loyal to me." Hall also was told, emphatically, to limit Stassen to the prescribed two minutes. Hall, in turn, assigned Campaign Director Humphreys to "keep behind" Stassen on this.

As Stassen sat stonily on the platform ready to be recognized, an assistant distributed mimeographed copies of his speech in the press section. Humphreys got one and was flabbergasted to see it was a full-length document that appeared to be longer even than Nixon's acceptance speech. He rushed to Stassen, knelt behind him, and whispered, "Governor, I've got to have an answer. . . . Are you going to take more than two minutes?" Stassen was noncommittal, so Humphreys dashed off a note soliciting the help of Adams, who was sitting nearby on the dais. Adams read the Humphreys note, and without a flicker of an eyelid, he scribbled on back of it, "I've done my job, you do yours."

Meanwhile Rogers and Hall had sidled up to Stassen to remind him of the two-minute restriction. Stassen nodded, in solemn understanding, to each of them, then went ahead and delivered every word of his prepared talk, plus a few more not in the text.

Later, as Nixon came before the wildly cheering convention to accept the nomination, he said in an aside-whisper, as he passed Rogers on the platform: "You really fixed that one, didn't you!"

A day or so afterward Nixon wrote to Herter: "I tried to reach you after I returned to the hotel because I thought we ought to have a little celebration before we returned to southern California. It would have been a particular pleasure to have had you and Mac [Mrs. Herter] with us.

"Pat and I are deeply grateful for your superb nominating speech. I am sure that you are as glad as we are that these last several weeks are behind us, and it has meant more than I can express adequately to have had you in our corner during this time. If I can borrow a phrase that the President used in his address, I'd just like to say that I only hope that what is past is prologue to an ever-deeper and enduring friendship."[8]

While reflecting on it two years later, Herter told me that one incident in the Stassen affair actually brought him "great joy." It had to do with the "Ike and Chris" buttons Stassen's helpers were distributing in San Francisco. When it was all over, Christopher Del Sesto, the enterprising young Republican candidate for governor of Rhode Island, salvaged several boxes of the buttons from Stassen headquarters and spread them throughout his tiny state.

[8] In 1957, on the anniversary of his renomination, Nixon wrote Governor Dewey, who in 1956 had been one of Nixon's most powerful backers, as he was in 1952: "Dear Tom: I wanted to tell you again how much I appreciated your loyal support preceding [the actual renomination]. It is hard to realize now that all the flurry created by the Stassen incident is almost completely forgotten. You can be sure, however, that I remember vividly the actions of those who were staunch friends both before and after the Convention."

That particular Chris got a surprisingly large vote in normally Democratic Rhode Island in 1956—then was elected governor by an impressive majority in 1958. Herter likes to think the "Ike and Chris" buttons helped.

Among Nixon's supporters was Nelson Rockefeller. "You and Pat won the respect and admiration of all at the convention—the way you both carried on despite every form of adversity," Rockefeller wrote Nixon on September 7. "I can't say how much I admired you both, and your acceptance speech was superb—positive, simple and direct, with such understanding and perception regarding the future—and then the moving way in which you spoke of your father in closing was so wonderfully typical of you.

"Together, you and the President have set the tone for the campaign and charted the course for the future of our country. . . ."

In a note after the election Rockefeller wrote on November 7: "Dear Dick: A great campaign and a great victory—more power to you.

"Under you and the President the Republican party is now emerging, at home and abroad, as the great liberal party of the future."

Nixon said in reply: "I particularly appreciated your letter because of our close association and friendship over the past four years. I hope that whenever you are down this way you will stop by the office for a visit because I would appreciate the opportunity to talk to you about some of the recent developments on the world scene."

When Stassen revived his "Dump Nixon Movement" after the 1958 Congressional election, it was like replaying the weird old record. His forum was again the White House. The pitch was altered only slightly. Stassen still was saving the Republican party from Nixon by magnanimously promoting others, but now he had also dumped Herter. He imparted his blessings on Nelson Rockefeller, Henry Cabot Lodge, Secretary of Interior Fred Seaton, and Secretary of the Treasury Robert Anderson. That was in Washington, November 12. By November 14, in Harrisburg, Pennsylvania, he had narrowed the field to Rockefeller and was implying, knowingly, that he would control the Pennsylvania delegation to the

1960 Republican Convention. A week later he was confiding to political reporters in Cleveland that he might run himself—not as a selfish matter, of course, but to help Rockefeller win the nomination, just as he had run in 1952 to help Eisenhower win it.

The former "Secretary of Peace" had no way of knowing that Eisenhower had telephoned Nixon the day after Stassen's visit to discuss that visit. The President emphatically absolved himself and the White House from any part of what Stassen said and did. So did the Republican leadership in Pennsylvania, which is currently Stassen's political home port. But Washington's so-called political observers varied somewhat in their interpretations of this newest operation.

The Washington *Evening Star*, noting Stassen's previous failures, said: "There's one thing about Harold E. Stassen—he likes to go down with his ship, and he doesn't care how many times it's sunk."

The New York *Post*, which isn't very tolerant of Nixon, said that "Stassen's record commands respect for him as a political planner and operator." One of its Washington political experts added, "Stassen has played an interesting and important, if secondary, role in national politics in recent years. He is likely to do so again in 1960."

12

Nixon's conduct during the weeks after President Eisenhower's heart attack raised his prestige in the administration. Previously, Eisenhower had always spoken well of his deputy, referring to him usually as "a comer" and "a splendid type of the younger men we want in government." Afterward Eisenhower declared flatly, "There is no man in the history of America who has had such careful preparation . . . for carrying out the duties of the Presidency." Several of Eisenhower's personal intimates who had serious misgivings about Nixon, including Dr. Milton Eisenhower, became supporters of the Vice-President. After the first month of Eisenhower's illness the judgment of a number of colleagues was summed up by Nelson Rockefeller, then a special assistant to the President. "All of us in the administration," he wrote Nixon, "are proud indeed of the job you have done during these truly difficult days, and are proud to be associated with you as the leader who is carrying on in the President's absence." Only a few friends were aware of how acutely uneasy Nixon was about his capacity to meet the challenge. He aged the equivalent of quite a few years during those three months—in his own estimation, as well as that of those with whom he worked.

It started after the Big Four chiefs of state had exchanged smiles and declarations at Geneva in July. Then Eisenhower had gone to Denver for a long vacation. The soothing aura of peace and plenty that late summer and autumn of 1955 inspired the Republican National Committee to unfurl the slogan: "Everything is booming but the guns." Nixon was to make a good-will tour of the Near East in the late fall—welcome duty, especially since there was no election campaign in 1955. On September 26 Nixon was to join Eisenhower in Denver at a conference of educators, sports figures, government officials and civic leaders to launch a nationwide physical-fitness crusade.

On Saturday, September 24, the Vice-President and Mrs. Nixon attended the wedding in Washington of a stenographer in his office. They were back home at about five, and Nixon read in the *Evening Star* that Eisenhower had an upset stomach. That didn't disturb him for he remembered that only a year earlier the President also had a slight digestive upset in Denver. It had made him uncomfortable, but hadn't prevented him from appearing on a campaign television program. Nixon was musing about this and turning to the editorial page when the telephone rang. It was Jim Hagerty.

"Dick, are you sitting down?" asked the President's press secretary.

"No, what is it?" was the reply.

Slowly, Hagerty said he had bad news. The President had suffered a heart attack. The press would be told about it in a half hour or so.

"My God!" Nixon whispered hoarsely. He caught his breath, then proceeded to tell Hagerty that heart attacks aren't necessarily serious any more, that victims frequently recover completely.

"I don't see how I could describe those first few minutes except as a complete shock," he recalls. "I remember going into my living room and sitting down in a chair and not saying anything or really thinking of anything for at least five or ten minutes. For quite a while I didn't even think to tell Pat, who was upstairs."

The numbness receded gradually. Nixon went back to the telephone and called his friend, Deputy Attorney General William P. Rogers.

"I wonder if you could come over, Bill?" he asked. Rogers arrived in fifteen minutes by taxi.

Meanwhile the news was released in Denver. Nixon's telephone began to ring, and people showed up—reporters, photographers, sightseers. The white-brick house in the residential Spring Valley

(189)

section of Washington had never before attracted such attention.

Nixon decided to say nothing to the press. Questions kept coming, however, and practically every move from one room to another in the house could be noted from the street. The commotion became such that after dinner Nixon suggested that he and Rogers go to the latter's house in nearby Bethesda. Mrs. Rogers was asked to come pick them up a block away. The two men slipped out a side door, moved quickly down an alley and reached the car undetected. Their escape was aided by one of Nixon's children who had gone outdoors at the other side of the house to look at the crowd. The crowd looked at her—instead of the door from which her father and his friend left.

Rogers and Nixon soon were joined in the Rogers large living room by General Wilton B. Persons, an assistant who was in command at the White House because Sherman Adams, the Chief of Staff, was vacationing in Scotland. The three men reviewed pending business and tried to figure what, if anything, could not be put off. Informally, they decided there was nothing. Nixon suggested, and the others agreed, that all the principal administration officials should be informed at once that the "team" was to operate as Eisenhower had planned it should and that there should be no precipitate comments about politics or administration affairs. It was decided that the administration should continue to function on a business-as-usual basis if possible.

Throughout the night—and for the next two months—Nixon was kept posted on every development in Denver, and every medical bulletin was read to him before being issued publicly. Persons left Rogers' house at 12:30 A.M. Sunday. Rogers went to bed at 1:30. About an hour later Nixon drifted up to the spare room where a pair of his friend's pajamas were laid out for him on the bed. He washed, slowly, then stretched out on the bed and scanned several magazines, reading without seeing or knowing what he read.

The guest bedroom was beneath a room in which Tony Rogers, fifteen, competed in a continent-wide amateur radio contest. But the Vice-President was as oblivious of the sounds above as he was

(190)

of the printed words. At four o'clock he went downstairs to take a telephone call from Denver. It was Hagerty. The situation was grave, but hopeful, because Eisenhower appeared to be reasonably comfortable under his oxygen tent.

Richard Nixon got no sleep.

After church Sunday morning Nixon stated, "The business of government will go on without delay. . . . The President's team will carry out his well-defined plans." That night he met again with Persons and Rogers at Rogers' house. They decided that a meeting of the National Security Council would be held, as scheduled, on Thursday, and Nixon said it would be a good idea to call a Cabinet meeting on Friday to demonstrate further that the government was continuing to function in an orderly way. The Vice-President spent that night in his own home, and he invited the press corps keeping watch in the chill outside to use his basement.

Within a week a political caldron was boiling. Nominating conventions were less than a year off. Republican plans had focused on Eisenhower. Now, as he fought for survival under an oxygen tent, everyone was certain there would have to be another candidate, including National Chairman Hall, who amazed political experts by insisting otherwise in public. Governor Goodwin J. Knight, one of California's three shadow contenders, was the first to move. He proceeded to aim verbal kicks at Nixon, his most formidable competitor. The Vice-President's adherents prepared a counteroffensive, but he sent word through Robert H. Finch, the Los Angeles Republican chairman, that there was to be absolutely no political activity for him, not even by indirection. Nixon meant to negotiate the trying days and weeks ahead with a maximum of naturalness and a minimum of fuss. He intended to encourage understatement of his role during Eisenhower's inactivity and to avoid any action that might substantiate a charge that he was trying to benefit politically from the situation. Therefore he continued to come early for administration conferences and meetings and presided from his customary chair, instead of the President's. He worked mostly in his own office. At the White House he used a conference room, and avoided the President's office. When Cabinet members wanted to talk with him, or he with them, he insisted on going to their offices, turning aside their suggestions that they come to his.

Adams flew in from Scotland on Monday morning and had lunch at the White House with Nixon, Persons, Rogers and Gerald D. Morgan, special counsel to the President. There was another evening meeting in the Rogers living room. Nixon, Rogers, Persons, Leonard Hall and his public relations aide, Lou Guylay, sat in a circle, and Adams sat slightly off to one side. The news from Denver late that afternoon had been bad. Someone in the circle mentioned nervously that the mistakes made when Presidents Wilson and Cleveland were incapacitated should be avoided. Calls kept coming from Denver and were received in the kitchen. Each report was analyzed, and Hall emphasized several times that administration officials should be careful not to do or say anything that would set off a premature battle for the presidential nomination. Nixon stated that things should not be permitted to fall apart for lack of decision. Adams seemed to be in a daze, possibly as a reaction to the shocking news or weariness from his rush across the Atlantic. For four hours, whenever he spoke—even in reply to questions—it was about his fishing in Scotland, and nothing else.

On Wednesday Nixon signed several papers "in behalf of the President." None was of legal significance. At the National Security Council meeting on Thursday it was agreed that Adams should operate from Denver as boss of the White House staff.

The highlight of that first week was a 2½-hour Cabinet meeting on Friday. Nixon opened it with a silent prayer and read the latest medical bulletin from Denver. The report that Eisenhower had spent his first night out of the oxygen tent and had slept without interruption for nine and a half hours brought smiles of relief in the large White House conference room. The meeting then proceeded at almost a normal clip. As the session ended, Dulles, the senior member, turned to Nixon and said:

"Mr. Vice-President, I realize that you have been under a very heavy burden during these past few days, and I know I express the opinion of everybody here that you have conducted yourself superbly, and I want you to know we are proud to be on this

(192)

team and proud to be serving in this Cabinet under your leadership."

Next day a letter came. "Dear Dick," the President wrote, "I hope you will continue to have meetings of the National Security Council and of the Cabinet over which you will preside in accordance with the procedure which you have followed at my request in the past during my absence from Washington. As ever, Dwight D. Eisenhower."

On Saturday, October 8, exactly two weeks after the President's seizure, Nixon visited him in his eighth-floor suite at Fitzsimmons Hospital, the first time a vice-president had been at the bedside of a seriously sick president. Meanwhile, the Cabinet and National Security Council, after marking time, proceeded to undertake serious business. With members having strong opinions on legislative programs and budget items, some sessions were spirited. Arthur Flemming, who was then the defense mobilizer, recalls a heated argument over the budget at one Cabinet meeting. He was impressed with Nixon's tact. When he complimented the Vice-President afterward, Nixon said he realized that some Cabinet members talked longer than they would have if the President had been present, but he intended to be especially careful because "it isn't my Cabinet; it is the President's Cabinet. I am just the presiding officer."

Nine months after the heart attack Hagerty had to break the news of another serious presidential illness to the Vice-President. It was early in the morning of June 8, 1956. The press secretary reached Nixon in his limousine as the Vice-President was heading for his office.

Eisenhower was operated upon late that night for ileitis, an abdominal ailment. When he recovered sufficiently to see members of his administration, the President asked that Nixon be the first official visitor.

Eisenhower's third illness—the stroke of November 25, 1957—resulted in an unprecedented agreement by which the President

(193)

commissioned the Vice-President to assume the powers of acting chief executive should the President ever become incapacitated again. The stroke was not severe, and the President was back at his desk within a couple of weeks. It had a singular side effect, however, in that Nixon now showed the self-assurance he had acquired since the period of the heart attack two years and two months before.

During the first few days, while the full extent of Eisenhower's seizure was still uncertain, it appeared that Nixon might have to represent the United States at a pending session of the NATO chiefs of state in Paris. There were also other important matters to which he was prepared to give his immediate attention. They had to do with the budget, the legislative program, the spreading economic recession, the Sputnik challenge, and so forth. Nixon required no special briefings. He was already intimate with the issues, problems, and administration policies. Dewey estimated that Nixon had obtained twenty years of experience in his first five years as vice-president.

Eisenhower created the stand-by office of acting president because Congress dallied on his suggestion that it repair the flaw in the Constitution that leaves in doubt a vice-president's constitutional status during a president's disabling illness. Eisenhower worked out his plan with advice from Dulles and Attorney General Rogers: Eisenhower's third illness convinced him not to wait for Congress any longer. He thought the matter through in great detail on his trip to Paris for the NATO Conference just a week or so after recovering from the stroke. Originally he believed the Cabinet should monitor the agreement and decide the question of a president's inability to do his job if, for some reason such as unconsciousness, the President himself could not. After weighing alternatives, however, he decided in January, 1958, that the Cabinet would be too cumbersome. He felt it would be simpler and more practical to make the agreement directly with the Vice-President. In essence, the plan is this:

If Eisenhower finds himself unable to perform his duties he will

(194)

tell Nixon and Nixon will become acting president with the full powers and duties of the office until Eisenhower, himself, determines he is able to resume his responsibilities. If for some reason Eisenhower is not physically able to tell Nixon to take over, Nixon will do so on his own authority and serve as acting president until Eisenhower decides he can go back to work.

Eisenhower committed the agreement to writing in the form of a letter to Nixon. A copy was given to Secretary of State Dulles, and another to Attorney General Rogers. Rogers requested that his be kept at the White House.

"When you read it, you realize that President Eisenhower would have made a very fine lawyer," says Nixon. "He has a mind that sees all alternatives, all possibilities of a problem. He doesn't have what usually gets a poor lawyer into trouble—the one-track mind, the inability to see the various possibilities on every question. He has the ability to think it all through and then put it into excellent form. One of the interesting things about the President is that, like many great men in the nation's past, he is a very fine letter writer. He likes to write letters, and he dictates them fast and well. As far as I am concerned, I can write a good letter if I must, but I dislike to do it. To me it is such a time-consuming job. The chitchat has to flow smoothly and easily and that is my great difficulty. For me it is a hard chore."

Eisenhower and Nixon are probably closer to each other than any president and vice-president have ever been. The relationship had already passed beyond the "my boy" stage of the 1952 campaign and the early administration months when Eisenhower was angered by a rumor in 1956 that he wanted to dump Nixon as a running mate. "Anyone who attempts to drive a wedge of any kind between Dick Nixon and me has just as much chance as if he tried to drive it between my brother and me," he snapped. In turn, Nixon's adulation of his chief—especially in campaigns—is surpassed only by that of an admirer of a previous Republican president who declared, "To doubt General Grant is to doubt Christ."

From time to time Eisenhower writes friendly notes to his deputy.

(195)

In one late in December, 1957, thanking him for his services during the year, Eisenhower added this postscript: "In view of the intimacy of our friendship this letter may seem to you a bit on the formal side. It is not meant to be. I am simply trying to make of record an expression of my grateful thanks." A highlight of every Nixon birthday is the warm expression of good wishes which the President sends, usually a couple of days early so he would be sure not to forget.

"As I look ahead to Friday and your birthday anniversary, I can only wish we could find some way to celebrate it rather than the agony of the State of the Union Message," Eisenhower wrote on January 7, 1959. "But my dislike of that chore doesn't detract in the slightest from the large measure of felicitations I send you, and certainly I hope that 1959 will be for you a happy and successful year." Nixon was to be forty-six on January 9.

Occasionally Eisenhower also invites Nixon to join him in a round of golf. Not long ago the Eisenhower-Nixon party happened upon a foursome of prominent Democrats, including National Chairman Paul Butler. The game of both groups went to pot.

The President is twenty-two years older than the Vice-President, and their backgrounds, training and interests are quite different. Furthermore, Eisenhower seldom associates privately with his fellow-workers. That is true also for Nixon. Thus, despite their unusually cordial and friendly relationship, the association is mostly business. Prior to the President's heart attack it was entirely business. When Nixon flew to Denver for a conference with the President two weeks before he was stricken, for instance, he was met at the airport by Hagerty and taken to a ninth-floor suite at the Brown Palace Hotel. It was about nine in the evening, and Eisenhower was entertaining a few personal friends in the hotel's Presidential Suite on the eighth floor. Although only one flight of stairs (or a very short elevator ride) separated them, there was no exchange of visits or indication of welcome from the President until the appointed hour for the meeting the next morning at Eisenhower's headquarters.

The bond between Eisenhower and Nixon has weathered some

serious strains and twists. A few of their respective adherents are still irked by slights dating from the 1952 campaign, particularly the "fund" episode. Some of Nixon's partisans are not unhappy now when the President himself becomes the target for criticism. A close friend of Eisenhower's, who has been one of his constant off-duty companions, rates it as "a gruelling relationship, all things considered." But Nixon has "developed more than any fellow you ever saw," he adds. "The President appreciates what a whale of a job Dick has been doing."

When troubles over Sherman Adams' fellowship with Bernard Goldfine threatened to get out of hand in July, 1958, Eisenhower turned to Nixon for advice. Adams, the President's most trusted assistant since the campaign in 1952, seemed to epitomize Yankee reserve and morality. Now a House investigating committee disclosed that Adams had accepted gifts, including a vicuña coat, and considerable hospitality from Goldfine, a wealthy fringe-operator in textile mills and real estate. The investigation also revealed that Goldfine listed his largess as a tax-deductible business item and that Adams made phone calls for him to executive agencies which were sitting in judgment on alleged law violations by Gold-fine.

This was a serious blow in an election year. The Republicans had campaigned vigorously against the mink-coat and deep-freeze operations of Democrats in the Truman administration. It was a handy issue, and now it was gone. Yet President Eisenhower was reluctant at first even to think of what the White House would be without Adams. On June 18, a day after Adams voluntarily appeared before the Congressional committee and admitted he had been imprudent but insisted he had broken no laws, Eisenhower stated firmly at a press conference that he needed Adams, and Adams would stay.

At the outset Nixon's opinion was not requested by either Eisenhower or Adams, and he didn't offer it. But the Adams sensation harmed him more than it did most other Republicans because it reopened the wounds of the old "Nixon fund" squabble. Invariably, stories about Adams mentioned that the fund affair had been Eisenhower's first problem in political ethics. (A Miami newspaper checked the hotel where Nixon stays on visits to Florida, and a wealthy friend whom he visits. It found Nixon pays his own bills.) Nixon and Adams had worked together in the administration rather effectively. Although some of Nixon's friends believed Adams was antagonistic toward him, the Vice-President saw no evidence of it. He charged rumors to the fact that Adams had many enemies and few friends among the Republican politicians in Washington, mostly because of his frigid demeanor and his readiness to say "no," flatly and without embellishment.

(The role Adams played in keeping Eisenhower from deciding to retire from politics after his heart attack is known to only a handful of party leaders. The recuperating President went into the pros and cons of his continuance in public life when Leonard Hall visited him at his Gettysburg farm on November 28, 1955. After clearly indicating that he had had enough of politics, Eisenhower all but dared Hall to explain to him fully what his, Eisenhower's, duty was; why he hadn't already performed his duty to his country; and why he should be called upon to do even more. Hall fidgeted nervously in his chair. And just as he was bracing himself to hear the dreaded words—"I won't run"—Adams popped into the room. Hall was relieved that the visit was over.)

Two days after Eisenhower declared he needed Adams, Nixon lectured a private gathering of Republican state chairmen at his home on the wisdom of Republicans sticking together and helping each other instead of acting like "cannibals" whenever one of their number was wounded. He discussed the Adams troubles quite candidly: there was no question about the presidential assistant's honesty. Then, for the benefit of those who continued to demand Adams' dismissal, Nixon said: "It doesn't take much guts to kick a guy when he is down."

Afterward Adams thanked Nixon and asked that Nixon keep him posted on any adverse effect his continuance at the White House might have. The Nixon association with Adams always had been "not close, not unfriendly, but just correct." He explained it further as "solely a business relationship."

Meanwhile Eisenhower invited Nixon's views. As the Adams situation worsened, the President leaned more and more heavily on his vice-president's counsel. In August Nixon reviewed the problem with Eisenhower on three occasions. "He brought it up each time," said Nixon. "The President seemed to have confidence in my judgment as to the effect of this case and how best it should be resolved. He asked me to advise and help resolve it."

After Congress adjourned on August 24, Nixon had two sessions with Adams. "I indicated that, while I doubted it would have a decisive effect on the voting in November, the great majority of candidates and political leaders would, for their own self-interest, repudiate him and this probably would make his position in the White House untenable," said Nixon. "I also told him that, because candidates elected to Congress would have taken this position, his relationship as the President's principal assistant would inevitably become difficult. He would not be able to carry out his assignments with senators and congressmen and political leaders as he used to do."

Nixon and National Chairman Alcorn kept in constant touch with each other and swapped ideas and information. At the President's request, Alcorn quietly made a nationwide check of the attitudes of Republicans. His survey was completed at a National Committee and National Finance Committee meeting in Chicago. Then Alcorn notified the President that there was an overwhelming feeling among Republicans that Adams should be replaced. That was August 28. Eisenhower reluctantly agreed—and asked Alcorn to tell Adams. When Adams returned from a vacation on September 15, Alcorn was his first visitor at the White House. A few days later, after cleaning out his desk and making certain that his successor would know where to find everything, Adams resigned. From the seat of power in the White House he retired to his home in New Hampshire to write a book.

Nixon's willingness to pitch in and help caused him to start off on the wrong foot in the 1958 campaign and also lost him a sizable amount of the good will he had gained from former skeptics since

(199)

Eisenhower's heart attack. The problem involved letters to the State Department about the administration's decision to stand firm at Quemoy and Matsu, the tiny offshore Chinese islands which were being bombarded by the Chinese Communists. There was considerable pressure for softening the administration's stand, and Eisenhower found it necesary to explain his position on television. On Saturday, September 27, the *New York Times* had a story reporting that about 80 per cent of the mail coming to the State Department still opposed the administration's policy. This encouraged the opponents and infuriated the administration faithful. After talking it over with Undersecretary of State Herter, Nixon was convinced the story had been leaked by a staff member who was in a group that invariably carped at Dulles' decisions. Nixon felt that an evaluation of the State Department mail would show, as it had at the White House, that bona fide messages from concerned citizens favored the administration's position by approximately two to one, while most of the others were contrived appeals or form letters.

After further discussions with Herter it was decided that something should be done and that a statement from the Vice-President would be more effective than one from the State Department. Therefore, Nixon stated, in part: "What concerns me primarily is not the patent and deliberate effort of a State Department subordinate to undercut the Secretary of State and sabotage his policy. What is of far greater concern is the apparent assumption on the part of those who put out the story that the weight of the mail rather than the weight of the evidence should be the controlling factor in determining American foreign policy."

There was an immediate uproar. The *New York Times* declared that the story on the letters was news, and therefore should not be "suppressed." The Chicago *Daily News* said, "Nixon goofed." And a Baltimore *Sun* columnist asserted that the statement unmasked Nixon's Fascist tendencies. Before his statement Nixon received only 20 letters on the Quemoy-Matsu issue. During the week following he received 982. Forty per cent favored his position and also the policy, and 60 per cent disapproved, many of them

(200)

violently. The president of a book publishing firm wrote that he recently had agreed with Senator Ives that the only hope for the nation and the Republican party was the "election of Dick Nixon in 1960." "Now I am not so sure," he said. "You have committed an egregious blunder. . . . My advice to you, sir, is to eat crow promptly and in a big way."

In reviewing the incident later Nixon told me that his statement was directed at "a group in the State Department that keeps trying to undercut Dulles' Far Eastern policies." He weighed the personal risk of "saying what I did" and decided that someone had to take it. "I believe the statement had the effect I intended it to have." Nixon believes the warning implicit in his statement will discourage State Department personnel who disagree with administration policy from assuming the right to buck it publicly.

After the Republican party's general defeat in the 1958 election Nixon reviewed the debacle state by state, and the summary of what he determined is a model of what can happen to a party burdened by a maximum of hard luck and stupidity in the same campaign year. He put it this way:

Half of our loss was due to the fact that the issues ran against us from the time of the second term inauguration in 1957 until the campaign began. We started with the issue of the budget. For four or five months in 1957 we were on the defensive about it. This split the Republicans right down the middle. That was the beginning, and just as we began to recover from it, and as the budget trouble was dead as an issue—what happened? Sputnik! This made people begin to lose confidence in us on national defense. Then just as that began to be cured by the fact that we got a couple of things in the air ourselves—what happened? The recession! That whipped us down and down. It had the worst effect of all, of course. We already had been starting down, and the recession gave us a push. But just as the good news that the recession was ending began to come out in July, there was another bad break—the Adams case. That kept us on the defensive so much that we couldn't play up the good news of improved economic conditions.

Now, all the bad news was over by the first of October, but you can't

(201)

undo in a month what had happened all this time. Some of our losses might have been prevented—we could have been saved to an extent in dealing with all of these issues if we had been more effective in stating our case, if we had used more showmanship as well as leadership. There's been no question of leadership in this administration. It's only been a question of showmanship. And despite the opposition charges that we are supposed to have been taken in by Madison Avenue, we have been awfully inept sometimes in presenting our case to the people. Take the farm issue, for example. What we have proposed and what we have done has been right for the farmer and the nation. The farmer has never had it so good. But, someway, somehow, our Democratic friends have done such a job on Ezra Benson that they have the farmers thinking he and the Republican party are against them. We took the worst shellackings in the farm states. That's where we lost the three Senate seats that I didn't think we would lose. That also denied us a couple of governorships, and lost us two. We had good candidates there. Incidentally, one thing I'd like to make clear is that all the speculation that I've been out trying to get Benson fired is wrong. I have never advocated any changes in the Cabinet, and it would be inappropriate for me to do so. The Cabinet membership is the President's prerogative alone. I praised Benson for working hard in the '58 campaign, and I praised him for his courage for standing for what is right although it is obvious that the Democrats have made him the symbol of "agin the farmer" just as they made Herbert Hoover the symbol of the depression.

As I said, the bad breaks we had on issues cost us half of our losses. The other half we are responsible for ourselves. We might well have taken the whole state of California—everything—if we hadn't gotten into such a fight among ourselves there. We lost in Ohio because of the right-to-work issue. The Ohio Republican organization is good and our candidates in Ohio were good. Senator John Bricker tried to persuade its sponsors against going ahead with the right-to-work initiative. He asked me to help, and I tried. But they went ahead anyway, and we lost everything. In Indiana the Republicans beat themselves by fighting each other. That cost us six congressmen and a senator. Furthermore, Republicans beat themselves in other states because of poor organization and failure to run stronger candidates.

13

R~ICHARD~ N~IXON~'s most unusual role in the administration—his overseas missions—stemmed from an offhand suggestion by President Eisenhower. "What are you going to do this summer?" Eisenhower asked him early in 1953 during one of the new administration's first National Security Council meetings.

"Anything you say, Mr. President," Nixon replied.

"Well, I think you should take a trip to the Far East. Take Pat . . . ."

So Nixon added diplomacy to the extra chores he was accumulating for his once-tranquil office and launched his newest career with an around-the-world tour of nineteen countries on three continents.

In the mass of welcome home messages after his return was a note scribbled on blue White House stationery:

Dear Dick. Proud as I am of the record you—and Pat—established on your recent visit to a number of Asian countries, yet I must say that I am glad to have you home. We, by which I mean all the principal figures in the administration, have missed your wise counsel, your energetic support, and your exemplary dedication to the service of the country. On the personal side it was fine to see you both looking so well after the rigor of the trip that must have taxed the strength of even such young and vigorous people as yourselves. I look forward to some quiet opportunity when I can have a real recital of your adventures and accomplishments.

With warm personal regards . . . Sincerely . . . D~WIGHT~ D~AVID~ E~ISENHOWER~.

Nixon had been abroad only twice—in the war and in 1947 with the Herter Committee of Congress.

The assignment was vague enough. President Eisenhower urged him to get to know world leaders. The State Department provided charts, briefings and a proposed statement for each stop, all of which added up to an implied plea that he avoid trouble and stick to the paths worn smooth by previous VIP junketeers. Nixon's political cheerleaders were of mixed minds. Some advised that an international sheen was just the thing he needed; others warned him to stay away from "internationalism" and "foreign do-gooding."

He and Mrs. Nixon headed for distant horizons much as they had often taken to the hustings back home. The first tour, covering 45,431 miles in seventy days, included one 24-hour rest stop at Melbourne, Australia. Off time on the next, a 30-day trip through Central America, was an afternoon in San Juan, Puerto Rico. A three-week African tour included a detour to Rome for a day of relaxation. But before Nixon reached the Eternal City he had scheduled visits with the Pope, the President of Italy, the Prime Minister and a few other people, and Rome became the busiest stop of the trip. There were no rest periods at all on the itinerary of the South American tour and visit to England in 1958.

Nixon learned from continent to continent. Problems are not solved "by smothering them with polite language," he discovered. An old-timer who watched him operate behind the ornately paneled doors in South America declared, "Why, Nixon tells them 'yes' or 'no' instead of 'mañana.' " Over the miles and years Nixon stuck by the informal campaign smile and handshake as his basic weapon. In West Africa the *Daily Mail* of Accra urged its own "officialdom" to treat newspapermen as Nixon does. "Every photographer had the opportunity to shoot at the Vice-President of the United States, as they pleased," wrote the editor. "Bless him."

In retrospect, Nixon feels the handshaking foray—the matter of meeting people on the street and exchanging a personal greeting— works as well internationally as in domestic campaigns. "The State Department was petrified before my first trip," he told me. "They seemed to be a little less frightened before each trip since. But each time they give me statements designed to avoid trouble by saying nothing at all. In my opinion, they were so colorless and ineffectual as to be worse than no statements at all. When you are abroad, speaking a language the people do not know, you cannot read, you must speak from the heart. So I improvise, and I've gone out and made a little news, a little color."

As a matter of fact, Nixon has made plenty of news, most of it in off-the-cuff observations. For instance, he told a gathering in a backwoods village of Ghana, "I hope the breezes continue to be friendly and cool as they are today, and the crops to be good, and all the people to be happy"; then pointing to the children, he added, "particularly these." The villagers were delighted and somehow the story of Nixon's simple wish for them spread through Africa and was mentioned and written about for months after his departure.

Applause for a speech in London on November 26, 1958, extended across to the Kremlin. The Vice-President said the free world should "speak less of the threat of Communism and more of the promise of freedom [and] adopt as our primary objective *not* the defeat of Communism, but the victory of plenty over want, of health over disease, of freedom over tyranny." Premier Khrushchev declared it a "welcome" statement. He added, however, that he and Nixon differed on their "concepts of tyranny."

Official reaction to the British trip was typical. Prime Minister Macmillan said: "Your speeches have deeply impressed the public . . . your personality and that of your charming wife has 'got over' in a wonderful way." Sir Winston Churchill wrote: "If I may say so, your visit to this country has been a great success and has strengthened still further our close friendship with the United States."

But not all the aftermath has been sugar and spice. While the British beamed at his observation that British colonialism wasn't as bad as it is sometimes depicted, for instance, Congressman Frank Thompson, Jr., a New Jersey Democrat, complained that that kind of talk would horrify new and uncommitted nations which "view anybody's colonialism as a hateful thing." Nixon has riled the French by seeming to imply that Algeria should be free. He infuriated Nasser by stating that Ethiopia and the Sudan should have as much to say about Nile River projects as Egypt. The Kremlin became so annoyed by Nixon's domination of the headlines during the African tour that Radio Moscow announced that Nixon and everyone in his entourage, including the American press, were drunks and bums. And some American industrialists have been less than joyful about his insistence that firms doing business overseas be more responsive to the welfare of host countries.

Nixon has been trapped in a Mexico City elevator, picketed in Burma, called "son of a dog" in Casablanca, and plagued by dysentery and other maladies in Ethiopia, Afghanistan, Indonesia and elsewhere.

But nothing was so spectacular as the violence in Peru and Venezuela that turned his South American visit into a commando operation. Riots in Lima and murderous attacks in Caracas provided an urgent, split-second test of Nixon's brainpower, backbone and luck. He handled it with the deliberate coolness of a battlefront strategist who looks to the future as well as the present.

None of the governments, ours or theirs, had foreseen violence prior to his tour in May, 1958.[1] Exhaustive investigations later indicated that the perpetrators themselves did not have violence in mind, at first. Economic adversity on the Latin continent, much of it a backwash of the recession in the United States, simplified the task of inflaming South America's latent dislike for its overrich Yankee neighbor. But even the Communists originally planned nothing more lethal than demonstrations and heckling. They began by emphasizing items such as America's "discriminatory" trade policies and its "friendship" for dictators. Nixon was depicted as a typical Yankee warmonger and an exploiter. It was when the Vice-President looked, talked and acted the opposite—and twisted each incident during his first stops in Uruguay and Argentina to his own advantage—that peaceful demonstrations were abandoned. The "warmonger" infuriated bedrock anti-Americans and delighted

---

[1] Nixon told some reporters who were hesitant about covering the trip that they would probably miss little since he doubted there would be much solid news in it. This influenced several to stay home.

the masses by his talk. His theme was freedom and progress for both Americas. He mentioned the atom only while urging nations to co-operate in harnessing its marvels to better the lot of mankind. The word "war" figured often in his public remarks, for he declared repeatedly that the only war the United States wanted to win was against poverty, disease and misery. On labor, he said that strong unions were vital to freedom, and union organizations in a half dozen countries made him an honorary member. He dealt with the dictatorship allegation by endorsing recent revolutions against one-man rule in Venezuela, Colombia and Argentina. He enraged critics by claiming that Hungary showed Communist dictatorship to be worse than the brand so well-known in South America.

He dealt with every question asked him, regardless of source. He ignored some provocations and acknowledged others with friendly words. During often tense days he permitted himself only one public display of outrage—he shook his fist and shouted "Coward!" at a rock-throwing mob in Lima.

By degrees it was decided to get rough to stop Nixon. Meaner, obscene insults were tried before saliva, rocks and murder were agreed upon. Near the end of his stay in Argentina, "racist" was shouted at him instead of the old standby "imperialist." A couple of countries later "racist" became "lyncher," and Nixon was warned in thousands of leaflets to "Go back to the U.S.A. where you enjoy the lynchings of Negroes and the massacres of Indians."

Organized crowds attacked the Vice-President physically in Peru and Venezuela. Violence was averted in Colombia by police vigilance, and in Bolivia by blowing up a railroad track.[2] The railroad was cut to isolate a mining town. Agitators had convinced the miners that the United States was responsible for Bolivia's economic chaos, and they planned a protest march on Nixon, wearing bandoliers of dynamite sticks.

La Paz is two miles above sea level, the highest city in the world. Its rarefied air slows down visiting lowlanders. But Nixon refused

[2] Most of the conspiracies cited in this chapter and the next were uncovered by security investigations and are still classified as secret, mostly because political leaders in the Latin-American countries want no embarrassing revelations.

(207)

a bracer of pure oxygen at the airport, and bounded around the city shaking hands, making speeches and joining native dances, while his traveling companions gasped for breath or went to bed with throbbing headaches. (Bolivians marveled at the performance. They also speculated that stamina at high altitudes must be a prerequisite for the American Vice-Presidency since their last such guest, Henry Wallace, began a good-will visit in 1943 by playing two sets of tennis.) Had Nixon known about the track-blowing he would have better understood why President Hernán Siles Zuazo opened their first conference with a reference to two portraits on his office wall. They were his predecessors, the President explained. One was driven mad by the nation's economic dilemma and committed suicide. The other was hanged from a lamppost outside the Government Building. "I often wonder what will be my fate," he said.

Trouble was fomenting at Lima and Bogotá before Nixon left La Paz. A group of students, most of them Communists, met secretly on May 5 to plan a riot during a scheduled visit at San Marcos University on May 8. Operational orders were expertly drawn, with maps of the university area that pinpointed the deployment of hecklers, group demonstrators, loud-speaker equipment, wheelbarrows of throwable fruit, and intersections at which fake traffic accidents were to bottle up the official motorcade. American intelligence agents had copies of the map the next day. So did the Lima police.

Meanwhile activists in other Latin capitals also were buzzing with ideas. They fell over each other in Bogotá, where officials were still jumpy because of an abortive revolution the week before. Joining the usual schemers in Colombia were the militant, right-wing Leyvistas. They had no particular quarrel with the United States, but felt the Vice-President's visit was a grand time to embarrass and perhaps overthrow their own government.

On May 6, five days before Nixon was to arrive, the Union of Communist Youth of Colombia posted plans for their demonstrations on university bulletin boards and invited everyone to participate. Elsewhere in the city Leyvista leaders were talking business with a brace of *parjos,* or hired assassins.

(208)

On May 8, the day of riot in Lima, twenty-four individuals congregated at the Bogotá home of a Peruvian exile named Pulgarvida. Among them were Communist leaders and three tight-lipped *parjos* who announced they were short on words but long on action. The conversation, often loud enough to be heard by intelligence agents eavesdropping outside, touched on several proposals, but centered on assassination. All agreed that killing the Yankee Vice-President would delight South America's long-suffering people and generate an upheaval that, in the end, would benefit the Latin Hemisphere at the expense of the Northern "imperialists." Next day a gathering of forty students and instructors representing Communist and like-minded organizations agreed to concentrate their activities at four points: the airport, Nixon's hotel, and his two wreath-laying ceremonies. Their plan required the "troops" to fire coffee beans from slingshots, toss fruit and eggs, and arouse maximum commotion. Late that night the Colombian Communist party, adult division, and its ally, the *Fronte Liberal del Pueblo,* ordered the younger wing leaders to headquarters, and decreed that everything should be co-ordinated, otherwise competing demonstrators would create havoc among themselves, leaving the Yankee enemy unscathed and victorious. Raoul Almadaospina, secretary of agitation and propaganda of the party's Bogotá regional committee, was appointed generalissimo. To punctuate their authority, the adults produced cash to pay for incidentals such as slingshots and 55,000 leaflets summoning "the people to the streets"—the traditional call to violence in Colombia, where incredibly, more than 250,000 people have been murdered since 1948.

Unfortunately for Señor Almadaospina and his compatriots, the turmoil earlier that week in Lima had inspired exceptional police vigilance in Bogotá. Thus the chief conspirators were rounded up the night before Nixon's visit, and their elaborate schemes evaporated. Even the slingshots and coffee beans went astray, and the only things thrown at Nixon were rose petals, by school children singing "The Star-Spangled Banner" in Spanish.

Peru was number five in the eight-nation itinerary. On the eve of arrival, Lima was blanketed with leaflets: "Students, Workers,

Employees—Join Us—Gather to Shout with All Your Forces—
Out Nixon—Death to Yankee Imperialism." The leaflets described
Nixon as "the most insolent representative of monopolistic trusts"
and invited all to take part in violence at San Marcos the next
morning, beginning when Nixon tried to enter the university.

Although trouble was in the air from the moment he landed, the
Vice-President was welcomed cordially along the city streets. But
at nightfall a screaming, fist-shaking crowd gathered as he and Mrs.
Nixon left the hotel for a formal reception, and the University
Student Federation's leadership called an emergency meeting. This
group, which a few days before had demanded the right to fire
professors and veto university regulations, adopted a resolution
stating that Nixon "personifies the plutocratic and imperialist designs of the United States" and therefore would not be welcome
at San Marcos.

Rumors of impending uproar grew wilder during the night. At
his reception Nixon conferred in a side room with advisers while
Lima's starchy set sipped Pisco Sours and denuded the huge buffet
tables. Security officers, diplomats, and political figures, American
and Peruvian, urgently recommended that Nixon cancel the San
Marcos appearance. One firm voice to the contrary was that of
Ambassador Theodore C. Achilles, a mild-mannered, professorial
man. He said United States prestige would suffer if its vice-president permitted a Communist-led mob to keep him away from the
Western Hemisphere's oldest seat of learning. He proposed that
Nixon at least "make a pass" at the university. But reports of
trouble continued to multiply, and predominating opinion was that
the Vice-President should confound the plot by going instead to
Catholic University.

"I was told San Marcos had given me a reason for not coming
by calling me *persona non grata*," Nixon recalled. "But I said,
'Wait a moment. What group did that, a Communist-dominated
minority? It may be a tough minority, but it is hardly representative
of the student body. You get hold of the university rector. If he
withdraws his invitation to me, I will not go. But he must do it
personally.' "

(210)

An embassy official called the university. He reported back that the rector admitted, privately, that there was danger and that he was fearful of what might happen. But he would not withdraw his invitation since that might cause people to think he had lost control of the university. Nixon then instructed John Sherwood, the Secret Service agent in charge, to inform the Lima police chief that "if he will allow us to say that he advised us not to go, we will cancel our appearance at the university." But the police chief was like the university rector. He admitted to Sherwood, in confidence, that there was great danger and he hoped Nixon would stay away from San Marcos. But he would not dare imply such a thing publicly because he would lose face if word got around that he doubted his ability to handle "rabble rousers."

"So it got right down to the fact that the buck had been passed," said Nixon. "The rector wouldn't take the responsibility; the chief of police wouldn't take it; so there it rested, with me."

The Vice-President slept fitfully that night. The conspirators never went to bed. By daybreak anti-American slogans covered the university walls like a rash. Banners were distributed, loud-speakers were up, and the wheelbarrows were at hand. Riot chieftains collected in knots at their designated spots and squads of special police were posted nearby an hour before Nixon was to come.

Four blocks away at the hotel, Nixon had early appointments in his suite. Then, at ten o'clock, he walked across the street to place a wreath at the San Martín monument. A thousand men and women silently stared as he crossed the wide avenue toward the shrine of Peru's greatest hero. Many had been waiting for hours to see how he would meet the challenge. Nothing was said. No one seemed even to breathe. Only the shuffle of shoes on the pavement disturbed the stillness. Nixon brushed aside two policemen and reached into the crowd to shake a hand. Someone half-shouted, "Welcome." Nixon laughed and shouted, "Long live Peru!" There was a wisp of applause. Another "Long live Peru!" from Nixon was echoed by bursts of "Long live Nixon!" "Long live North America!" Tension had eased. Nixon noted that the Lima police chief was absent from the entourage for the first time.

(211)

"When I walked out of the hotel I knew the day was going to be a hard one," Nixon said later. "The whole thing was a battle. Consequently, I was mentally and physically alert. I was on edge, the kind of 'on edge' I feel before a big speech or when going into a very difficult press conference, but more so. My mental and physical resources were mobilized and ready to use.

"I had several alternative plans in mind. I always leave myself a chance to change plans when dealing with Communists. If you fool them, you confuse them. My inclination the night before was to go [to San Marcos]; that was my inclination as I walked from the hotel. But I had not reached the point of no return. I think it is best to make decisions in which great risks are involved at the latest possible moment. I don't believe in waiting until the moment of decision passes, but it is important to allow all the time possible for improvising . . .

"When dealing with this type of situation, your mind must always go, even while you're shaking hands and going through all the maneuvers. I developed the ability long ago to do one thing while thinking of another, and as I walked with the wreath that morning I thought of various things. I realized the buck was with me. If I canceled the rector and police chief would say that it was not on their advice. Also running through my mind was what Achilles had said when I asked him, 'What would you do, Mr. Ambassador?' He said Spanish people despise fear and have great admiration for courage. 'If you don't go, the Communists will say that you are afraid,' Achilles said.

"As I was standing there after laying the wreath, I made the decision to go. You know, you step back and you have five minutes to think while you stand at respectful attention. That's when I decided."

When the wreath-laying ceremony was over, Nixon asked his Secret Service aide and the ambassador to tell the motorcycle escort it would be San Marcos. The security man scowled; the ambassador smiled. It took coaxing to convince the police cyclists. Their chief had instructed them to lead Nixon to Catholic University. The advance motorcade was practically there when Nixon ordered it turned around. The mob's roar rose as Nixon approached San Marcos University Square. He stood in the convertible, waving and smiling, as though expecting a friendly greeting.

"I hadn't determined as we drove up whether I would get out of the car," Nixon told me later. "But I saw a few in the crowd were not participating too much. With all those signs and the shouting, I decided we would not accomplish our purpose if we drove away. I wanted to try to talk to them, and to go into the university building. So I jumped out of the car and walked up. Everybody must have been surprised. As I walked, the mob backed up a little. Some took the hand I stretched out to them."

The Vice-President called for the leaders to come out and explain why they would deny him freedom of speech; he defied them to listen; then he accused them of fearing the truth. The rioters pushed and shoved, and the fruit and rocks began to fly.

Colonel Vernon Walters, the interpreter, said, "Mr. Vice-President, they are throwing stones." "I know. One just bounced off my shoulder," Nixon replied. Then a rock hit a Secret Service agent, John Sherwood, in the mouth, and the Vice-President said, "All right, let's get out of here."

"We were being pushed around, and it was getting noisier and noisier," as Nixon tells it. "I figured at that point there was a great possibility the mob might get out of hand. That's when I gave the order to leave. As we moved back to the car and got in, the mob milled around and the rocks fell. I thought it was important to do something else. I didn't want any of them to think that we were putting our tails on the ground and being driven off. So I stood up in the car, faced the noisiest of them, and smiled and waved, in trust. Then the rocks really came down because I think it was at that point that the Communists realized they were really defeated. They lost their heads. That was a mistake. They should never have thrown rocks. If they hadn't thrown rocks, it wouldn't have been so bad for them.

"I will admit that I was excited. I felt the kind of tension you experience in any kind of battle. But when I shook my fist at them and called them 'cowards' I still had control of my temper. The

(213)

kind of treatment I was getting was pretty hard to take, but I knew the greatest mistake I could make would be to lose my head. I realized that that was exactly what they wanted and expected me to do, and this realization, I am sure, helped me to keep my temper under circumstances when I ordinarily would have lost it."

From the riot area Nixon dashed off to Catholic University. The hard core of the San Marcos mob headed for the hotel, where they hoped to have another, more telling demonstration. These two hundred individuals, led by Hector Bejar and two other Communist party functionaries, showered saliva on the United States Embassy windows and seized the wreath Nixon had placed earlier at the San Martín tomb, ripping out flowers that formed a likeness of the United States flag and the North American continent.

Nixon had a rewarding hour of talk with the surprised, but pleased Catholic University students. When he started back for the hotel it was noon, just two hours since he had walked onto San Martín Plaza. Now he had the feeling of having done well. He reflected on the disgrace this would be to the Communists and their cohorts, then saw remnants of the San Marcos mob waiting near the hotel door. He halted the motorcade and jumped out of the car.

"I didn't think that we should try to drive up because the police would have to force them out of the way, and that is probably what they expected. It is always best to do the unexpected if you can get away with it. I knew we had them on the run, and it was essential that we bust right through, walking. So we walked through them, waving and smiling and even shaking a few hands."

Rocks, fruit and spittle began to fly as the Vice-President neared the hotel door. Saliva and debris spattered on Nixon's head. "That guy must have had some chewing tobacco or something," he told me. "It covered my face."[3]

[3] The spitting is still a mystery. There was enough in common about the pattern of all the violence to suggest central direction. But no field order, not even the meticulous San Marcos map, called for spitting. Furthermore, experts insist that Peruvians and Venezuelans seldom spit, even when agitated. Nevertheless, the barrages spewed on Vice-President and Mrs. Nixon in Lima and Caracas came from disciplined mouths, not from lone hotheads.

(214)

Nixon paused in his suite long enough to bathe and change, then went to a luncheon with Peru's business leaders. He delivered an extemporaneous lecture on the responsibilities of modern capitalism. He warned "businessmen who believed in free enterprise" that nations where a few Communists can lead hundreds of willing non-Communists into violence are in grave danger.

"As long as free enterprise seems in the minds of the people to be designed primarily to keep the status quo, to keep the rich rich and the poor poor, we give the Communists the very opening they need," he said. "There is a great difference between individual enterprise in this twentieth century and the kind we knew fifty years ago. We must recognize that in the past its proponents made mistakes. We pay for them today. . . .

"If individual enterprise is to survive, it will do so only if it is enlightened, only if it proves to the people that it is the best way to raise living standards, increase wages, and better working conditions."

The Vice-President made only one change in his schedule that day. He held his press conference at four o'clock instead of six, at the request of reporters anxious to meet early evening deadlines in the United States with the full story. Nixon stated that he risked the visit to San Marcos to demonstrate "how important it is not to allow a minority element to appear to have the power to deny freedom of expression. . . . The greatest cowardice of all is intellectual cowardice, being unable to hear facts and truths." Furthermore, no apology was needed from Peruvians, since responsibility for the incident which would bring so much shame to aristocratic Lima rested with Communists, who owed allegiance to no country other than Russia. Instead of questions, Peruvian newspapermen concluded the press conference with speeches of praise.

Papers elsewhere in South America made similar statements: *El Tiempo*, of Bogotá, declared: "Mr. Nixon behaved with courage and elegance before the frantic mobs." It charged that San Marcos students had been "victims of saboteurs and ill-bred people" who had been trying to mix with Lima society, "one of the most refined of the societies of our capitals." *El Colombiano* found the Vice-

President "an unassuming, self-made man, whose political career is not the fruit of improvisation or favoritism, but of his efforts and skill in the public service of his country." The local Communist magazine, *1958*, announced that the Communist party was blameless for the eruption. The finger of scorn should be pointed at Hollywood, the magazine said, for American movies taught cultured Peruvians to be violent.

An official and secret report to the State Department stated that Peruvian authorities actually had been "prepared to see mild anti-Nixon demonstrations carried out." It cited these reasons: the President was "annoyed" because President Eisenhower had not invited him to Washington; the schedule itself angered the Prime Minister since others monopolized it and left little of the limelight for him; an American major-domo affronted the Foreign Minister by putting a press car ahead of his in the motorcade; and the government, generally, was displeased by Nixon's insistence on meeting with university people, labor leaders and opposition politicians, instead of attending only official functions as Argentine President Frondizi had done so graciously two weeks before. Furthermore, some government officials felt that a dramatic hint of Communist growth in Peru would frighten the United States into enlarging its Peruvian aid and trade programs.

Ecuador, the sixth stop, was a comparative paradise. Leaflets had been distributed throughout Quito, stating, "The Communist party, the most articulate voice of the authentic popular and national interests, protests the presence of the monopolistic oppressor and warmonger Nixon." Furthermore, "Death to Nixon" and "Go home, Nixon" were scrawled on fences, walls and sidewalks, and the Communist Youth Group had planned a demonstration for Nixon's visit to Central University. But it was clear the people wanted to hear Nixon out before permitting a second Lima. They ignored the leaflets and scrubbed off insulting slogans, and when Nixon canceled his university appearance, student delegations protested that Ecuadorians were not "uncivilized" like their Peruvian neighbors. They urged him to reconsider. He did and, after a lively roundtable session with student and faculty representatives, the Law School seniors voted him honorary membership in their class.

It was obvious that Nixon had made an excellent impression in Quito; the whole city seemed bent on proving it. Nixon caught the spirit and enjoyed it. Opening a championship soccer match, he couldn't bounce the ball well enough off his head, but was instead permitted to kick it. Spectators roared when he told them over the public-address system, "I've always been better with my feet than with my head."

A stamp and a haircut climaxed Nixon's two days in Quito. To commemorate the visit, Ecuador issued a two-sucre airmail stamp. It was the first to bear the Vice-President's picture. The haircut was less ceremonial. Nixon decided he needed it during a handshaking expedition, so he walked into the nearest barbershop— an establishment that charged fourteen cents. A crowd gathered, the barber snipped away nervously, Nixon praised the result. The next morning Ecuador's most influential newspaper featured a cartoon of the barber standing in front of his shop, saying proudly, "I'm the only one who could skin Nixon." The cartoon was entitled "Democracy in Action." That same day practically all of Ecuador's non-Communist press showed enthusiasm: El Comercio said, "Without doubt the Vice-President won the greatest triumph to which a man in public life can aspire: the affection of the people." The Diario del Ecuador found Nixon "a man of tremendous charm, who in his direct contacts with the people, perfectly acts the role of ambassador; one can read in his eyes the desire to make friends; to clear up misunderstandings."

Then came Bogotá, Colombia, a prelude to Caracas. Every extremist organization, left and right, was out to get Nixon. But police decapitated each plot by arresting thirty-four chief conspirators before the Vice-President landed, and following his motorcades with an armor-plated paddy-wagon for plot leaders plucked from the crowds. (The police concentration on anti-American conspirators was a boon to Bogotá's notorious pickpockets. They netted the wallets of two Secret Service agents, Samuel C. Waugh, the president of the Export-Import Bank, and several others in the Nixon entourage.) The night Nixon was to leave, Secret Service headquarters in Washington announced it had information of a pending assassination attempt in Caracas. William Key, the Vice-President's administrative assistant, confirmed this at a press conference in Colombia. Nixon seemed unperturbed. He had been hearing reports of that kind since his good-will activities began in 1953, he said. "It's just one of those routine things. I'm going to ignore it."

Later, during an interview for this book, Nixon admitted the reports from Caracas were more disturbing than any he had ever received. "I felt that it was going to be bad. I thought the reception would be the coldest we ever had. But I believed it would be proper. That was my feeling about Caracas—proper, but no violence."

14

CARACAS was the last stop on the Nixon tour. It was also the most important. The tough core of Venezuela's Communist organization had survived suspiciously well under the Pérez Jiménez dictatorship, and after the January 23, 1958, revolution, it burst like a spore and its influence spread in all directions, particularly through the press, the university, and the wobbly and inexperienced ruling Junta. While always touchy about possible Communist domination of any hemisphere neighbor, Washington was doubly so about Venezuela for ample commercial, strategic and political reasons.

Thus Nixon's visit was really a specific mission to bolster the Junta's prestige and stability and privately convince the new rulers that their benign attitude toward the Communists would ultimately bring grief to Venezuela and perhaps both American continents.

Nixon was invited to Caracas on March 14 after a United States diplomat hinted to the Venezuelan Foreign Minister at a reception that the Vice-President might come in mid-May if asked. The Junta and Cabinet happened to be meeting at the time, and a note was rushed to Admiral Wolfgang Larrazabal, the President, who announced immediately that Venezuela would "greatly welcome" a Nixon visit.

The Communists reacted instantly. With aid from most of the non-Communist newspapers they revived and expanded upon the most damning anti-Yankee propaganda: the charge of long and profitable intimacy between the United States and the ex-dictator as "proved" by a medal President Eisenhower awarded him, the

(219)

Secretary of State's high praise for his regime, and the luxurious asylum afforded him in Miami.

Within a week the Labor Minister suggested that Nixon not risk a meeting with labor union leaders. By mid-April the ferment engulfed the university. Student groups passed Stay-Away-Nixon resolutions, all stemming from a common source. By April 24 Ambassador Edward J. Sparks told a Junta member he was becoming disturbed. Venezuelan authorities summoned political party and student organization leaders, including the Communists, to a secret meeting April 29. Each of them solemnly pledged "to co-operate in not disgracing Venezuela by doing dishonor to a distinguished visitor." That night Ambassador Sparks was assured officially that "all elements of danger had been counteracted."

While that assurance was being conveyed, Communist party officials were instructing their high school and university subchieftains to accelerate the anti-American drive. Two days afterward the Vice-President was the star, *in absentia*, of the May Day parade in Caracas. Placards and slogans portrayed him as a world villain *sans pareil* and the symbol of North America's lust for war and profits at the expense of downtrodden Venezuelan workers.

On May 3, after the Vice-President had inadvertently put violence plots in motion by getting the better of the first waves of hecklers elsewhere on the Latin continent, *Tribuna Popular,* the official Communist newspaper in Caracas, announced there would be no more pussyfooting with Nixon. He now would face "vigorous" demonstrations in every Latin capital, it stated, and Venezuela would top them all. The paper proclaimed the party's battle-cry— "Nixon, No!"—in huge red letters atop page one, and sidewalks, walls and fences blossomed overnight with "Nixon, No!" in red.

The Vice-President's advance Secret Service agent came to Caracas the next day to review the schedules, travel routes, precautionary arrangements, and other details.[1] The seasoned Caracas

[1] The overseas host country is always responsible for Nixon's safety. But two Secret Servicemen normally accompany his party, and one precedes it to double-check arrangements and serve as a contact with local security agents. Twelve Secret Servicemen were on the South American assignment. After an assassination report all were ordered to Caracas as part of the routine emergency procedure. This saved Nixon's life. Each agent was later commended by President Eisenhower and awarded an Exceptional Civilian Service Medal.

policemen had been killed or dismissed in the revolution. The new force was not only green and untried, but it was also the target of a psychological campaign. The Communists tried to instill an attitude of softness toward mobs in the new force by reminding individual cops repeatedly about the fate of their duty-conscious predecessors. But Army officers supervised each unit and vouched for their discipline, and Nixon's advance agent found few flaws in the plans outlined by the Venezuelan and American embassy people.

He briefed them on Nixon's dislike for shows of martial strength and his abhorrence of police brutality against friendly crowds during his handshaking expeditions. And the agent also requested that an open convertible be available for the Vice-President at the airport.

On May 6 Nixon's roundtable session at the university was canceled at the request of two prominent Venezuelans. They said the "peaceful demonstration" being cooked up by students might not unduly disturb the Vice-President but would reflect on Venezuela's good name. The press then quickened the tempo of agitation by competing for the wildest yarns about Nixon and the United States government. One publication featured a picture of a Negro being lynched, entitled "American Way of Life." Another "exposed" Nixon as a friend of dictator Pérez Jiménez.[2] *Tribuna Popular* proved its superiority in the venom contest with a 24-page issue on May 10 devoted to the United States and its Vice-President. Communism's official voice recognized each Venezuelan interest individually with special articles. The business community was informed that United States monopolists had designs on firms controlled by South Americans. The intelligentsia was reminded that America denied visas to certain "intellectuals" while welcoming the ex-dictator and his chief of secret police. There was also a nod to the patriotic Simón Bolívar. The liberator was quoted as having prophesied more than a century ago that "the United States seems to be destined by Providence to plague the Americas with miseries in the name of liberty."

[2] The Caracas press ignored or pointedly underplayed Nixon's subsequent statement that he and most Americans heartily disliked Pérez Jiménez and his ilk and the United States would gladly extradite the ex-dictator if the Venezuelan government would institute the proper legal proceedings.

Dominating page one was a large photograph expertly altered to picture Nixon as a snarling beast with sharp fangs for teeth. It was labeled "Tricky Dick," an appellation borrowed from the Vice-President's political opponents back home. Many copies of this picture showed up as did other gems from the *Tribuna* on the banners and placards that were flaunted like battle-standards in the violent doings of May 13. As that day approached, slogans previously plastered all over the city were systematically altered. An "M" was painted over an "F" and "Fuera [go home] Nixon" became "Muera [death to] Nixon." Rumblings in the slum and university precincts intensified. Youngsters gossiped excitedly about their plans and flippantly ignored the shushing of their elders.

Non-Communist newspapers that had parroted the *Tribuna Popular*'s line and even featured articles by well-known Communists seemed suddenly shocked by their own power to inflame. They sobered up with last-minute appeals for calm in the city, while the government Junta flooded radio and television airwaves with spot announcements pleading that the distinguished guest be treated courteously or Venezuela would be dishonored.

The government also ordered the commander of the Caracas Army garrison to review and oversee all security precautions. His first major change involved the Nixon motorcade. It would form in the street beyond the Airport Terminal rather than at the customary place on the flight line, he decreed, since the line of sleek limousines might otherwise detract from the splendor of the honor guard.

Caracas, a city of ultra-twentieth-century skyscrapers and neolithic hovels, and 1,200,000 people, many of them destitute, throbbed with activity on the eve of Nixon's coming. High school children paraded downtown breaking windows and street lights. University plotters bragged openly about their pending heroics. American security agents hurriedly changed Nixon's route in the city to avoid streets within shooting range of the huge campus, and the Vice-President's schedule of activities was whittled down. A visit with the Municipal Council of Caracas was canceled when the councilmen pleaded they could not be responsible for "events" if the Vice-President appeared at a public session, as planned.

(222)

Nixon's stroll through Plaza Bolívar to chat with the people and shake their hands also was scratched, and a hush-hush tip about a poison plot created panic in the nation's high echelons. The report was that the murder potion was to be served at the Junta's welcoming luncheon for the Vice-President. This affair was hardly subject to cancellation, so the crisis was solved by firing the caterer.

A coded message from the State Department warned of an assassination scheme unrelated to the one Secret Service headquarters in Washington had announced. Venezuelan security chieftains noted the message and declared their grand strategy would cope with every possible situation. Wherever Nixon went, the streets and buildings around him would be so saturated with security agents that every fourth hand he shook would belong to a plain-clothes cop, they said.

At nightfall on May 12 the Junta notified the American Embassy that "everything is under control—all is well." At three the next morning—eight hours before the Vice-President was to land—that assurance was repeated, and the embassy conveyed it by radio to the Vice-President in Bogotá and the President and Secretary of State in Washington.

The deputy American ambassador in Caracas flew to Bogotá with a dispatch case of up-to-the-minute information and briefed the Vice-President during the 640-mile flight over the Andes from Colombia to Venezuela.

"I stressed the strong probability or even certainty of unfriendly demonstrations," the diplomat wrote later in a memorandum to the Secretary of State. "I spoke of the increased activity of the Communists in Venezuela during recent weeks; I said that the two points on which the agitation was almost certain to be based were the presence of Pérez Jiménez and Pedro Estrada [the former secret police chief] in the United States and our restrictions on imports of petroleum. I also showed the Vice-President aboard the airplane a copy of *Tribuna Popular*, May 10, which contained unrestrained propaganda against Nixon. I said, however, that on the basis of reports we've received from responsible Venezuelan authorities, both directly from members of the Junta and the Foreign Office, and through the Secret Service representatives in Caracas and [U.S. intelligence agents], we were satisfied that any attempt at violence could be effectively disposed of."

As his plane touched down at Maiquetía Airport, Nixon realized his principal job in South America—to bolster the government and spotlight Communist danger in Venezuela—would be tougher than he had expected. A cold, unfriendly atmosphere chills positive diplomacy, even for the usually chillproof Nixon. This bothered the Vice-President more than "probable" demonstrations.

Nixon had no idea, of course, that, whether he liked it or not, the history he was about to live would deal with showers of spitting attacks by mobs, revolutionary stirrings, emergency deployment of United States air, sea and land forces, and his own reactions, verbal and physical. Furthermore, he could hardly foresee that among his novel experiences of the next day and a half he would even be "kidnapped" by his host, the provisional President.

Two hours before Nixon was to land, a swarm of people descended on the airport, snapping the hot, listless Terminal Building to life. Adolescents, soldiers, government officials, reporters, photographers and policemen were in the melee. The soldiers came in trucks; the boys and girls and their middle-aged leaders in buses; the United States government officials, in nine black limousines rented from a mortician for the Nixon motorcades; the United States press corps, in a chartered Panagra airplane. Unnoticed in the bustle was an open Chrysler convertible driven by a United States Army master sergeant. It was there for the Vice-President, who had used open cars everywhere in his seven previous South American stops, including the riot in Lima. As it developed, however, he found a closed limousine preferable in Caracas, despite the torrid weather, and would have switched to a tank if one had been available.

The sight of press photographers set the airport activities off long ahead of schedule. When the cameras pointed at the mob on the Terminal balconies, adults gave a signal and their flock of five hundred boys and girls unfurled the anti-Nixon banners and proceeded to shake fists and shout insults at the open air. A thousand soldiers then fixed bayonets and formed ranks in four battalions, and policemen scurried to posts atop and around the Terminal Building, with carbines at the ready. Once they had started, the demonstrators would not stop. Their frenzied screaming, stomping and banner flailing continued after the photographers pointedly put away cameras. The adolescents paused once, however, to gasp and wolf-whistle when Jinx Falkenburg, who covered the Nixon tour for the Tex and Jinx radio and television programs, shook a disapproving finger at the hooligans, and they switched back to their previous noises.

When the Nixon airplane landed and the Vice-President and Mrs. Nixon emerged, smiling and waving, the mass screech rose several octaves to a pitch that drowned out a Venezuelan Army band and a battery of 105mm artillery firing a 21-gun salute.

"I was very surprised in one respect," Nixon told me afterward. "I expected placards, but I was surprised that they allowed the airport to be completely dominated by the Commies and their stooges. The minute I stepped off the airplane, while getting the salute, I cased the place. I always do that when I walk out. I looked it all over and watched the kind of crowd, thinking where will I make an unscheduled stop, where will we move out and shake hands, and so forth. And as I looked that one over, I just simply saw that here was one place where we would have an altogether different situation than we ever had in any other country I visited. The crowd was all unfriendly. I could see it; I knew it immediately. I whispered to Walters [the interpreter], 'What are they shouting?' I had asked him to check it before we got off the plane. He said, 'Mr. Vice-President, this whole crowd is against us.'

"So we walked down the steps from the airplane, and I quickly made a few mental notes and decisions. As we trooped the line [inspecting the honor guard] I decided not to wave to the crowd, but to ignore it since they were showing disrespect for their flag and their national anthem as well as ours."

A knot of airplane mechanics standing far off beyond the honor guard was the only demonstrably friendly group of nonpolitical

Venezuelans Nixon was to see that day or the next. Their shouts of "Welcome" and "Long live United States" broke through an occasional lull in the racket from the Terminal, and Nixon wondered if it was a mirage. Happily, he shunned protocol to shake their hands before he was formally presented to the local officialdom.

"As we were walking back [to the officials], I turned to Walters and said, 'Look, we're not going to do the mike scene,'" Nixon said. A microphone had been set up, as is customary, and the Vice-President was prepared to tell his hosts: "It is gratifying indeed to know that the Venezuelan people have embarked once again upon the road to democratic government."

Nixon said he "was not going to be put in the position of doing something undignified. It would have been stupid to have tried to speak and be shouted down. I wasn't going to let that happen. And so we walked in."

Thanks to the Venezuelan police and security chiefs, he walked into trouble. The head policeman had refused an embassy attaché's request that the mob be cleared from Nixon's path. "They are harmless," said the police official. "They have a right to demonstrate." The security chief directed the motorcade to form in the street beyond the Terminal. Thus the Vice-President and his wife had to push through a hundred yards of agitated humanity instead of boarding their cars in safety on the airport ramp.

The organized spitting and garbage throwing commenced as the party approached the landing-field side of the Terminal. Before they could reach the shelter of an awning, the band once again struck up the Venezuelan national anthem. The Nixons froze at respectful attention, and the mob on a balcony overhead spat down on them.

"I think that was the time when I felt as irritated as at any time on the trip," said Nixon. "I thought, What a really lousy thing this is." Midway in the anthem he reached down to pick up a rubber noisemaker that had bounced off his cheek. "I was tempted to give it back to the guy. But then I figured that they might think I was throwing something at them. You have to be very careful in a situation like that. You have to think all those things through. My first impulse was to throw it back. If I had done that, it would have been a good move, provided it didn't start something. This was an emotional crowd, and they might have thought I was being unfriendly."

Mrs. Nixon also relaxed her rigid attention at one point to reach through a line of soldiers and shake the hand of a girl who had spat and shouted obscene insults at her. The teen-ager was startled. Tears filled the eyes that had blazed with hate, and she turned away in obvious shame.

Before the anthem had run its course, the adult mob leaders hissed, "Go, go, go," to their charges, and the youths melted away from the balcony and formed ranks on the street to block the Yankee visitors when they emerged from the building. Venezuelan authorities watched solemnly. The soldiers stood erect and at perfect attention, fixed bayonets gleaming in the sunlight. Police disappeared. And a few Secret Service agents and United States military officers cleared paths to the cars through spitting, tripping feet, garbage and swinging fists.

A little girl was elbowed by two escorts through the mob to give Mrs. Nixon a flower bouquet. This was the first token of friendship shown the Vice-President's wife since she had landed. Mrs. Nixon hugged and kissed the child and whispered, "Thanks," in her ear, hoping she heard it above the noise. In the confusion a teen-ager grabbed Mrs. Nixon's hand and screeched a question about the Vice-President torturing "little black boys" in Little Rock.

"He was one of the very mean young boys," Mrs. Nixon told me later. "I pretended that I didn't understand him. I just said, 'How are you? So nice to be here,' and a few things like that which I thought he and the others might understand. . . . They must have been told that we were horrible people."

Mrs. Nixon and the wife of the Foreign Minister were assigned to the second limousine of the motorcade. Its back seat was spotted with saliva. Mrs. Nixon wiped it away while her Venezuelan hostess expressed mortification. Major James D. Hughes, the Vice-President's military aide, and two Secret Service agents joined the ladies and rolled up the windows as several of the youngsters surrounded the car to spit and kick at it, while the main mob concentrated on Nixon and his number one car. Secret Service agent Sherwood had long before banished any thought of permitting the Vice-President to use the open convertible. But its driver, Master Sergeant James W. McAtamney, was a handy addition to the thin ranks protecting the visitors. The sergeant and Sam Moskowitz, second secretary at the embassy, were kicked and spat on while protecting the Venezuelan and American flags attached to the Nixon limousines. They got it again while helping to shield the Vice-President as he climbed in behind Foreign Minister Oscar Garcia Ventuni, Nixon's official greeter. It was an unpleasant day for Señor Garcia. The mob treated him as though he, too, was vice-president of the United States.

Caracas was twelve miles away. Carloads of the demonstrators slipped into the motorcade. Some rode alongside the Vice-President's vehicle, shouting, spitting and throwing things at forty miles an hour. Motor scooters joined the melee at the city limits. They zigzagged around the Vice-President and Mrs. Nixon's cars, almost colliding with the police escorting the motorcade on motorcycles.

In the lead limousine the Foreign Minister and the Vice-President were on the back seat, Colonel Walters and Agent Sherwood were on the jump seats, and Wade Rodham, the advance Secret Service agent, sat up front with the Venezuelan chauffeur. With Mrs. Nixon and Señora Garcia Ventuni in the next car were Major Hughes and agent Dale Grubb with agent Ernest Aragon sitting beside the Venezuelan chauffeur. A large open truck for photographers[3] went ahead of the procession. Seven limousines for others in the party followed the lead cars. Fortunately for the Nixons, a half dozen Secret Service agents were in them.

"When we left the airport, I had a chat with the Foreign Minister right away," Nixon said. "He wiped the spit off me with his handkerchief and said he was sorry but the people are very expressive because they have not had any freedom for so many years and the

---

[3] I was among the half dozen reporters who scrambled aboard the truck and witnessed the day's violence from a perch superior to any theater or stadium seat imaginable.

new government did not want to suppress freedom. I told him that if his government did not learn how to control the type of people that I saw there at the airport and control the excesses in which they were indulging, there wouldn't be any government, and there wouldn't be any freedom either. I spoke with great feeling because I was disturbed.

" 'These are Communists,' I pointed out. 'I've seen these same signs and placards all over Latin America. These Communists will deny Venezuela the freedom it deserves and should have.' I also pointed out that they wouldn't let me speak or even him, that they denied both of us freedom of speech and shouted throughout their own national anthem as well as ours.

"He told me that I was right. He said he, too, thought they were Communists. 'But I urge you, if the press should ask you about this, I urge you not to say that they are Communists,' he said. 'You see, here in this country we judge freedom differently.' Then he went off into a long rigmarole from which I gathered that the government wanted to get along with the Communists because the Communists had supported them in the revolution. The Foreign Minister was afraid that my identifying these Communists as such would embarrass the government."

The Foreign Minister changed the subject. "This is an interesting highway," he said. They were on the Autopista, a magnificent dual-lane highway built by Dictator Pérez Jiménez to connect the airport and Caracas. In the ladies' car Señora Garcia Ventuni apologized repeatedly. "It's a minority, it's a minority," she said. Mrs. Nixon hoped that was the case, and turned the conversation to children. While flying to Caracas that morning she and the Vice-President had talked to their daughters in Washington by way of an amateur radio hookup. The Nixons used the portable radio rig of Colonel Thomas E. Collins, Jr., the pilot, who carries his hobby along wherever he goes. (In the emergency that afternoon the Colonel's hobby provided the only direct link between the Vice-President, in Caracas, and the White House, Pentagon and State Department, in Washington.)

When the attack began in the city proper Major Hughes and

(229)

agent Grubb decided that Mrs. Nixon would remain in the locked car, and not walk with the Vice-President, as scheduled, to place a wreath at the Simón Bolívar tomb. It was to this ceremony at the Pantheon, Venezuela's most sacred shrine, that the motorcade was headed. The Pantheon was to be the Vice-President's first stop in Caracas.

While the motorcade neared city limits, an advance party at the Pantheon several miles away tried frantically to warn Nixon, by radio, to stay away. The scouting group, which included the Vice-President's administrative assistant and a Secret Service agent, had seen the mobs waiting at strategic corners on the Avenue Sucre. They had to park two blocks from the Pantheon and "look as anti-American as possible" for their own protection while pushing their way to a place where they could observe what was going on at the shrine. They sent back three separate warning messages, in code, over a prearranged radio network centered at the Caracas Police Headquarters. None ever reached the Nixon party.

"We got into town," Nixon said. "What concerned me was that I saw no friendly people on the street. The stores were locked and shuttered. I knew then that we were in very serious trouble. Before we reached the first roadblock the rocks began to hit the car. That is a frightening sound, incidentally—the crack of rocks against a closed car."

The barrage came from a crowd waiting on a slope where the Autopista curves into the city and becomes the lower end of the Avenida Sucre, a modern six-lane roadway with a center divider. Its lower end bisects a neighborhood where policemen were torn apart, trampled and set afire in the revolution four months earlier. The Nixon greeters at this gateway to Caracas waved placards with Nazi swastikas alongside the photograph clipped from the Communist newspaper. They also shouted obscenities in English, the mildest of which was "son of a bitch."

The avenida reportedly had been cleared of all traffic an hour before, and the motorcade rolled along at quite a clip—until it became ensnarled in a solid mass of buses, trucks and cars.

(230)

A shouting mass of people surrounded the stalled lead cars and performed the long-since customary rites with spit, garbage and rocks. Some tore the crossed Venezuelan and United States flags from the limousines, and kicked the fenders and doors. One hefty fellow threw himself in front of the vice-presidential car, and was tossed aside like a medicine ball by a Secret Service agent. Six agents had leaped from their cars farther back in the motorcade and rushed up to screen the Vice-President. Half the Venezuelan police escort vanished when the attack began. The other either sat frozen to their motorcycle seats or scurried about making a pathway through the traffic snarl.

The motorcade again clipped along the avenida at a fair pace, until it was stopped short by another tie-up, this one just four blocks from the Pantheon Plaza. "Here they come!" someone shouted. Masses of men and women, young and old, poured from a dingy alley a hundred feet away shouting and waving banners, placards, pipes, clubs and bare fists, like a scene from the French Revolution. At least five hundred of them swarmed around the Nixon car, the excess overflowing to envelop the other cars. Practically all of the remaining Venezuelan police quickly disappeared. But one plain-clothes officer, a Yugoslav immigrant who is related to a Democratic congressman from Minnesota, stayed to help the thin line of Secret Service agents.

The agents operated with cool, contrived skill. Even while being hit at and spat upon they avoided any appearance of antagonism or violence that would stampede the frenzied mob. Agent Robert Taylor was knocked flat by a shell casing. He wiped the blood from his head and resumed the job of trying to keep the mob from the Vice-President, using his shoulders, feet and open palms, instead of a fist or a weapon. It was like a fantastic ballet. Without appearing to do so, agents would trip up an attacker in a way to make a dozen fall. They would gently nudge one individual so that he in turn pushed the others away from a door handle, like sweeping away clusters of flies. The car doors were the principal objective of the gang bent on dragging the Vice-President from his limousine to tear him apart—the most degrading death possible, by Vene-

(231)

zuelan standards. In the number one car, agents Sherwood and Rodham unlimbered their pistols, and the Foreign Minister mumbled, "This is terrible," as the attackers hit the windows and doors with clubs, pipes, their fists and their feet.

The onrushing horde reminded Sam Waugh, president of the Export-Import Bank, of a flood in Plattsmouth, Nebraska, when he was a child. "I felt helpless, like I did when the flood rushed down the main street of our community sweeping all before my eyes."

Nixon turned apprehensively to see, through his back window, if his wife was all right, since she was in the limousine behind his. "It was a relief to find that the mob was concentrating against me," he said. "I felt they would continue that way, and therefore she would be all right." He was thankful for that, Nixon added, because "I knew it would be hopeless for me to try anything anyway." Nixon also noticed that the number two limousine had driven smack up against his and he thought, That is pretty wise of the driver, since the maneuver kept attackers away from the back of his car and the front of Mrs. Nixon's.

"I saw the mob descending on us, and I knew that this was planned," Nixon told me. "I was surprised to see how many teenagers there were, young ones. Then I saw the collection of the old ones, and I saw they were leading it. It was the same story. I just thought, How could people do this? Then when the first window broke, I realized we were in very serious trouble and I began to think, Well, now, how do we get out of this situation? and How do we recoup? How do we get back at them? Nothing much was said in our car. I knew that the important thing was to find a way to go some place where they weren't expecting us. I was thinking that all along."

The attack intensified. A motorcycle policeman threw a tear-gas bomb. It landed aimlessly behind the milling crowd. Some fled, then came right back, throwing dirt and horse dung. Then the mob started rocking the Vice-President's vehicle.

"It looked as though their tactics were to turn the car over and burn it," Nixon said. "I figured that this was what they were going to try. I wasn't concerned about their smashing the windows and getting me out. But I was concerned that they might get hold of the car and smack it over. I also noted that the police had gone, except for a couple of them who weren't doing a thing.

"We just sat there," the Vice-President continued. "I looked right into the face of the guy who was smashing the window on my side with a club. He smashed it and smashed it, and finally busted it. He hit it about ten times before it cracked. It's hard to hit a window like that. You have to hit it with a good crack. It won't cave in with just a nudge."

Nixon said the man with the club looked to him like a combination of Gerhard Eisler, Eugene Dennis, and all the other Communists he had faced in various places.

"What went through my mind was the complete unreasoning hate in their faces—hate, just hate. I'd never seen anything like that before. Never. This mob was a killer mob. They were completely out of hand, and I imagine some were doped up to a certain extent.

"I thought, How are they able to stir up the people to this pitch? Then I realized as this was going on that right here was the ruthlessness and the determination, the fanaticism of the enemy that we face. That was what I saw in the faces of the mob. This is really Communism as it is. Some people had been telling me, including the Foreign Minister sitting there at my side, that Latin-American Communists were different, that they were 'theoretical Communists' and really nationalists. Well, I figured, they should know better now."

As the window beside Nixon gave way, Sherwood pulled his gun. "Now is the time to get the sons of bitches," he snapped. Rodham drew his gun, too, and said coldly that he and Sherwood would each "get six of them before they get us." The windows on both sides of the car were now being bashed in. Slivers of glass flaked off at each blow and shot back and forth inside the car, making hissing noises. A man tried to poke a pipe at Nixon through a hole in a window.

A large rock hit the window beside Colonel Walters and stuck there. "Are you all right?" Nixon asked. "Yes, except I have a mouthful of glass," replied the interpreter. "Spit it out, you've got interpreting yet to do today," said the Vice-President. Something smashed the back window, showering glass over the Foreign Minister. "It's in my eye," he yelled. "This is terrible, this is terrible."

"Spit was dripping off the windshield," Walters recalled. "From where I sat it was like watching a horror movie. I kept thinking that we were going to move on and get away from it. Then I saw this boy with what looked like a shell casing in his hand. I knew he was going to throw it. I hoped it was a shell casing and not a bomb. Frankly, I was prepared in my mind all along that we would be bombed, particularly when we stopped so long. They could roll the bomb underneath. That was the thing. The gasoline tank would have gone up. I watched this boy, and after what seemed like an awfully long time, he finally threw it, and that is what hit the back window and splattered glass in the Foreign Minister's face.

"When my window broke, I felt to see if I was bleeding," added Walters. "A piece of glass was bedded in the side of my mouth. I pulled it out, and there was blood in my hand. I thought, God, how are we going to get out of here? Then I saw a man, not two feet away, trip up. A pistol fell to the ground. He picked it up and put it into his pocket."

In car number two Mrs. Nixon tightened the mental grip by which she controlled herself and wondered if the windows would hold in her husband's car and whether the doors would be broken open and the occupants dragged out, or the car tipped over.

"I had visions of all those things," she told me. "We got a few good knocks on our car, but that didn't frighten me. I kept watching what went on ahead. I couldn't believe that nobody, none of the police, would do anything. I tried to calm the Foreign Minister's wife. Of course her husband was in the other car, too. And she felt horrible that this was happening in her country."

A huge rock glanced off a window near Mrs. Nixon. She gritted her teeth. Agent Grubb cursed to himself and loosened the pistol in his holster. Major Hughes put his hands back to shield the ladies and swore to himself that he would never travel again without a weapon. Señora Garcia gasped.

Back in limousine number nine shattering glass injured Rose Mary Woods, the Vice-President's executive secretary, and others.

Twelve minutes after the violence had started—and just as it seemed to be reaching a murderous climax—some Venezuelan soldiers showed up. They made a narrow opening in the traffic tie-up, and Nixon's car shot through it. Mrs. Nixon's car followed close behind. Both headed for the Pantheon, but just before reaching it they swerved off to the right into an alley. Nixon had decided in that split second to abandon the wreath-laying ceremony and to head for safe territory where mobs would least expect him to go.

That decision saved his life and Mrs. Nixon's. It also spared his entourage and many of the eight thousand screeching Venezuelans who crammed the plaza. Subsequent investigations showed that two well-disciplined groups were in the plaza crowd. Each had a special mission. Vice-President and Mrs. Nixon were their targets. The largest group of a hundred or more, including high school and university students, was to barrage the visitors with rocks and fruit. A unit of hardened experts was then to follow through with homemade bombs. Venezuelan investigators discovered the murder plot while searching the home of a female Communist functionary a stone's throw from the plaza. A cache of about four hundred Molotov cocktails was found under the steps, stacked neatly and primed for reissue.

Earlier, two American officers had got a taste of what was in store for the Vice-President at the Pantheon. Lieutenant Commander Louis Scliris, naval attaché, made this report on his experience with the wreath that Nixon was to place at the Bolívar tomb:

"I picked up the flowers at 11:05 A.M. and put them in the back of the embassy pickup truck. Then I proceeded directly to the Pantheon followed by the florist's station wagon with the floral wreath. Upon arrival I started to take the flowers out of the station wagon. Police did not bother to come down and give protection from the crowd. Individuals who looked like students grabbed the flowers and ripped them apart. I was personally kicked, spat upon and generally manhandled. They broke the window of the station wagon. I proceeded back to the embassy with the station wagon. The florist was ordered to make a new wreath. The crowd was made up of youngsters interspersed with forty- to fifty-year-old men who were directing them."

Lieutenant Colonel Gerald M. Daily, the Army attaché, reported: "When I arrived at the Pantheon at 12:05 P.M. a crowd of six to eight thousand were demonstrating in a disorderly fashion. There were no police in sight. Soldiers from the San Carlos Guartel were stationed there as an honor guard. Military police with fixed bayonets were also present and tried seriously to keep the steps of the Pantheon clear of the surging mob. They were fairly successful until about 12:20 when the crowd got in behind them.

"The military police retreated to join the honor guard which remained fixed in its designated position. The military police and honor guard were jeered and stoned. It was evident that they were molested because they were giving protection to Captain Huse [a naval attaché] and myself.

"The Venezuelan officers accompanying us were themselves hit with flying objects, eggs, fruit, sticks and stones. The soldiers were formed up in two ranks, with Captain Huse and myself in the center, and with fixed bayonets they marched up to San Carlos Guartel where we were given sanctuary. These soldiers were responsible for our safety, for otherwise we would have been seriously set upon by the crowd."

Teen-aged girls in the plaza mob were particularly aggressive, at least verbally. They had the time of their lives screeching filthy words in English and Spanish. In its account of the day's highlights the Communist newspaper said: "A valorous girl, easily recognizable as a student of the Andreas Bello High School because of her red and white uniform, jumped into the truck, seized the wreath and carried it back among the students where it was torn to pieces."

The motorcade disintegrated. The two lead cars managed to keep together, however, and stopped near a medical center to take stock. No one in the ladies' limousine was injured. All in the Vice-

President's were scratched or cut. No hospital attention seemed necessary, however, and the road ahead was clear, so the Nixons went to the Embassy Residence atop a steep, easily defensible hill in the city's exclusive Las Lomas section.

"I felt a great sense of relief, naturally," Mrs. Nixon recalled. "On an occasion like this it isn't personal fear that you think of particularly. It is the long-range thing. You just feel sick that anything like this could happen to mar what was meant to be a goodwill trip. You think, What is going to happen now? What is the eventual outcome of this? What is the public opinion on it? So many things go through your mind."

Anger boiled inside the Vice-President, but he was outwardly unruffled and composed. "These incidents are against Venezuela," he said to reporters who caught up with him as he entered the ambassador's house. "No patriotic Venezuelan would have torn down his country's flag as the mob did to the Venezuelan flag and also to ours. I don't feel it at all as a personal offense. If anything, the future relations of the United States and Venezuela will be better than ever." To a university group which hurried up the hill to apologize, he said, "As far as I'm concerned, the incident is closed."

Major Hughes, one of the first jet pilot heroes in Korea, said, "It was a little bit like heaven," when the emotionally exhausted vice-presidential party reached the comparative safety of the Embassy Residence. Gin and tonics were waiting. Nixon nodded pleasantly to several guests already there for a luncheon, then walked off by himself to look pensively out a window. He slumped in an easy chair and beckoned to Hughes. "I can risk my own life, but I have no right risking anybody else's," he told his military aide. "We will stay here. Tell my appointments I would be pleased to see them if they would come here." The Nixons were scheduled to stay at the Circulo Militar, the sumptuous military club which Pérez Jiménez had built for $35,000,000 to ensure the devotion of his Army officers. Mrs. Nixon had a two-day schedule filled with visits to orphanages, hospitals and women's organizations. The Vice-President canceled that and all other plans which required movement outside the embassy quarters, technically United States territory. As Hughes took notes, Nixon outlined a completely new operational plan for the hours ahead. The Vice-President was literally wrung-out, so he went to bed. It was Nixon's first afternoon nap in twelve years of public life. He slept for forty minutes.

As he napped, his staff quietly transformed the ambassador's house into a fortress and developed a plan for leaving Caracas the next day, and Washington began to throb.

A preliminary flash report to the State Department said the mobs were still at large in the city, the security system obviously had broken down, and while no American was seriously injured, the situation was still unclear. Undersecretary of State Christian Herter concluded from this that the Vice-President and his party "were virtually prisoners in the embassy . . . and the situation was gravely serious," so he alerted the Joint Chiefs of Staff. At the White House, President Eisenhower was furious and apprehensive. Nothing like this had ever happened before. It was the worst mob action ever directed against either of the highest-ranking United States officials. John Foster Dulles, just back from Copenhagen, Paris and Minneapolis, rushed to the White House. By now there was alarm in the administration hierarchy because efforts to reach Nixon by telephone and even via an Air Force radio network had failed.[4] At 2:50 P.M. Washington time (2:10 Caracas time) President Eisenhower ordered the Pentagon to prepare for action. The Joint Chiefs of Staff happened to be conferring with Secretary of Defense Neil McElroy on troop-movement problems in small wars when the White House called General Nathan Twining, the chairman. By nightfall America's military might was poised for the liveliest and most bizarre rescue mission of all time. A naval force of six destroyers, a guided-missile cruiser and an aircraft carrier equipped to land Marines by helicopter moved flank speed toward

[4] Washington could hardly be blamed for suspecting foul play. Actually the overseas circuits from Caracas were tied up, mostly by correspondents, and the operator on the Caracas end of the Air Force network happened to step away from his receiver when Washington flashed. Later, direct communications between the Nixon party and Washington were established by way of Colonel Collins' amateur radio setup.

(238)

Caracas with orders to stay just beyond sight of the Venezuelan coast until directed to move in by the President. The Air Force alerted jet-bomber, fighter, and fighter-bomber units and evolved a plan for instant action which was informally assigned the code name "Operation Poor Richard." And one thousand picked fighting men—two companies of paratroopers and two companies of Marines —were rushed to bases in Puerto Rico and Cuba, within easy striking distance of Venezuela.

At 6:05 p.m. the Pentagon announced the Marine and paratroop activities. A communiqué stated: "The movement is being undertaken so these troops will be in a position to co-operate with the Venezuelan government if assistance is requested. This is purely a precautionary measure, and there is no indication that such assistance will be required."

The Navy and Air Force activities were kept secret. Nixon would have preferred no public disclosure of the paratroop and Marine movements, as well. He learned of the troop movements three hours after the Washington announcement, when a Venezuelan government official came to plead with the ambassador for a statement denying that it happened.

Rioting mobs were still loose in the city proper. The Vice-President was dubious about the government's ability to keep order or provide his entourage proper protection. But he also knew that, if the situation worsened to the extent that American troops were needed, it was doubtful that they would find any still-living members of the vice-presidential party to protect. Furthermore, he foresaw a terrible propaganda reaction to Washington's sword rattling and even a possible revolution in which the Communists might take complete control of Venezuela.

(President Eisenhower later defended his action as "the simplest precautionary type of measure in the world." At the time it was taken, he said, "we knew nothing of the facts. We could get no reports from the outside . . . and not knowing what was happening, and not knowing whether the Venezuelan government might not want some aid from us, we simply put it at places where it would be available.")

(239)

At 9:15 P.M. Nixon had his ranking diplomatic aide, Assistant Secretary of State Roy R. Rubottom, Jr., call the State Department for an explanation. Rubottom was told that Secretary Dulles had cabled Nixon all the details. (The message was never received.) The Pentagon announcement was read to Rubottom and a secretary in Caracas took it down so that the Vice-President would know at least what had been said officially. "This whole matter will take a lot of undoing," Rubottom informed the State Department.

At the urgent request of Venezuelan authorities, Nixon and Ambassador Sparks then issued a joint statement declaring their faith in the Venezuelan government's power to maintain law and order without outside help and pointing out that the military action announced from Washington was nothing more than a movement of troops between American bases. The statement added that America had no intention of sending those troops to Caracas unless the Venezuelan government requested it—which Venezuela was not expected to do.[5]

Nixon's staff set up a rigid security system at the Embassy Residence and completed a tightly integrated departure plan for the next day. Sixty American Army, Navy and Air Force men on duty as instructors of the Venezuelan armed forces were mobilized to join the embassy's five Marines and Nixon's twelve Secret Service agents as guards at the vice-presidential residence. A battalion of heavily armed Venezuelan soldiers manned the streets for blocks around. Everything brought to the house by anyone—flowers, packages, even notes—was carefully checked by security men. At the airport thirty-five United States and Venezuelan guards were stationed around the Nixon airplane and the private aircraft chartered by the American press group.

[5] The troop announcement was a boon to the Communists and allied anti-Americans. Their violence against the Vice-President had boomeranged, throwing them decidedly on the defensive. Revulsion spread through South America, and already was strong enough to kick the Communists from control of organizations like the Student Federation in Lima. But Latin America is extremely sensitive about "big stick" threats from the United States and, overnight, organizations, newspapers and individuals who had been apologizing all over the place resumed the offensive. The discourtesies to Nixon and his wife became old stuff; the demonstration of "Yankee imperialism" became the hot news.

Meanwhile the Vice-President had a busy afternoon and evening in his fortress. He met with several groups, including the non-Communist Venezuelan political leaders. Dr. Romulo Betancourt, anti-Communist chief of the leftist Acción Democratica party who subsequently was elected president of Venezuela, insisted the asylum given Dictator Pérez Jiménez in the United States was the root of the trouble.

Nixon smilingly recalled that he had heard the same thing from the Pérez regime when the United States gave Betancourt asylum after the uprising which brought Pérez to power, causing Betancourt to flee. All the political moguls insisted they were upset about the morning's violence, but none cared to point a finger at the Communists, whose leader was a colleague on the committee of political chieftains which had an important advisory role in the government. When Nixon outlined evidence that proved the Communists inspired and led the mob attacks, Dr. Rafael Caldera, secretary general of the Christian Socialist party, protested, "But the Communists issued a statement just a while ago saying they were not responsible." Although the official Communist newspaper gloated over each morsel of the violence, the Communist party headquarters indeed issued a communiqué absolving itself and blaming followers of the ex-dictator, known as "Pérez Jimenistas." But Nixon was amazed that any hardheaded political veteran would believe it.

Later the ruling Junta and the Venezuelan Cabinet came to pay their respects. Nixon interrupted their flowery apologies to say there would be no ill will, personally or officially, and to suggest that they forget the incident and discuss affairs of state with him. But Admiral Larrazabal, the provisional President, said he was too dispirited to talk. He apologized again and left, and as he rode down the hill his car was stoned. But little damage was done its bulletproof glass and armor-plated hide.

Nixon told me afterward there was no question but that "the greatest danger of my whole life was in Caracas."

"Picketing is not new to me; the throwing of stones and that sort of thing, of course, is new. I was prepared for debating. I was prepared for Communist tactics. I was prepared for picketing and

(241)

usually know how to handle pickets. But I was not prepared for what happened in Caracas," he said.

The Vice-President also said that "the most difficult period in one of these incidents is not in handling the situation at the time. The difficult task is with your reactions after it is all over. I get a real letdown after one of these issues. Then I begin to think of what bums they are. You also get the sense that you licked them . . . though they really poured it on. Then you try to catch yourself . . . in statements and actions . . . to be a generous winner, if you have won.

"Most importantly you must think of what the lasting impression is going to be. You are writing some history here. You are affecting international policy. You must consider the sensibilities of the people. Those are things I thought about before the press conference that evening."

Nixon met the press at six o'clock on the Embassy Residence veranda surrounded by an army of security agents.

On his overseas tours the Vice-President customarily recognizes local reporters ahead of the United States correspondents accompanying him. On this occasion, however, the American contingent led off, and the first question was: "Never before in the history of the United States has one of our important officials suffered the indignities and violence you suffered in this city today. What is your reaction to this horrible and shameful incident?"

His reaction to the obvious first question was, in effect, to turn the other cheek. He reiterated his friendship for the government and people of Venezuela. "The Communist planners of today's outrage were able to gain a great deal of support from students and other groups because of what happened in this country during the past ten years," he said. "What we saw here was the terrible legacy of the dictatorship of Pérez Jiménez. Dictatorship breeds violence, and violence in turn breeds other dictatorships when allowed to go unchecked."

Nixon urged that the nations of North and South America join to "fight and strive in every positive way against the poverty, misery and disease on which dictators of both the right and left feed to gain

(242)

power." Then he said, "If this day serves no other purpose than to bring clearly to the attention of officials the character and tactics of those who would overthrow freedom, it would serve a useful purpose."

After the press conference three of his staff members sat with the Vice-President and Mrs. Nixon awhile in an upstairs bedroom. In the intimacy of those closest to him, Nixon released the bitter anger that he had submerged during that hard day of frustration and trouble. As is his custom after long periods of public self-control under trying conditions, he opened the safety valve and blew his top. Once relieved, he went to bed. It was the last night of Richard Nixon's three-week good-will tour of South America—and the first on which he was asleep long before midnight.

A report to Washington at 7:00 P.M. said: "It is relatively quiet everywhere. The Residence is under full protection."

Elsewhere in the city, Junta President Larrazabal had turned over to the Defense Minister complete responsibility for the Vice-President's safety with authority to take any measures he thought necessary. This, in effect, rescinded his directive of a few days before that ordered soldiers and policemen not to shoot at rioters.

The next morning President Eisenhower telephoned at ten o'clock. The whole country was proud of the Nixons, he said, and a great welcome-home ceremony was being arranged. Furthermore, Eisenhower said he would be there with the two Nixon children despite advice from the State Department protocol people that his presence would violate a rule. The President made it clear that he intended to head the welcoming delegation "because of my admiration for [Nixon's] calmness and fortitude and his courage in very trying circumstances."

Prominent Venezuelans apologized to Nixon through advertisements in morning newspapers. One asked, in huge type: "What would happen to Poland if the Poles did to Khrushchev what we did to Nixon?" Delegations came to the Embassy Residence to pay their respects and express mortification. Twenty-five women repre-

(243)

senting Venezuela's principal women's organizations brought flowers to Mrs. Nixon and wept with embarrassment.

Nixon's departure plans were secretly set. He was to leave Maiquetía Airport at three o'clock—nine hours ahead of schedule. But he did not want to land in Washington before the airport reception at eleven the following morning—Thursday, May 15—so an overnight visit to Puerto Rico was arranged with Governor Luis Muñoz Marín.

Major Hughes and Colonel Collins worked out the intricate evacuation plan in compliance with Nixon's wish not to risk another ride through the city. Three sturdy old twin-engine C47's were flown to a small landing strip near the Embassy Residence. The Vice-President and his entourage were to be whisked to the strip by automobile, then flown to the main airport. An Air Force helicopter was brought in for emergency use if the short automobile ride to the landing strip was found to be dangerous. In addition, four large military airliners were flown to fields a few minutes from Caracas for use should anything happen to the Vice-President's DC6 or the American press plane at the airport. Two of the stand-by liners were poised for immediate take-off at Plesman Field in Dutch Curaçao, and two at Maracaibo, the Venezuelan oil city. Shortly before noon the Junta invited the Vice-President and his party to lunch at the Circulo Militar. Nixon replied that he would like to lunch with the Junta—but at the Embassy Residence. Eugenio Mendoza, a civilian member of the ruling body, pleaded with him to reconsider or the government would be disgraced, so Nixon relented, and he and Mrs. Nixon were spirited across the city in limousines surrounded by five hundred soldiers in buses and trucks. There were no incidents along the way.

The luncheon was a large and outwardly gay affair. All the important Venezuelan officials and their wives had gathered hurriedly for it. Admiral Larrazabal asked if the Vice-President was aware that Pérez Jiménez had escaped via the landing strip from which he meant to leapfrog across the city. No, he wasn't, said Nixon. He ordered the landing-strip operation canceled immediately, and his aides substituted the helicopter plan. But it was evident as the luncheon dragged on that the government wanted to prove, with a motorcade departure, that it could protect foreign visitors. After the meal Admiral Larrazabal asked Nixon to tour the spacious military club, obviously to kill time. It was already past three, and the Vice-President resigned himself to being "kidnaped" by the provisional President. "I guess they are going to take us out through the city," Nixon whispered to his military aide. "I was sweating blood," Major Hughes confided later.

At 4:15 a plump Army colonel intercepted the inspection party in the club locker room and told Admiral Larrazabal, "All is ready." This, it developed, was the signal that the city was secure. The Admiral cut short the tour and led Nixon outside to a motorcade that resembled an armored column coiled for attack. There were hundreds of troopers in an array of military vehicles, and five armor-plated, bulletproof limousines for the dignitaries. Nixon joined the President-Admiral in car number one. Mrs. Nixon, directed to car number two, almost tripped over a submachine gun, extra clips of ammunition, and a tear-gas canister as she got in. Major Hughes pushed the arsenal aside but kept the tear gas handy. The Venezuelan security chief, sitting with the chauffeur of Nixon's car, assured the Vice-President that peace had been restored to Caracas. As the armada started off, however, he took a pistol from a holster and a tear-gas gun from a pocket, and kept one in each hand during the 22-mile ride from the Circulo to the Airport.

Without asking for his consent, the government was taking Nixon out the hard way—via the Avenida Sucre. Its military might had been deployed along the route during the morning. Tanks and armored cars were posted at intersections. Soldiers and police armed with machetes and tear gas lined the sidewalks. Knots of people that hesitated when ordered to disperse were sprayed with tear gas. So were the alleys from which the mobs had streamed the day before.

The armada whizzed along at sixty miles an hour through what looked to Nixon like a "ghost city." The few people still on the streets held handkerchiefs over their noses. Nixon thought this was

(245)

"a new way to express their contempt" until someone explained about the tear gas.

The airport and its Terminal Building were empty except for the honor guard, the band, and the artillery battery which had performed in the previous day's welcoming ceremony. The artillerymen fired a 21-gun salute and the band struck up "The Star-Spangled Banner" as the vice-presidential airplane taxied off. The music and booming that had been swamped by mob screeches the day before now came through loud and clear.

When the airplane soared away from Venezuelan soil "everyone was relieved at once," said the pilot. "There was a completely new attitude in the crew and the official party." It was 5:05 P.M.

At eleven the next morning—May 15, 1958—Nixon got the heartiest home-coming welcome ever staged in Washington for a vice-president. President Eisenhower was at the airport with the Cabinet and administration leaders. Senate Democratic leader Lyndon B. Johnson headed delegations of senators and representatives. Thousands of university students were there, including Latin Americans carrying banners with slogans of friendship and praise.

"Through this entire trip the Vice-President has conducted himself effectively, efficiently and with great dignity," said the President. "There have been some unpleasant incidents, and he and Mrs. Nixon have faced real danger and risk of harm and even worse . . . [but this will] in no way impair the friendship of the United States and our sister republics to the south."

The outpouring moved Nixon to say: "Certainly there is no greater experience than to return home to see our friends, our family, and to realize how blessed this country is—blessed with freedom, economic opportunity, stability in its government, and with fine leadership, whether that leadership is furnished by one of our great parties or the other. Never forget what a great privilege it is to be an American citizen and to live in the United States."

While en route to the White House for lunch with the Eisenhowers, Nixon was reminded that a recent predecessor once turned down an offer of Secret Service protection because "no one would take the trouble to shoot a vice-president."

15

On September 3, 1957, President Eisenhower sent Nixon a memorandum which for the first time in history assigned a vice-president a major role in foreign policy.

"My basic thought is that you might find it possible—and intriguing—to be of even more help in our whole governmental program dealing with affairs abroad than you have been in the past," Eisenhower wrote, in part. "By your extensive travels you have been of inestimable assistance to the Secretary of State and to me. In addition you have gained an understanding of our foreign problems that is both unusual and comprehensive. My belief is that this knowledge and comprehension, supplemented by your special position of having one foot in the Executive branch and one foot in the Legislative branch, can be advantageously used in helping to lay out advanced programs and schedules . . ." and for the next page and a half the President outlined additional responsibilities he wanted the Vice-President to assume in helping to shape trade, mutual assistance, technical and direct aid, and monetary and defensive policies.

This increased influence of Nixon's was reflected in the speed with which many of his subsequent proposals for South America were carried out. It had been different before. Nixon had spoken of "new" policies on three official visits to Latin countries during his first term as vice-president, for instance. "Our policy toward Latin America in the past has been characterized by starts and stops, by big talk and very little action," he said after his Central American tour in 1955.[1] "United States policy toward Latin America must have consistency, continuity, and follow-through. This administration recognizes the necessity for that type of policy, and we are determined to carry it forward."

But for three years there was NO follow-through, except for a speedup in fund appropriations to complete the Inter-American Highway. Not until 1958, when Nixon returned from the chaos of Caracas, did deeds begin to catch up with words. In the next six months there was more positive action than ever before in United States relations with its southern neighbors. Emphasis was on cultivating increasingly influential elements in universities and labor unions, promoting economic development, and pointing the impact of United States information projects and propaganda at the worst sore spots of misunderstanding. The Student Exchange Program was doubled—and then some. Seminars were formed to permit great numbers of South American university students at least a month of undergraduate study per year at a North American institution. San Marcos University in Lima, the scene of the first anti-Nixon riot, became the first school in Peru to establish credit courses in North American literature and language. Added status was given labor attachés to maintain closer liaison with workers' organizations in each country. After years of reluctance, the United States joined the international agency for stabilizing coffee prices. The Export-Import Bank was authorized to lend an additional two billion dollars. There was quick approval by several United States monetary agencies of loans throughout the continent, many of which had been pigeonholed for months, including varying sums to settle immigrants from Europe and elsewhere. There were also loans and grants to build technical schools, expand technical assistance, provide drought and disaster relief, particularly in Brazil, and other programs. Nixon struck at the belief of South Americans that the United States encourages dictatorships by stating that the United States government hereafter would base its relationships with Latin government officials on this dictum: "For dictators, a formal hand-

[1] Nixon also said then, "I am convinced that Communism has passed its high-water mark in Latin America."

(248)

shake, nothing more; for free governments, an embrace."

To Caracas, Nixon's mission was a failure.

Hopes of salvaging it were lost in the outcry against Eisenhower's maneuver with Marines and paratroopers.[2] The result was to aggravate problems in Venezuela: government was weakened; the five-man Junta ousted two members considered most friendly to the United States; Caracas papers stopped printing news critical of Communism, and, as a candidate for president, the popular young Admiral Larrazabal lent his respectability to the Communist party in return for its votes. (He lost; they won impressive representation in the Congress.)

Before and during Nixon's visit to England six months after the South American tour the London *Daily Worker* broke out the slogans and diatribes of party papers in Latin America. Mass anti-Nixon demonstrations were proclaimed. The people were urged to rise and "take anti-nuisance" measures against the visitor. "Tricky Dicky—Traveller in Death" was the banner headline over one lengthy article. "Tricky Dicky—Abominable Showman" was another. None seemed to pay much heed; Nixon's *real* challenge was more difficult than facing a Communist mob. It stemmed from hostility toward the Eisenhower administration because of the Suez troubles in 1956 and general antipathy toward Nixon as an individual. As one newspaper put it, the British view of Nixon was "a haze of impressions left by his political speeches and fostered by his political opponents."

Nixon's London speeches, his televised press conferences, his private and extremely candid sessions with leadership groups of all kinds, and his general activities put him in better focus quickly. "Good for Nixon! He had to do well, and he did brilliantly," wrote Randolph Churchill. An American diplomat who witnessed practically the whole performance told a friend: "Nixon almost succeeded in making Britain feel that our foreign policy is both intelligent

[2] The "troop movement" gave the Communists another opportunity. The party newspaper (in Caracas) featured a calendar of United States "aggression" in South America, listing a page of incidents that supposedly occurred during the past one hundred fifty years.

and flexible." Suspicion of Nixon in some quarters was indicated, however, by a letter to the Baltimore *Sun* in which Lord Winster said that "by and large he did a solid good job . . . [but] he is not what we would call our cup of tea."

From the start Nixon has seen every overseas tour as a "graduate course," with subjects encompassing a gamut of government and human relationships. Before leaving Washington he studies the history, problems, leaders and peoples of the countries he will visit as if cramming for final examinations. En route to each capital he reviews material brought along in a traveling library and gets a briefing from an embassy official who boards the plane at the stop ahead. (This is identical to the procedure Nixon uses in campaign tours.)

Six years of study and firsthand experience have made Nixon a crusading internationalist. He has become the administration's most forceful advocate of aid programs for underdeveloped countries, including the neutralists; one of its strongest voices for freer trade, expanded student, professional and cultural exchanges—the view that THOROUGH defense and international assistance are more vital to America's future than a balanced budget. Through his travels Nixon has come to know more than a thousand foreign statesmen outside the Communist bloc.

Despite Nixon's efforts to be totally prepared before every trip, he has faced frequent tests of ingenuity. On the very first tour, for instance, President Syngman Rhee greeted him in Korea with a threat to reopen the war if North and South Korea were not quickly unified. Nixon had to convince the crusty old patriot to keep calm and trust the United States government. In the process he shed several layers of his diplomatic inexperience. He has had a variety of unpleasant surprises over the years. He arrived in India the day the United States revealed it would supply arms to India's enemy, Pakistan. While he was in Formosa, Secretary Dulles intimated in Washington that the United States might sooner or later recognize Red China. In Paraguay, leaders of the underdog Liberal party were delighted by the opportunity to confer with Nixon behind closed doors. But joy turned to gloom when the

Vice-President indicated it would be improper for him to join their crusade to oust the country's dictator, General Stroessner.

Some tours have had embarrassing aftermaths, typified by the Dominican Republic's distribution of a large photograph of Nixon and the dictator Trujillo, smiling at each other over raised wine glasses, with Nixon quoted as saying, "A toast to this great country and its illustrious ruler." But what the Vice-President and Mrs. Nixon call their "people-to-people operation"—handshakes on the streets and visits to union halls, hospitals, schools, etc.—apparently overshadowed the embarrassing incidents.

Nixon's overseas tours also gave him an opportunity to do quite well for himself, politically. In fact, nothing else he has undertaken as vice-president has helped so much to enhance his chance of being elected president. Politicians now realize a man has to prove himself in international affairs to win the Presidency. World-traveler Adlai E. Stevenson is the only possible opponent in 1960 of either party who could seriously match Nixon in prefacing an observation with: "On my world travels . . ." as Nixon often does.

Few potential opponents for the Presidency have won the open or implied endorsements given Nixon in many lands. That of Archbishop Riccardo Pittini, of Santo Domingo, the Roman Catholic primate of the Antilles, was typical. After a visit with the Vice-President the archbishop said, raising his voice so that all could hear, "You must come back . . . . we want you back as a full-fledged president." The Rev. Martin Luther King, Jr., one of America's foremost Negro leaders, told me he "strongly opposed" Nixon before he met the Vice-President in Africa. Now King sees him as "a superb diplomat."

Before Lima and Caracas, political response to Nixon's overseas operations was subtle. The tours were noncontroversial, the only Nixon enterprise that enjoyed an Eisenhowerish immunity from partisan attack. South America changed that. Democratic National Chairman Butler saw it as a cleverly concealed propaganda scheme to keep Nixon in the headlines. "All the sympathy the Republican high command is trying to squeeze out of it cannot conceal the fact that the Vice-President gained his reputation as a master of the smear technique," he said. Robert C. Albright reported in the Washington *Post:* "Before Vice-President Richard M. Nixon's triumphant return from Latin America, Democratic politicians quite frankly considered him easy to beat in the 1960 presidential election. They don't talk that way now." The House of Representatives on the day after Caracas unanimously passed a resolution commending Nixon "for his courageous and dignified conduct." On the other hand, Walter Lippmann declared the tour a "fiasco" and a "diplomatic Pearl Harbor"; the Boston *Globe* called it "one of the most ineptly handled episodes in this country's foreign relations"; and William V. Shannon wrote in his New York *Post* column: "Because North Americans tolerate Nixon's behavior is no reason why South Americans must also accept it. South Americans may have more self-respect than we do."

Meanwhile the Gallup poll claimed that Nixon's popularity increased substantially. (Nixon received 25,000 letters, telegrams and postcards. All but a handful were highly commendatory. "You'll never top that trip, Dick. Don't try," advised J. Edgar Hoover. Another friend, Nelson A. Rockefeller, wired: "Your courage and determination have inspired democratic forces throughout the hemisphere. We all feel a great sense of pride in your action. Congratulations.")

16

THE Constitution specifies nothing more for the Vice-President than that he should preside over the Senate and be ready if the President dies. Nixon's interpretation is that "the first function of a Vice-President—his first responsibility—is to support the President and the administration." As a result, he has spent less time at his duties in the Senate Chamber and more at various chores and activities in the executive department than any of his thirty-five predecessors.

He has been President Eisenhower's representative at everything from a golf trophy presentation to a state dinner for the King of Morocco and a conference of governors. Early in the administration his influence was restricted to legislative liaison and politics. His operations have since spread to the whole range of government, but he still finds that some associates listen more intently when he stresses *political* significance. This is one of Nixon's secret annoyances.

Jim Hagerty says, "Dick felt his way at first. One of his great strengths is that he knows when to keep quiet. He didn't go horning in. When he did speak, he spoke on things he knew about. Gradually, as he developed, he grew in status in the eyes of all the administration. And his judgment became more and more respected." White House wiseacres have long since stopped referring to him as "Junior."

Nixon's power in the administration comes more from his persuasiveness than his limited amount of administrative responsibility. It was at his urging that President Eisenhower called in bipartisan

Congressional leadership to discuss the Berlin crisis early in March of 1959. In the summer of 1958 it was Nixon's idea that the President ask legislative leaders for their advice on the Lebanon crisis, and not just present his decision to send in American troops as a *fait accompli*. His argument was that President Truman's mistake in the Korean crisis was to inform Congressional leaders *after* he had already ordered troops to move. Furthermore, it was Nixon's idea that Ambassador Murphy be sent to the Middle East as America's top-level trouble-shooter until the Lebanon emergency had passed. Federal aid to school construction is still part of Eisenhower's program because of Nixon's arguments at a Cabinet meeting in early January of 1959.

He also has lost some important battles. One was his and Labor Secretary Mitchell's proposal in the winter of 1958 that taxes be cut to fight the recession. That earned him dark looks from some administration colleagues and a quip from Senator Lyndon Johnson. Johnson and Speaker Sam Rayburn had a firm agreement with Secretary of the Treasury Anderson regarding tax reductions. When the White House announced, firmly, that there would be none, Johnson said to Nixon, "You and Mitchell got on that high horse, and here Eisenhower and Bob Anderson rode off and left you."

Nixon seldom disagrees with an administration policy in public. When he states an opinion that is not necessarily that of the administration—as he has been doing more frequently in the second half of the second term—he is careful to point out that he speaks for himself. Also he is cautious to avoid criticism of the administration, which would be dangerous politically and contrary to his belief that "advisers to a president must vigorously present their views" within the family circle but not outside if it conflicts with a presidential decision. In fact, Nixon believes that any Cabinet member who "cannot forthrightly agree" with an important administration decision should resign.

The Vice-President sits across from Eisenhower at Cabinet and National Security Council meetings and at other sessions with Congressional leaders—a difference from the status of Vice-President Calvin Coolidge in President Harding's administration. Coolidge was placed at the foot of the table.

Nixon has access to the President whenever he wants it. But the visits are infrequent because he usually sees Eisenhower three times a week at White House meetings, and he makes a point of calling on the President otherwise only when there is important business to discuss.

Although both men have volatile tempers, they have not exchanged a cross word since taking office. But there have been irritations difficult to repress. Eisenhower uttered his tart words, in private, for instance, when he read that Nixon had referred to Earl Warren as "a great Republican chief justice." And it was obvious to his friends that Nixon was not happy about Stassen's use of the White House, after a talk with Eisenhower, as a platform from which to reopen the "Dump Nixon" movement.

Nixon prefers the printed word to spoken briefings and is seldom satisfied with predigested, one-page memorandums. He insists on going into details himself. This is a throwback to his nine months as a junior lawyer with the Office of Price Administration. "Those were very valuable," he says. "I saw the way the information was bundled up. By the time it got to the top there was nothing left. Many times the richest and most important material was taken out. You simply have to go down below and get the raw material yourself if you want to know the whole story." Often in briefings Nixon takes notes and has them transcribed for study when he returns to his office.

He has made his share of mistakes. Perhaps the worst was his effort to keep peace between Senator McCarthy and the administration. One *gaffe*—which he is unlikely now to repeat—happened on April 16, 1954, while France appeared to be losing its war with the Communists in Indo-China. Eisenhower was vacationing at the Augusta Country Club; Dulles was attending a conference overseas. Nixon appeared before a convention of newspaper editors. There were six hundred editors and seven hundred guests in the room, yet Nixon established the ground rule that his remarks on foreign policy would be "off the record"—they could not be attributed to him. His exposition of world problems was well received. Then Nixon proceeded to answer questions. One that he might well have passed over as being purely hypothetical caused trouble. Would the United States send troops to Indo-China if the French pulled out?

Nixon replied: "If in order to avoid further Communist expansion in Asia and particularly in Indo-China, if in order to avoid it we must take the risk by putting American boys in, I believe that the executive branch of the government has to take the politically unpopular position of facing up to it and doing it, and I personally would support such a decision."

Soon news tickers throughout the world crackled with urgent messages, many of them garbled. In essence, they reported that the United States threatened to send troops to Indo-China. Experts speculated that Nixon had planted the question to launch an administration "trial balloon," testing American feelings about fighting in Indo-China, and at the same time warning the country that all-out war was at hand. Because of his "off the record" rule, there could be no official recognition that he had said anything, and therefore it was difficult to make quick and proper clarifications. The State Department issued one the next day, but it didn't clarify anything; nor did speeches in Congress charging that Nixon was "whooping it up for war."

Meanwhile Nixon asked a columnist close to Eisenhower's staff to call Augusta and explain. He also had a long session with General Bedell Smith, the Undersecretary of State. A day or so later Eisenhower telephoned from Georgia and told Nixon not to worry about the uproar. The President said he was not at all concerned and, anyway, his controversial comments might have the good effect of alerting the country to the seriousness of the Far Eastern situation.

Far less publicized is Nixon's duty as head of the Government Contracts Committee, the agency which tries, by persuasive methods, to end racial and religious discrimination in firms doing business with the government. Among other assignments he has been directing preparation of the administration's Mutual Security and Reciprocal Trade Programs for transmission to Congress and is in over-all charge of a study of the world economic struggle developing between the Communist bloc and the West. He also is chairman of a Cabinet committee recently established to deal with price stability and the nation's growth and development. In Eisenhower's opinion, Nixon's three most valuable contributions to the administration have been his confidential advice to the President, his liaison between Congress and the executive department, and his good-will and fact-finding tours overseas.

In the Cabinet Nixon's closest friends have been Dulles, Secretary of Labor James P. Mitchell, and Attorney General William P. Rogers. Nixon and Mitchell have an affinity for each other's ideas and sometimes have stood practically alone on the "progressive" side of social and economic issues. They agreed in the summer of 1957 that the greatest danger to the nation's economy was not inflation but recession and proved to be right. While their convictions often jibe, in labor matters Nixon is more conservative than Mitchell. It was through Mitchell that Nixon adopted Dr. Arthur Burns as an informal adviser on economics. Dr. Burns formerly was the principal economist on Eisenhower's staff.

Rogers has somewhat the same background as Nixon, who is his senior by six months. A New Yorker, Rogers got his start as a bright young lawyer on Tom Dewey's racket-busting staff in Manhattan. The Vice-President says Rogers has "a very keen sense of timing, but he is more cautious than I am as to what ought to be done in most instances. I will take chances and move aggressively sometimes when he would not. This is good, for I know that he can always see the pitfalls of any course of action, and therefore his advice is very valuable. Also, he keeps his counsel."

Only a few have known that the relationship between Nixon and Dulles has been perhaps the warmest in the administration. Although the Secretary of State was thirty-five years old and already an established attorney in New York when Nixon was born, their friendship has been both personal and professional. Dulles has been Nixon's behind-the-scenes adviser in many crises, especially during Eisenhower's illnesses. "Dick is the best person we have, outside of the President himself, for overseas good-will missions," Dulles has said. "I don't know anybody who so effectively represents abroad the best qualities of America, and the kind of dedication to the ideals of our nation which have made it respected and admired." The Dulleses and the Nixons frequently had dinner together and then just sat around and talked—sometimes into the early morning hours. In his paternal way Dulles even tried to convince Nixon that he should take shots, as he had, for hay fever. (Nixon always agreed, but never got around to it.)

Practically every time Nixon was impressive at a Cabinet or National Security Council meeting, Dulles would later telephone the news to Mrs. Nixon. "Beneath this austere, sometimes forbidding exterior is one of the most thoughtful and sensitive characters in public life today," says Nixon of his friend.

"Just before he took his last trip to Europe I had lunch with him in his office. He customarily has a very light lunch and on this occasion he had only a couple of fresh figs and some cottage cheese. I happened to drop the remark that fresh figs were Pat's favorite delicacy but that they were hard to get in the winter months. The next morning his driver came to the door with a package containing a dozen fresh figs and a friendly, handwritten note from the Secretary. He had ordered them airmail from California. To think he found time to be so thoughtful on a day when he had the gravest world crises on his mind made us realize again what a really fine man he was."[1]

[1] Three or four months before Dulles was hospitalized for cancer treatments in February, 1959, Mrs. Nixon sensed that he was not well from the way he picked at food instead of eating heartily and in his normal good humor. He never complained, but to Mrs. Nixon it was obvious that he was constantly in pain. Dulles admitted after his hospitalization that he had been suffering for many weeks. On his recent trip to Europe the pain was often so excruciating that he could hardly move or keep any food in his stomach. Somehow his intense interest banished the agony when he was discussing the Berlin crisis with De Gaulle, Adenauer and other European leaders. But when he returned to his quarters everything inside him seemed to fall apart. He had given his personal assistants two directives. One was that they were not to mention to anyone that he suffered periods of vomiting and near collapse from pain; the other was that they were to watch him very closely and to inform him the instant they suspected his illness was in any way impairing his effectiveness.

As president of the Senate, Nixon has been a stickler for observing the prerogatives of the majority and minority leaders. Technically, he has the responsibility of appointing members to committees and special projects. But he always names senators recommended by their party leaders. Lyndon Johnson believes Nixon has shown greater fairness to him and other Democrats than previous Democratic vice-presidents showed to Republicans. In dealing with members of his own party, Nixon has had to be even more careful. No statesmen guard what they believe to be their privileges by tradition more than senators do. Thus when Nixon invited members of the Senate to luncheon discussions with Cabinet members, the Republican minority leadership objected, privately, and the luncheons ceased.

Although some members are his friends, Nixon has never been popular in the Senate. For one thing, the small group of senior members who constitute the "club that runs the Senate" prefers to view him as a tenderfoot since he hadn't completed his apprenticeship in that body when he was elected vice-president. Thus the Senate, through its appropriate committee, provides Nixon with a smaller staff and facilities than he had as a freshman senator. The suite set aside for him in the new $35,000,000 Senate Office Building was so inadequate that he preferred to stay where he was in the old building.

On at least one occasion his Senate position assumed great importance, however. It was at the opening session in 1957 when he made it known that he would disagree with a long-accepted interpretation of Senate rules that permitted filibusters. This implied threat was a major factor in the passage that year of the first civil rights legislation enacted since Reconstruction.

It is no secret that Nixon regards his constitutional duty to preside over the Senate as the least important he performs. Usually, he opens the session, then, in effect, turns the President's chair over to Robert G. Baker, an assistant of Senator Johnson's, the secretary of the majority. One of Baker's tasks is to inveigle Democratic members to preside in Nixon's absence. It is no compliment to the office of president of the United States Senate that even novice

(259)

senators grumble that someone should "make Nixon preside—he gets paid for it."

Yet Nixon would not suggest that the duties of the Vice-President be changed by law. He sees the contact between president and vice-president as something "very personal" and he believes every vice-president's responsibilities should be left to the discretion of his chief. In the continuing debate over whether a vice-president should be more a part of the legislative than of the executive branch, Nixon says, "I think the Vice-President should do anything the President wants him to do."

One of the most interesting relationships in Washington is that of Nixon and Johnson, who are often said to be the smartest politicians in their respective parties. There is no particular personal friendship between them, but their association is cordial, mutually respectful, and ever-watchful. A veteran of many political battles, Johnson feels he has been the victim of so much unmerited propaganda that he is careful about the reputation of someone else who may have been in the same circumstances. Johnson has often said that one of the biggest lifts to his morale after he suffered a heart attack in July, 1955, was a personal visit to his bedside by President Eisenhower. Only the President, the Vice-President and Robert G. Baker, through whom Nixon kept in daily contact with Johnson's condition, were probably aware that Nixon had arranged that visit.

Although he doubts that a Southerner could be nominated, Nixon considers Johnson the best qualified Democrat to be president. Johnson doesn't return the compliment, but he has the highest opinion of Nixon professionally. As pillars of their respective parties, neither would hesitate to trip up the other politically—and Johnson seems to get more opportunities than Nixon. The vote on raising the interest rate on veterans' loans is typical. Most Republicans favored the increase, and most Democrats opposed it. The vote was 47-46 in favor of raising the rate, but Johnson wanted to put Nixon on the spot by making him break a tie. He asked that the final tally be delayed for ten minutes until Senator Fulbright could come to the floor and cast his ballot. Several Republicans rushed forward and privately urged Nixon not to permit the delay. Nixon did, however, and after Fulbright made it a 47-47 tie, Nixon voted with his party. Johnson then nodded to Senator Wayne Morse who leaped to his feet and declared that Nixon's action "will make political history. . . . he inflicted the final *coup de grâce* to the cause of low interest rates in America."

Nixon does make time for more than politics. An avid sports fan, he reads the sports pages every morning before the regular news and is more intimate with the scores of games going back many years and relative standings and percentage point averages of ball players than he is with specific election returns, even in his home state. He is not much of a performing sportsman, however. He plays golf occasionally, and has brought his average down from 130, when he taught himself the game in 1951, to the mid-80's. He does not hunt or fish, is a nonjoiner of clubs and organizations, and would much rather read than take exercise. Nixon almost always wears a vest. Often he relaxes while talking or working in his office by cocking his feet up on the edge of the desk. One of his favorite dishes is cottage cheese and ketchup.

But new ideas and solutions to problems may enter his head after he has gone to bed and just before he normally would fall asleep. He keeps a pad to jot them down. The inside breast pocket of his jacket is a repository for scraps of paper with ideas and notes to himself. He scribbles them down as they come to mind during conferences and National Security Council and Cabinet meetings. He empties the pocket periodically. One sifting of its contents revealed a range of notes dealing from ideas for a speech to be delivered at Harvard to a reminder to congratulate an old friend (who happened to be a Democrat) on being nominated for an office in his home state. As to the arts, he prefers light classical music to either the heavy classics or the modern and he has no concept of modern painting, which he admits is over his head.

Whereas politicians are often shameless egotists Nixon tends to deprecate himself, even in speeches. He makes a point of reading editorials that are critical of him or of a policy he favors but he often passes over or just scans the laudatory comments. He has never watched himself on a filmed television program, and though he has a kinescope copy of the spectacular "Nixon Fund" telecast, he has never taken it out of the can.

Nixon gets as many as 22,000 invitations to make speeches in one year. The average in the first couple of months in 1959 was thirty a day. A member of his staff whose hobby was trying to keep track of the fees offered him for public appearances, articles, books and speeches estimated that he could have earned at least $300,000 in that way during his first two years as vice-president. (He has received no money for speaking and writing as vice-president. Fees that have come anyway have been given to charities or educational institutions.)

On election nights, when he is a candidate, Nixon has a superstition about listening to early returns. In campaigns, crowd reactions assume great importance to him during the final hectic days. Friends recall his reaction the Friday night before election day in 1952, when the large Hollywood Legion Stadium was less than half filled for a final rally. Attractions included Esther Williams, Virginia Mayo and other Hollywood stars, and Nixon wondered why people hadn't come to see them, if not him. All he could think of was a similar turnout for the last home state rally in 1948 for Governor Earl Warren. Warren was vice-presidential candidate on the Dewey ticket, and it not only lost nationally, but also failed to carry California, though polls then showed the Republicans much further ahead than they did in 1952.

Nixon is a doting father and thoughtful husband. He never forgets a birthday or anniversary in the family. He and his two daughters—Patricia, thirteen, and Julie, eleven—are always cooking up surprises for Mrs. Nixon, when Mrs. Nixon and the girls are not cooking up surprises for him. Breakfast is often a ceremonial meal because Nixon is always home for it. His daughters sit on each side of him, sometimes squabbling over which can get closer. The Nixons have tried to shield their children from the flattery and barbs a public family normally must learn to live with. They have

(262)

never subscribed to the Washington *Post*, for instance, to avoid having their children see the Herblock cartoons. Mrs. Nixon was especially pleased when a teacher remarked, in apparent surprise, that the "Nixon girl" in her class was so "normal, natural and unpretentious."

Some of Nixon's talents have been revealed to his wife during diplomatic tours to foreign lands. He never would fix things around the house in Washington, pleading that he didn't know how. But an experience in Liberia convinced Mrs. Nixon he was either fooling or learned very quickly. When they found out on returning to their quarters late at night that the plumbing didn't work, the Vice-President sighed, rolled up his sleeves and managed to fix it.

Mrs. Nixon never talks politics publicly, and seldom at home. The Vice-President discusses some ideas with her, however, and respects her judgment. "We might disagree on some small points, usually in how to approach something, but actually I have found that Dick is usually right," Mrs. Nixon has admitted.

17

Mᴏsᴛ of Nixon's colleagues in the administration, including some who were once skeptical and even suspicious of him, agree with John Foster Dulles that Nixon is "uniquely experienced" and qualified for the Presidency. Nixon, himself, is confident that he has what it takes. He undoubtedly would like to move over the threshold at which he has stood so long, and into the White House. But his avowed ambition is not so fierce as many think. In fact, if he is not thoroughly satisfied that he is wanted, if he feels that he would have to strong-arm his way to the nomination, he will not run. His decision probably will be made sometime after the 1959 session of Congress adjourns.

Meanwhile, since Nelson Rockefeller's triumph in the New York election cast him as *the* serious rival, Nixon has been willing to share or even shed the glory of being front-runner—and also the abuse. Furthermore, he wonders why "the Democrats continue to make me their major target if, as Truman says, I am the easiest man to beat." It is well known in the political brotherhood that when there is still time for precampaign maneuvering the objective is to kill off the toughest opponent you might have to face in the general election, not the easiest.

"Rockefeller will be a good governor of New York and could potentially be a strong candidate for president," says Nixon. "He is photogenic, has a good voice, and he likes people and shows it in the way he meets them. In addition, he showed the ability to select and use expert professional advice in his campaign for governor."

The Rockefeller-Nixon amity that developed when Rockefeller

was an Eisenhower assistant continued after he left the administration. He went out of his way to encourage Nixon, for instance, during Stassen's drive to block Nixon's renomination for vice-president. Following his own nomination for governor in the summer of 1958, Rockefeller was anxious to have Congressman Kenneth Keating, a strong vote getter among orthodox Republicans upstate, as running mate. At Rockefeller's request, Nixon helped convince Keating to forsake sure re-election in his Congressional district and run for senator, an exceedingly risky business for a Republican in New York State at that time.

Afterward there was no indication until October 22, the day before Nixon was to campaign in New York, that Rockefeller preferred to be dissociated from him. Since Nixon refused help from national Republican leaders in 1950 when he ran for senator, he could understand why an individual candidate, sensitive to voter sentiment peculiar to his state, would rather run on his own. But in this case the timing and the manner of notification had the earmarks of a public snub.

The decision was made by the Rockefeller strategy board, on which Keating was not represented. A key point of Rockefeller's strategy was to avoid any issues above the state level. For that reason he had passed up an opportunity to appear on television with Eisenhower. His advisers feared that Nixon's visit would inevitably inspire discussion of national issues and frighten off many Democrats and liberals who might favor Rockefeller despite his party. It was also whispered that the endorsement of the New York *Post*, a Democratic newspaper with influence among liberals, hinged on Rockefeller's attitude toward Nixon. L. Judson Morhouse, Republican state chairman, was assigned to ease Nixon out of his plans to speak in New York. Less than a half day before the Vice-President was to arrive, Morhouse contacted his party in Connecticut. But everyone was busy and the conversation was somewhat confused. It got more befuddled as it continued, sporadically, that afternoon from telephone booths wherever the Nixon campaign entourage stopped—in Vermont, Rhode Island, and finally New York City. At one point the impression was that Rockefeller

(265)

strategists were asking Nixon to bypass New York; at another point it was felt they wanted to censor a speech the Vice-President was to make on a state-wide radio-television network; at still another point the message was that the otherwise lavish Republican campaign could not afford to carry Nixon's speech to every part of the state.[1] Discussion ended after the astonished Vice-President sent word that he would, of course, forgo the television speech but would have to make a public statement as to the reason, since his speech had been advertised and was expected. It remained a Republican family affair, but the fact that Rockefeller avoided Nixon during his brief stay in New York could not be kept secret. Newspaper speculation about a rift caused party leaders to scramble over each other trying to arrange a meeting. Finally, Rockefeller's son called the Nixon suite at the Waldorf Astoria late on the afternoon of October 23 and arranged for his father to have breakfast with the Vice-President the next morning.

In the aftermath, Rockefeller declared that Nixon's visit "is going to be a tremendous help in New York." Governor Harriman, Rockefeller's Democratic opponent, charged a "deal" had been made whereby Rockefeller would have a part in Nixon's subsequent campaign for president "to tend to give Nixon respectability." Mrs. Dorothy Schiff, publisher of the New York *Post*, explained in a column that her newspaper "might well have endorsed Nelson Rockefeller" had he not breakfasted with Nixon because "to us, Nixonism has replaced McCarthyism as the greatest threat to the prestige of our nation today."[2] Governor Dewey rated Nixon's speech as the best political telecast he had ever seen.

On election night Rockefeller was the first successful Republican to whom Nixon telephoned.

Considering the Republican party's poor showing, a French newspaper summed up the initial interpretation of the elections

[1] When that information was relayed to Leonard Hall, who was to be Nixon's host at a Theodore Roosevelt Centennial observance in Oyster Bay, he hurriedly solicited several friends and rushed to the Batten, Barton, Durstine and Osborn advertising agency and plunked down, in advance, the whole cost of the network, including time, personnel and special facilities charges, which was $11,854.04.

[2] The *Post*, in a last-minute switch, withdrew its support of Governor Harriman.

with a picture of Rockefeller entitled "Victor" and one of Nixon called "Vanquished." Though he was not a candidate, Nixon recognized the damage he suffered by being tied in with his party's defeat —especially since the spectacular Rockefeller election provided a dramatic contrast and also the kind of new face that fascinates Republicans when they pick their presidential nominees. "There is no question but that a person in politics is always hurt when he loses, because people like to play winners," says Nixon. "But the one thing sure about politics is that what goes up comes down and what goes down often comes up."

The Republican outlook was so dark before the 1958 elections that most of Nixon's friends, including those in high echelons of the administration and the party, urged that he preserve himself for more promising times. They advised him to stay out of the campaign or, at most, restrict himself to token activities so that he might be dissociated from the outcome.

To Nixon, "that was impossible both from my own personal attitude and from the standpoint of the country and the party. I sincerely thought, and I still think, that the President should have a Republican House and a Republican Senate, and I was determined —just as I had been in 1954—to do what I could to get them. And, in any event, I believe that anyone with guts enough to run as a party's candidate for Congress ought to have national support."

Some have rushed to entomb Nixon prematurely in the past. Thomas S. Stephens, the President's appointments secretary, was the first. Scouting Republican newcomers after the election in 1946, Stephens, then a behind-the-scenes strategist in the Dewey organization, reported that California had two attractive freshman congressmen—one, named Nixon, would probably stay in the House forever, and the other, a Don Jackson, "would go a long way." In 1950 the *one* Republican victory of which House Speaker Rayburn did not wholly disapprove was Nixon's election to the Senate. Rayburn was glad to be rid of the Californian, and predicted Nixon would be "buried" in the Senate. Herbert Brownell, Jr., one of the Republican party's most talented politicians, never underrated Nixon, however. He judges Nixon to be "a master" at politics whose skill encompasses a knowledge of how the system works, an appreciation of the importance of personal contacts, an ability "to keep factions together," and the capacity "to win nominations and exert leadership."

One speculation about a Nixon-Rockefeller contest to which Nixon takes exception is equating it with the Taft-Eisenhower encounter in 1952. "That analogy is inaccurate," he insists. "It is inaccurate because Taft had certain great advantages over me, and I had certain advantages over him. . . . In another sense, Rockefeller has certain advantages over Eisenhower, and Eisenhower has many over Rockefeller. No one can say that Rockefeller would have all the so-called 'Modern Republicans' and that I would have the 'Old Guard Republicans.' The major difference between Taft and Eisenhower was in their attitude toward international affairs. On this issue Rockefeller and I have in the past had very little disagreement."

Nixon affirms that "the Republican nominee, whoever he is, inevitably must run on the record of the Eisenhower administration, just as the Democratic nominee must run on the national record of his party."

The big issue between Republicans and Democrats in the coming election will be the economic one, in Nixon's opinion. He believes the Republican party's fundamentally conservative position is a gamble and, from present indications, his own advocacy of it would result in "a loss to me politically of support both within the party and in the country at large." He adds: "I think this fight has to be made, and 1960 is the time to make it because if the country doesn't learn now, it will learn later the hard way [about the results of permitting] government to continue to get larger and the private sector of the economy to shrink. The fight may not be won this time, but it has to be made so that the people will know what their choice is."

When it comes to particulars about the next election, Nixon sees a hard, challenging road ahead for his party, with not a single state or section "safely Republican" and "the whole country now a battleground except for the South, where there are a few very hopeful,

(268)

but isolated spots of Republican strength, although the Democratic party is otherwise firmly entrenched." But he does foresee more unity among Republicans, nationally, than among Democrats. Nixon says his party has to concentrate on finding better candidates at all levels. He advises it to rid itself of the antilabor tag, to broaden the base of participation in all its party affairs, to work extra hard at winning back support in the great industrial sections lost in 1958, to make a major effort at regaining the farm vote, and to convince the business community "to recognize its responsibility to contribute to campaigning on a year-around basis." Furthermore, he believes the party needs to develop and rebuild its organizations everywhere, especially "in those states and counties where better professional help is needed, meaning, unfortunately, that some of those who have not kept up with the times will have to step aside." Nixon insists "the deadwood has to be cut out of our organizations at all levels if we are to develop the vitality and fresh ideas which are indispensable for victory.

"We should make no bones at all about our basic belief that private enterprise generally is more efficient and desirable than government enterprise as the best means of assuring economic and social progress," he says. "We should also emphasize that opportunity comes ahead of security with us. In other words, ours is the Greater Opportunity party. In standing for such sound principles as the balanced budget, we have to be intelligent enough to put the issue in terms of the dollars and cents of the family budget rather than in terms of the astronomical billions of the federal budget. In other words, we have to do a better job of relating our principles to the problems of people."

In addition, Nixon believes: "It is as wrong for the Republican party to become a far-right party as it is for it to become a radical party. As a matter of principle it can never look back and it must never put itself in the position of dividing Americans into classes. To take the far-right viewpoint would destroy it as a national party."

Republicans should not count on a serious split in the Democratic party, he warns, because there probably won't be one despite the cleavage among Democrats on civil rights. Nixon does figure, however, that the big problem confronting the Democrats—"to find a qualified candidate acceptable to the South and to the North"—is a mighty difficult one.

"I don't think either party could win with an extremist, whether of the left or the right," he adds. "The middle usually prevails in the United States because extremists have one thing in common: they push too hard and drive reasonable, fair-minded people away."

The quality of candidates could make the difference between winning control of Congress and losing it again in 1960, he believes. "On the average the Democratic candidates in 1958—particularly for the House and Senate—were younger, more articulate and more effective than their Republican opposite numbers," he admits. "As a result we lost in some places where we had the issues and the organizations on our side."

This is the way he sizes up the Republican problem and its solution:

"In order to win the House, we will have to hold the 152 seats we now have and pick up another 68. I'm inclined to think the ones we have will hold, because 1960 will not be as bad as 1958 under any circumstances. But we have to concentrate on keeping the seats we have, and then we should shoot for 100 seats that we don't have now. If we can win 70 per cent of them, we have it made. In picking the candidates for those 100 districts I would say the ideal age should be 30 to 40 years. They should not be ultraliberal or ultraconservative. They must represent the thinking of the people of their particular districts. For example, Barry Goldwater and Hugh Scott do not agree on all issues. But it is obvious from the election returns that Goldwater will speak for a majority of the people of Arizona in the Senate and Scott for a majority of the people of Pennsylvania. This is as it should be. There are, of course, certain general principles which I feel all Republican candidates should subscribe to. I believe all Republican candidates should have a broad-gauged understanding of and attitude toward the world conflict and international affairs. They should be united in their support of constructive programs in the field of civil rights. I also believe that they should be economic conservatives, but conservatives with a heart—they should be conservative not because they look upon conservatism as the best means of assuring that we stay where we are but as the best means of assuring maximum social and economic progress in a free society in the years ahead.

"I would like to see the Republicans select more candidates from the university communities, from the various racial and religious groups, and, where possible, from the responsible leadership of some of our local unions."

As to senatorial candidates, Nixon believes that "the ideal age" is between 35 and 50 except in the case of incumbents. "It doesn't make much sense to elect to the Senate for the first time a man in his sixties because, even if he wins, he won't serve long enough to gain the seniority which is essential if a senator is to represent his state effectively."

Furthermore, Nixon says: "I want to emphasize that I don't go along with the idea of selecting candidates just because they are pretty-boys who look and sound good on television. I think I am a pretty fair judge of political television, and I am convinced that being a smooth actor and a fast talker on television may appeal to the people in the short run but not in the long run. Sincerity counts above everything else on television. This is something, unfortunately, that many of the public relations experts simply don't understand. They put too much emphasis on how a man is going to look or sound and not enough on bringing out his basic character and his beliefs. I think they underestimate the intelligence of the American voters. They aren't fooled by the automatic smile every two minutes, or the contrived gimmicks and gestures. Above everything else, a candidate to be effective on television must know what he is talking about, believe deeply in the rightness of his cause, and speak naturally and sincerely just as if he were carrying on a conversation with two or three people in a typical American home which he had happened to visit."

The cornerstone of Nixon's political credo is: "Once a battle is over, don't hold grudges." He adds: "Obviously one can work more closely with those who were his friends in past campaigns. But I

(271)

never cut anybody because he opposed me for nomination or an election."

He considers party unity essential in campaigns and believes very few politicians develop enough stature to stand out above their respective parties. Most who attack their "own party will get publicity at the moment," he says, "but in the end if the party goes down, they will go down with it."

One extremely important fact of American politics is that neither major party is actually a majority party, Nixon points out. One reason he disapproves of categorizing Republicans as "Modern Republicans" or "Old Guard Republicans" is because it implies a desire to throw one or the other group out of the party. Furthermore, he says, "I don't believe in dividing Republicans into classes any more than I believe in dividing Americans into classes."

Considering the expense and effort, political campaigns are pitched to a limited clientele—not more than 20 per cent of the voters, in Nixon's opinion. He figures the vast majority—half Democrats and about half Republicans—usually vote their party affiliations or for a favorite individual, regardless of issues. Thus it is to the uncommitted, the "swing vote," that campaigners must appeal on the issues, while at the same time energizing their own party faithful sufficiently to interest them in going to the polls.

He believes in the need "for vigorous, sharp debate" in campaigns. "I do not go along with the current popular view that the primary aim of a political figure is to be all things to all men," he says. "The record of a candidate has got to be mercilessly exposed to light. You hear some yakkity-yakking that campaigns should be limited to ivory-tower, philosophical discussions of issues. I welcome that kind of discussion in a campaign, but if you are going to get your case across you must combine that type of discussion with simple, direct, hard-hitting, down-to-earth speeches which people will listen to and understand."

Nixon says the line he draws between what is permissible and what is not permissible in a campagn is simply this: a candidate's whole record, including all of his public utterances, the organizations to which he has given support, and all matters bearing upon

(272)

his philosophy are fair game. But, unless it bears directly on how he would do his public job, Nixon says a candidate's personal and family affairs "are frankly none of the public's business."

In each election the type of campaign he conducts "depends on what the times require," Nixon explains. "Suppose the Republicans were to lose in 1960, for example, and suppose as a result, you had corruption shot through the government, and you had a lack of imagination, ingenuity, everything that you thought was needed if the United States was to maintain its place as a first-class power. Then, in the 1964 election the people would need to be awakened, and the only way you can awaken them is to smack the opposition and the issues hard."

In his first dozen years of politics Nixon developed some common-sense campaign techniques. "There is no public relations gimmick that will take the place of hard work" is one tenet. "In a political campaign you've got to dramatize your case" is another. Then there are these: "You should fight the battle on the ground on which you are strongest, and avoid the tactical error of fighting on your opponent's strongest ground" . . . "I don't think anybody ever is as good on the defense as on the offense, but whenever anybody attacks, I believe the way to answer is not simply to defend, but to take the offensive" . . . "No one can tell in advance what the issues will be six months later" . . . and "You really find out who has what it takes when the going is tough. It is easy when you are on top."

A common mistake of many campaigners, including those running for high office, is to "shoot their ammunition too soon," Nixon observes. "Willkie, for instance, shot his wad too early in 1940. He had nothing left, or he might have won. I've noticed that with Stevenson also. In both his campaigns he made a brilliant start, but he didn't have staying power. He wore out. He made his mistakes when he was tired. Apparently he didn't know how to pace himself. That is something I guard against constantly. If I have made fewer than normal mistakes in the tag end of my campaigns, it is because I know that when you are tired you must be careful of snap de-

(273)

cisions. That's when you've got to weigh things even more carefully than usual."

While recognizing that he and other campaigners probably will have to continue to use them, Nixon feels that the use of labels and characterizations in campaigns is unfortunate. "They are more important than they ought to be," he says. "Unfortunately a great majority of people don't study issues, and they gain impressions from something they have read or heard about a candidate. Now, during the 1958 campaign the President and I used the term 'radical' to describe the economic philosophy of the Northern and Western wings of the Democratic party because we felt that the term 'liberal' has become so corrupted in recent years that it could not accurately be used in describing that philosophy. We did not use 'radical' with the objective in mind of calling names. We used it only as a descriptive term, a term which we felt was the opposite of moderate in so far as approach to economic problems is concerned."

While urging broader participation by young men and women, he also warns: "Don't go into political life if you have to be begged to." And sometimes he is tempted to pass on the advice Dewey gave him in 1952: "Don't get fat, and don't let your zeal lag."

Not since the controversial Martin Van Buren's victory more than 120 years ago has a vice-president been elected president on his own without first taking office by succession. Nixon broke a precedent when he became the first Republican vice-president to be re-elected. Of his predecessors, seven vice-presidents have been elevated to the White House on the death of presidents. Three of the nine presidents in this century alone took office by succession. Adlai Stevenson expressed the thoughts of many people about the delicate matter of a president's life expectancy when he declared on election eve in 1956 that "every piece of scientific evidence that we have, every lesson of history and experience, indicates that a Republican victory . . . would mean that Richard M. Nixon would probably be president of this country within the next four years." Stevenson's observation made sense on the basis of actuarial realities, for even before General Eisenhower's

(274)

three serious illnesses he often complained to friends that the cares of the Presidency were "eroding."

Nixon is satisfied that President Eisenhower and most Republican party leaders "appreciate the fact that my primary desire is to see the administration succeed, and to rebuild the Republican party so that *this* nomination would be worth something to somebody . . . . maybe somebody else." Eisenhower has told him several times of his "very strong feeling that it would be improper" for him to show any favoritism between potential candidates. Thus Nixon doesn't expect an endorsement from Eisenhower—either for himself or for anyone else.

Meanwhile, nothing is more annoying to Nixon than the persistent charges ("by people who know better") that he lacks convictions and that his positions conform to the political expediency of the day. He says: "I know that fighting cuts in the budget in 1957 was not the popular thing to do politically. My position on civil rights certainly does not go far enough to satisfy the extreme pro-civil rights people, and on the other side it has lost the Republican party strength and could hardly be helpful as far as getting the nomination is concerned because it is anathema to many Southern delegates whose votes are often very important at the convention. At the same time, up to this point the party has gained very little in the North because generally speaking our Negro voters as a group are still primarily more interested in economic issues than they are in civil rights.

"Take labor—I recognize it would be better for me as far as the nomination is concerned to go along with the more extreme views of the right on this issue, and from the standpoint of the election I am sure it would be better to knuckle down generally and soft-pedal any labor legislation.

"The Assistance Programs, which I regard as the most vital of all before us, constitute another area in which my stand can hardly be described as one conducive to getting votes. It is far easier and much more politically popular, believe me, to talk about more missiles, more guns, more space ships. People understand that. It is something concrete. I am for a strong national defense. But I

(275)

recognize the necessity for a greater national effort in the area where I realize the public is not adequately informed. We have to develop greater public support for these nonmilitary programs if we are to survive, and I intend to keep plugging it as hard as I can, politics notwithstanding."

In candor, Nixon admits to strong personal ambitions and wonders about the frankness of those who claim they have no such ambitions of their own. He also has a solid theory about the role of "fate" and "circumstances" in politics which sometimes makes a very honest Nixon observation appear to be coy or evasive. "It is not accurate to picture me as a fellow who is out seeking the Presidency every day of his life, because I'm not," he says. "I have been in a very fortunate position as a political man since the time I started. The positions that I've gotten—first the House, then the Senate, then the Vice-Presidency—generally have come to me. It happened that I was in the right place at the right time. This can change. The only thing that I will do so far as the future is concerned is to continue to do the most effective job I can for the country, and of course, for the party. And then, what should happen will happen."

Nixon states that he has "consistently resisted the efforts of many well-meaning people"—before the 1958 election and after— to set up Nixon-for-President clubs. "None of that will be going on around the country with my approval at least through the balance of this session of Congress," he says, "because my entire effort during this period will be devoted to helping the administration make a good record, helping to rebuild the Republican party throughout the country, finding candidates for Congress and other offices, developing the organization, getting the financing, and doing whatever else needs to be done. In addition, from a party standpoint, the major thing that I am going to do in 1959 is to try to articulate the basic philosophy on which I think the Republican party should stand.

"So far as 1960 is concerned, I think that the Republican candidate for president will be the man who happens to fit best the qualifications wanted at that time by the people who vote in Repub-

(276)

lican primaries and the people who attend the Republican Convention. This, too, can change. The only thing certain about a public figure's popularity, as well as an administration's, is that it is never stable, never static. It varies very greatly, up and down, sometimes very violently. Today they may want a man of one type; tomorrow they may want a man of another. I approach it almost impersonally in this sense: I realize that I could have been a political casualty any time since 1946. And I may have become one now. If I haven't, I may become one in the next year or two.

"I do not intend to get on the treadmill Taft was on or that Stassen has been on—of going out and seeking the nomination at all costs. I happen to think that the Presidency is the toughest job in the world. I also happen to have great respect for many of my Republican colleagues, and I think that there is no such thing as an indispensable candidate or an indispensable man. The times may require and demand a man with different qualifications. If that is the way the ball bounces, I will be completely resigned to it.

"I think, in other words, that if I happen to be the man that the party and the country needs, it will come. But if I don't happen to be, it will go to somebody else. Putting it in a nutshell, between now and the convention in 1960 I intend to do everything that I can to make the Republican nomination worth something to whoever gets it. That may help me; but it may not."

18

THE questions most often asked about Richard Nixon relate to his convictions, his political principles, the sort of president he would be, and his attitude toward people. A rigid evaluation of his whole record, the red and the black, his personal and political background, searching talks with scores of his friends and enemies, and a series of candid interviews with him between November, 1957, and January, 1959, supply answers as well as some surprises.

Essentially a cautious individual, he doesn't wish away risks. Few contemporaries can match his political boldness. Nixon has a taste for ideas and provocative conversation and is one of those rare politicians who would rather listen than talk. He constantly probes for opinions. Frequently, his friends, the elevator operators, maintenance men and clerks on Capitol Hill make more sense than his colleagues, the administration executives and congressmen. When it comes to witticisms, Nixon is no Alben Barkley or Goodie Knight. Neither is he as dour and humorless as he seems. He usually is quite the life of small parties and has even had his moments at large public affairs. At the first joint meeting of the Senate campaign in 1950 his Democratic opponent, Mrs. Helen Gahagan Douglas, charged that big-business interests were sending huge sums of money to California to beat her. When it was his turn to speak, Nixon revealed almost apologetically that he had gotten a contribution from New York only that morning. Then he pulled from his pocket a check for one hundred dollars and a letter which he read: "I am enclosing a small contribution to your campaign and

(278)

only wish it could be ten times as much. Best wishes. Signed, Eleanor Roosevelt." Mrs. Douglas and the audience gasped. The hubbub became a roar of laughter when Nixon admitted that he, too, was surprised until he checked the postmark. The letter was from Oyster Bay, not Hyde Park. The contributor was the wife of Theodore Roosevelt, Jr.

Nothing about Nixon's public image is less accurate than the view of him as a cold fish with little liking for people. His own reticence is partly to blame. In his personal life he is a man of consideration, and many have had cause to be grateful for his good works. For several years he has been sending his honorariums for speeches and magazine articles to private welfare agencies and educational institutions. He has given as much as $9,000 a year in this way. One episode that, typically, is little known occurred just before Congress adjourned in 1954. A young minister who had given the invocation in the Senate asked the Vice-President for an autographed picture, explaining that it was for his daughter, Susan, a victim of leukemia. The child was eight, the age of Nixon's older girl. When the Vice-President checked the hospital about visiting hours he was told that another child, Freda, suffering from the same disease, was in the room with Susan and that both were able to see visitors. The next morning Nixon called at the hospital, bringing two large walking dolls that a friend had sent to his office as gifts for his daughters. The Vice-President told stories, the bedridden little girls giggled, chattered and asked questions, and everyone had a gay time. That afternoon Susan's father wrote to Nixon: "You left two very happy little girls this morning and a father whose heart was warmed and comforted by the amazing kindness of one who, on the busiest day of his crowded year, would take the time to bring such joy to little children. May the Master who said, 'Who so receives one such little child in My Name, receiveth Me,' bless you and your dear ones as you have blessed us in this difficult hour."

Not long afterward Nixon was notified that Freda had died—"with your doll in her arms." He continued his interest in Susan's case until the end. She died in 1956.

Nixon is often said to have no interest in the welfare of minorities and to sail with the political winds on civil rights. It is symptomatic of one of his failings as a politician that one has to dig long and hard to become convinced of his sincerity in this area. His shyness and his obsession about the privacy of what he regards as personal matters obscure many attractive qualities. His intimates have always known that this man simply has no sense of racial or religious bigotry. Tolerance has been a way of life in his family. A Quaker great-grandfather running a station on the slave-rescuing Underground Railroad in southern Indiana symbolizes a heritage of opposition to human injustices. As a student Nixon wouldn't abide—indeed, he helped prevent—the exclusion of a Negro boy from a school club. Later, in law school, he was infuriated to learn that some officials of the American Bar Association had once attempted on religious grounds to keep Louis D. Brandeis, whom he greatly respected, from being confirmed as an associate justice of the Supreme Court. When a question was asked in a test about the then president of the association, Nixon replied: "If he is anything like his predecessors who opposed the confirmation of Justice Brandeis, he is a son of a bitch." This was extreme language for a 23-year-old Quaker.

That Nixon is sincere on civil rights is certainly not to say he would refrain from using the issue politically. He has done so and will do so again. But his position on specific facets of the problem, such as school desegregation and compulsory fair employment practices laws, clearly is not tailored to capture bloc votes, since he favors a gradual program of desegregation and opposes as unworkable the idea of a federal law to end discrimination by force. It is a common surmise in Washington that Nixon would welcome racial antagonisms to split the Democratic party and win in Eastern and Western states the Negro votes which could decide the presidential election. The fact is, however, that he wants tensions eased and the problem of discrimination solved—and he would welcome a bipartisan effort to bring that about, though knowing full well that removal of the civil rights issue would be a great boon to the Democrats.

Nixon disagrees fundamentally with Eisenhower on how to deal with this delicate issue. "I feel strongly that civil rights is primarily a moral rather than a legal question," says Nixon. Eisenhower sees it as a matter of .enforcing the law, whether you like it or not. "Laws play a necessary part, of course," Nixon points out. "But the approach of those who say 'Education alone is the answer' and 'Leave us alone and this thing will eventually work out' is not adequate. It is just as unrealistic to assume that passing a law or handing down a court decision will solve this problem. Where human relations are concerned, a law isn't worth the paper it is written on unless it has the moral support of the majority of the people. The only way we are going to solve the school segregation and other problems in the civil rights field is for our leaders in all walks of life—government, church, education, and the press—to use their great influence to help develop the moral support which a law must have if it is to survive. Just passing laws and trying to enforce them isn't going to work any better than prohibition did."

Nixon believes "the place to start mobilizing the moral conscience of America is among our young people; they have a minimum of prejudice." As for school desegregation, he thinks "the moderate approaches which have been put into effect in Nashville and Louisville are very constructive. They are reasonable and sensible and provide a possible formula which might spread all over the South in a way that would be workable and realistic."

Over the years Nixon has altered his position on some issues: his espousal of federal aid in certain fields of education and freer trade are typical. The most significant change, however, is that his overriding interest has become foreign affairs. In this field he is the administration's—and perhaps the nation's—leading advocate of Big Aid over Big Guns. "In the next ten years our greatest external danger will not be military, but economic and ideological," Nixon insists. Therefore, he believes, it is more important to provide money for people-to-people and cultural-exchange programs than for missiles and submarines.

"If we have to choose in allocating funds between military programs and the economic, information and other nonmilitary programs, I would put the emphasis on the nonmilitary programs and take a gamble on the military programs. If we continue to gamble, as we are now, on the nonmilitary we are sure to lose the ideological war for the world and ultimately this means that we will lose our freedom without a missile ever being launched."

This civil-over-military view extends to other areas where there may be competition. That applies particularly to the field of research, including outer space research. "Scientists must not be limited by military needs or military thinking," says Nixon. "There must be civil control of policy and the distribution of the funds for research. The emphasis should be science for peace, rather than science for war."

Nixon's domestic credo is conservative. He is, so to speak, a conservative with a practical yardstick. He is well acquainted with the internal and external forces that make the government's wheels turn, and he applies a simple—perhaps oversimple—rule of thumb to ideas and programs: "Will it work?"

"I'm a radical when it comes to the goals which I think our economy should shoot for," he says. "I reject and have no patience whatever with the approach of some ultraconservatives who defend the status quo and speak of going back to the 'good old days.' Conservatism at its best is progressive. The Republican party in its greatest years has been progressive, while at the same time following conservative economic policies. I will say honestly that because of my background—because I have experienced what happens in a family where there is catastrophic illness, inadequate wages, poor housing—if I thought the 'let-the-government-do-it' type of programs would work, would produce more, would in the long run be best for the great majority of the people I would probably be the most enthusiastic radical in these fields that you could possibly imagine."

He adds: "I recognize that in thinking otherwise I may be running against the tide in a way that may prove to be politically disastrous. I sense as I go about the country an increasing tendency on the part of the people, which I think most unfortunate, to want the federal government to solve all their problems for them. It would be very easy for our government to go that way. That is

(282)

why I think it is the responsibility of those of us who really know what would happen, who recognize the pitfalls, the terrible hazards of that course, to fight as vigorously, articulately and hard as we can against the phony pie-in-the-sky proposals of the economic radicals, and for the truly progressive programs of the economic conservatives."

In terms of specific issues, Nixon sums up his economic philosophy this way: "I am for a government living within its means—the so-called balanced budget. (We should approach this on a five-year basis rather than being bound to one year.) I firmly believe that private enterprise, generally, while not sacrosanct, is more efficient, more productive, and more desirable than government enterprise in assuring economic progress and providing for the needs of the people. And I believe the government should give more attention, more emphasis, to providing increased opportunities for our citizens than increased security. On that score I believe the government has certain real responsibilities to protect the people against the hazards of old age, unemployment, sickness, and ill-health. But that should not be its major function. To provide adequately for all, including those who are not able to care for their own needs, we must have a strong productive and growing economy. We cannot simply stand still and cut up the pie into constantly smaller pieces. That is why we must put our primary emphasis on providing opportunities—on promoting enterprise, growth and a maximum contribution by each individual."

Nixon sees a "critical need" for corrective labor legislation stronger than that proposed by Senator Kennedy in 1958 and again in 1959, but he firmly opposes the right-to-work approach. "All that the right-to-work movement accomplished in 1958 was to serve as a red flag in bringing out a tremendous organized labor vote which was predominately pro-Democratic," he says. "Right-to-work states a general principle that sounds good, but such measures in practice have been relatively ineffective. They don't touch the abuses that need to be dealt with. Those who supported right-to-work with their time and money would have been far better advised to have contributed to the election of candidates to the state and national legislatures who could be counted upon to consider and vote for necessary labor legislation fearlessly and independently."

There is a great danger, Nixon thinks, in the trend of management and labor to drift further and further apart. "Some differences are inevitable, necessary and healthy, in my opinion," he says, "but what is unfortunate today is that attitudes are hardening, each side is getting tougher, and there is less and less mutual understanding and mutual trust." Nixon would get at this problem through high-level off-the-record contacts and conferences between leaders of government, management and labor. "The conferences should be off-the-record because otherwise they could become just a sounding board for the extreme views of all participants," he says. "I don't know whether this approach would solve all our problems, but it might create better understanding, and I am sure each participant would learn something from the other."

Tax reform is another issue on which Nixon has firm personal convictions that do not necessarily jibe with administration policy. "While popular politically, the idea that we can get more tax revenue simply by soaking the rich is phony and unworkable because the tax rates now are at such a level that we have dried up that source," he says. "You couldn't squeeze any more taxes out of the people in the higher brackets at this point than you could get juice out of a cueball." Nixon favors a program that would lower taxes in the higher brackets which "have reached the point of diminishing return," reduce corporate taxes, and revise excise taxes. "This would have the effect of stimulating economic growth by unleashing capital and encouraging new capital," he says. "This, in turn, would lead not only to more revenue for the government, but even more important, it would inevitably produce more and better jobs for our people."

Timidity in politics and government is so distasteful to Nixon that he refers to neuter, play-it-safe politicians as "gutless wonders." He feels that conscientious candidates and public officials should view "this fetish about being noncontroversial" with skepticism. "There are many who believe, particularly with the advent of television, that the most effective way to win is for candidates to have

(284)

a public relations outfit take a very scientific poll of what issues interest the public and then avoid all which are controversial and speak out only on those which are what they call 'safe,' " Nixon says. "I will have to admit that this approach seems to work in some instances. What I believe, however, flies straight in the face of the advice of most of the public relations experts because most of them to whom I have talked throw up their hands in horror whenever a candidate suggests that he might take a strong position on an issue before they are sure that overwhelming public opinion is already in favor of his stand."

He concedes that "just saying what the public relations people tell you to say might win in any given election," but adds: "It is wrong because in the long run it not only will not win, but more important than that, I think in the long run that type of approach would be catastrophic for the country. Speaking as a Republican— and I would say the same if I were a Democrat—I think it would be catastrophic for our major parties if a majority of the leaders adopted that weak and spineless approach."

As a matter of advice to politicians, Nixon makes it clear he isn't recommending "throwing yourself on the sword." But he does advise this: "If you believe in certain principles of government, you have to take chances, you have to be willing to sacrifice yourself if necessary. It is very easy, I can assure you, to be a candidate when you're ahead or your party is ahead. It's easy to get money; it's easy to get crowds; it's easy to get the workers, the organizers and the recruits. When you are behind, when people think you might lose, the situation is quite different."

Nixon takes a special interest in American political figures, and his conclusions reveal much about Richard Nixon himself. "I don't think that a leader can control to any great extent his destiny," he says, discussing why some succeeded and others failed. "Very seldom can he step in and change the situation if the forces of history are running in another direction. That is why men like Taft, Clay, Webster, and even Stassen never made it, much as they wanted to be president, though all of them had leadership qualities that would have made them good presidents. They never

(285)

made it because circumstances, in each case, called for somebody else." As to the influence of individual leaders on their times, Nixon believes that "once a man gets into an important position of leadership—the Presidency, for example—his character can have a great deal of effect on how the stream of events moves one way or another. He can direct it, but he can't turn it around completely. In 1932 Franklin Roosevelt ran on a platform pledging to cut federal spending at least 25 per cent by streamlining the government and eliminating extravagance.

"It was a conservative economic platform if you ever read one," says Nixon. "Roosevelt probably honestly thought he was going to put it into effect. But he could no more have done that than fly to the moon because the times called for something else. The times called for spending, for government action to stop the depression. So when Roosevelt took office he became, in effect, a captive of circumstances. Since he couldn't turn the tide backwards, he had to go with it. By the force of his personality he directed the course it took. He turned it into the channels of the great social reforms of the 1930's, some of which were very admirable and others of which proved to be unworkable and undesirable."

In Nixon's judgment the problem of leadership in a democracy always has been how "to implement noble ideals and principles with practical accomplishments." He believes Jefferson—"an idealist with sense"—was the first president with the capacity to do it, followed by Abraham Lincoln, Theodore Roosevelt, and Woodrow Wilson. Lincoln was the greatest president, in Nixon's opinion, largely because the times offered "by far the greatest opportunity for leadership." Furthermore, Lincoln "had a very deep feeling for people, but on the other hand, he could be tough in a crisis. No one pushed him around. He was a very skillful political operator."

Theodore Roosevelt, whom Nixon regards as a model, "was probably as representative of the aspirations of the people as any president. Yet he was never a passive captive of public sentiment. He knew what the people would support, and got out front and led them and guided them at the same time."

Nixon admires Wilson and Franklin Roosevelt as "very effective

(286)

war presidents" and "dynamic leaders" in the international sphere, and he believes Herbert Hoover would have emerged as one of the finest presidents had he been elected in 1920, instead of 1928.

"Hoover had the misfortune to have held office at the wrong time," says Nixon. "As far as background, education, experience and administrative ability are concerned, he had no peer among the presidents. In spite of the fact that political opponents painted him as a black reactionary, he was a very progressive leader of the Republican party. There was considerable talk of nominating him in 1920. I'll never forget how strongly my father favored that. I've often thought that, had Hoover been elected then, the course of history might have been different. He had an international outlook. He was a humanitarian. He had superb administrative skill and a scrupulous sense of honesty. Under Hoover there never would have been a Teapot Dome. Unfortunately, he came to office in a period which, perhaps, no president could have survived without coming out more or less as the goat of the times."

As a matter of historical perspective, Nixon believes that Truman showed, by his commanding influence in international affairs, how wrong people can be in prejudging a prospective chief executive.

"I thought Truman followed a demagogic line in his attitude on virtually every domestic policy, particularly in his attacks on the Eightieth Congress," says Nixon. "I also take exception to some rather libelous things he has said about President Eisenhower, the administration, and myself as well. And I couldn't, of course, have disagreed with him more in his brushing off the Hiss case and the domestic Communist issue as 'red herrings.' There has never been any doubt in my mind about Mr. Truman's complete loyalty to the country and the fact that he detests Communism as much as I do or any other American does. But I felt that in this instance he allowed himself to be taken in by very bad advice."

On foreign affairs, however, Nixon regards Truman's decision to fight Communist aggression in Korea as "right and very courageous" and his praise is unqualified for Truman's "strong leadership" in behalf of such programs as the Marshall Plan and Greek-Turkish aid. All told, in Nixon's opinion, Truman "was a much more ef-

(287)

fective leader from an international standpoint than anybody thought he was capable of before he became president."

What kind of President would Nixon be?

Well, to begin with, he would be perhaps the hardest-driving chief executive and the most controversial since Theodore Roosevelt. There would be nothing haphazard, nothing bland about his administration, nor any doubt about its political identity. It would have holdovers from the Eisenhower regime, but under Nixon they would move more energetically. And when the party's call to battle sounded, Cabinet members and other administration chieftains would most likely take to the hustings instead of touring faraway places or tarrying in Washington, as has become customary.

While Nixon would head the Republican party in fact as well as name, the outright partisanship of his administration would be less rigid than many anticipate—and hope. The first cries of disappointment probably would come from party leaders lining up at the White House door for patronage.

Nixon would be a "strong president" in the tradition of the two Roosevelts. Lacking experience as an executive, he would of necessity have to stop writing all his own speeches, handling all his own press relations, being his own Sherman Adams, and trying to manage all the activities for which the President is responsible. In addition, he would be haunted by some episodes from his career as a razzle-dazzle campaigner and Congressional investigator. To uphold executive immunity in his administration after having demanded, as a congressman, that President Truman's people testify before Congress, for example, Nixon would need the best of his political skills.

In fundamental outlook, a Nixon administration would not differ radically from the Eisenhower administration. Essentially, it would maintain the familiar image of being conservative on domestic matters and internationalist in foreign affairs. But Nixon is not merely an "Eisenhower Republican"—he is a "Nixon-Eisenhower Republican"—and his innate tendencies are much less conservative than Eisenhower's.

An administration headed by Nixon would differ from Eisenhower's both in its approach to problems and in its make-up. It would have businessmen in some important positions, but would never be a "businessman's administration." It would also have braintrusters: "Frankly, Republican administrations and the Republican party need, above everything else, a broader intellectual base. We have not used adequately the talents available. We have not called enough on our educational leaders, the so-called eggheads." There would be labor leaders, scientists and individuals of diverse talents in high positions. Furthermore, Hoover, Truman, Eisenhower and maybe even Henry Wallace would be offered specific assignments. "Ex-presidents and ex-vice-presidents should be constantly consulted; their advice should be sought, and they should be asked to do special missions for the President." For all the bitterness of his past campaigns, Nixon, surprisingly, is not vindictive. He wouldn't hesitate to utilize his worst enemy if he felt that person was the best man for a particular position.[1] The Vice-President under Nixon would find himself burdened with even more than the record number of executive responsibilities which Nixon has received under Eisenhower.

There would be little room for speculation about a Nixon administration's position on any issue of consequence. This approach would be selective, however, since Nixon considers himself "practical in the sense that I don't believe in taking issues simply for the sake of a fight." His maxim on compromise is: "A leader must always conserve his resources for the battles that count. He must look at the major objectives of his administration . . . and must never become involved in a fight on a minor issue which might prejudice his chance to win on a major issue."

As president, Nixon's primary interest would be foreign relations. He would have a strong secretary of state, one who could best fit the mold of Dulles, whom he esteems. To deal with the Communists, Nixon is convinced American diplomats must have "a

[1] Nixon strongly endorsed Dulles' idea to have Adlai Stevenson serve as adviser at the State Department while plans were being made for the conference of NATO chiefs of state in 1957.

quality of unshakable conviction and character which an individual develops only through experience in handling the toughest practical problems." Nixon sees that quality in a few well-known political and diplomatic figures, and also in several labor leaders. A union official is often on the guest list when the Vice-President entertains for visiting statesmen, and some probably would have important State Department assignments after an overhaul of the government's overseas personnel policies, which would be Nixon's first major undertaking.

No one, whether in dismay or in admiration, can expect that Richard Nixon would be a weak executive.

RICHARD NIXON "OFF THE RECORD"

(These statements of Nixon's views about politics and many other matters are taken from more than two dozen interviews and conversations between November, 1957, and January, 1959. E.M.)

The line I draw between permissible and nonpermissible campaign tactics is a very simple one. The candidate's record is public property in so far as it indicates the position he might take on issues while in the office which he seeks. Now, this means his record in terms of all the votes he has cast if he has held public office, all the speeches he has made, all the organizations to which he has given his support. All matters of this kind which bear upon or might indicate his philosophy should be discussed openly and frankly by the candidate and by his opponent. I draw the line, however, on anything that has to do with the personal life of a candidate. I don't believe, for example, that a candidate's family is fair game. I never went along with those in the Republican party who criticized Mr. Truman on the ground that he had Secret Service agents go with Margaret Truman when she took a trip to Europe. I have never gone along with those who criticized President Roosevelt because of some aberrations of some members of his family. It seems to me that the troubles of a man's family are, frankly, none of the public's business. But as to the record, that has got to be mercilessly exposed to light.

As to my whole outlook on being "controversial"—I am aware that when you take strong positions on issues, knowing that the public may not at that particular time support the positions, you run a great political risk. In the short run it may result in your defeat. But in the long run it is the only way to build a sound party position.

Political success comes from a combination of hard work and breaks. But unless you have the guts to take chances when the breaks come your way, and the determination and stamina to work hard, you will never amount to much more than a political hack and a perennial "almost-ran" in your political career.

I am practical in the sense that I don't believe in fighting windmills. I don't believe in taking on issues simply for the sake of a fight. I believe a leader must always conserve his resources for the battles that count. He must not fritter away his energies by getting involved in every little struggle that comes along. In relatively unimportant matters a good public servant, an effective politician must compromise and should compromise to avoid bloodletting. He must look at the major objectives of his administration and keep them always in mind. He must never become involved in a fight on a minor issue which might prejudice his chance to win on a major issue. That is one of the best rules a politician could follow in political campaigns, too. It is one of the reasons Lyndon Johnson is so effective as Democratic Majority Leader of the Senate. They talk about Lyndon being a compromiser. But I admire Lyndon, although I don't agree with him on some things, because he is always able to keep in mind the major objectives. He will compromise on some things, but in the end he gets the major part of his program through.

There is too much of a tendency to leave the solution of civil rights problems to those who represent the minority groups on both extremes. If we are to progress in this field, people who are not members of either extreme would have to take the leadership.

I think it proper to emphasize that both of our political parties, Republican and Democratic, have a record in the field of civil rights that leaves much to be desired. Since the days of Lincoln a great deal of lip service is paid to the cause of civil rights during each political campaign and at the great party conventions. The same is true with legislation before Congress and the state legislatures. We have to admit honestly that too often speeches and statements supporting an enlightened attitude are made by individuals who know and are satisfied that nothing is going to be done.

Demagogues who advocate impossible legal approaches to the civil rights problem do more harm than good, and invariably set the cause back.

Congress should always be subject to criticism, but it should not be smeared or attacked as an institution that is incompetent or worse.

Untrue and irresponsible charges of that sort are harmful to the country and the people. I feel the same way about the Supreme Court. I may privately disagree with some of its decisions, but I respect the Supreme Court as one of our principal institutions.

We should not tie down our scientists to the specific inventions which military men or political leaders deem desirable. The greatest advances have been made not when scientists have been told to restrict themselves to certain objectives but when they had complete freedom in basic research to explore the unknown.

Basic research cannot be carried out on a crash basis. The practice of providing huge sums and declaring crash programs only when outside events generate a sense of urgency is dangerously irresponsible. A truth that we must never forget is that where new inventions and knowledge are concerned there are no monopolies by any people or any nation.

There is a great tendency in this country to go to extremes on things of this kind, and to worship science as an end in itself. It would be most unfortunate for us to try to ape the Russians, to believe that scientific materialism produces the best kind of society. I think all elements of American education—the humanities as well as the scientific—need additional emphasis.

With automation it is inevitable that the working day is going to be reduced. And I believe that we should plan for that day so that leisure time can be used not just for what is really the opiate of the people in the United States—television in its present form—but for developing the tremendous cultural possibilities—in the arts, music, literature—which are possible when our people have the burden of toil lifted from them.

The most fundamental weakness in many of our schools is that students are not allowed to face the challenge of failure. Passing is automatic. . . . The educators say it is more important to help students adjust to one another and feel the warmth of success than it is to demand rigorous achievement. This approach does not measure up to the reality of life. When students leave school they will find that success is not automatic. Knowledge and achievement will count, not good intentions. In the hard competition of life they will have to face possible failures.

(293)

What is wrong with the old Adam Smith philosophy and what should be completely unacceptable to any American (and I would say this particularly to my fellow Republicans) is the idea of the survival of the fittest. Let's put it this way: The fittest should survive, and also the fit should survive. Those who are "unfit" you have to have a social consciousness about, to take care of them. The "survival of the fittest" assumes "the hell with the rest of them." This is wrong, morally and socially, apart from being completely wrong politically.

Unless the system in which you have political freedom proves that it is the most effective in bringing about economic progress, Communism is going to gain increasing adherents throughout the world. We have to bear in mind this essential fact: the terrible poverty and misery that so many people suffer cannot continue to be endured. They know there must be a way out, and they are going to take the way that they think is the quickest and surest, in the long run.

The fear of a temporary budget deficit should not be allowed to put us in a straitjacket that keeps us from doing what is needed to insure economic growth. I am not rigid with regard to the balanced budget in this sense: I think we should approach the budget problems on a five-year basis rather than being bound to one year. There are some years—a recession year, for example, or one where you have a great international crisis—when we all know that it is inevitable and necessary for the budget to be unbalanced. There are other years when we can have surpluses to make up the over-all deficits.

Our position of world responsibility is new, and consequently we are very impatient every time anything goes wrong in the field of foreign policy. We assume that every policy, every action must immediately be crowned with success. We have to grow up in this regard. We must weigh long-range gains against the short-range defeats that we may suffer.

I would like for us to speak less of the threat of Communism and more of the promise of freedom. We should adopt as our primary objective not the defeat of Communism but the victory of plenty over want, of health over disease, of freedom over tyranny.

Our experience in Hungary is a warning of what we should not do regarding the liberation of the Communist satellites. We certainly should not encourage people to undertake violent revolutions unless we are prepared to help them, and it isn't likely that we will be because of the risk of a world war. What we can do and should do is to encourage at every opportunity those governments which do have the courage to assert some independence of the Soviet Union.

I think at the present time it is wishful thinking to predict a split between Red China and the Soviet Union. I believe they are partners with the same major objectives. That partnership will be bound together not by personal friendships between leaders but by a common adherence to the belief in the Marxist, Leninist, Stalinist theories.

Politics is an art and a science. Politicians are, in the main, honorable, above average in their intellectual equipment, and effective in getting action on problems that less practical people only talk or write about. An individual has to be a politician before he can be a statesman.

The political leader is important. Whether Republican or Democrat, it is his responsibility when running for office to study the issues, to determine what he believes to be in the best interest of the country, and then to take strong positions and to try to win the people over to his point of view. If leaders do not do that, the country will drift in its policies into following mass thinking that will represent in some instances the lowest common denominator. Considering the great problems that we face in the world, that is inadequate. Our decisions must represent not the lowest common denominator but the best thinking that America can produce. I don't think that you can lead from a position of vacillation. If you are going to lead, you've got to decide in advance whether the issue is one that you feel is worth fighting about. If it isn't, then you take no position at all. But if it is worth fighting about, you've got to take a clear-cut position and get all of the advantage that comes from being out in front.

In an election campaign party unity is essential. If I were asked how I can go out and support all Republican candidates for Congress if, in some instances, individual Democrats are better qualified, I would be very frank to answer that what you have to consider is the fact that ours is not a government of individuals. It is a government of majorities, of a group. An individual by himself can accomplish virtually nothing. I know that for the party to be an effective instrument of

(295)

government it needs to control Congressional committees and the House and Senate organization.

I don't believe in dividing Republicans into classes, such as "Modern Republicans," any more than I believe in dividing Americans into classes. I have no desire to throw out of the Republican party those who happen to disagree with me on certain issues. By the same token, I have very strong convictions as to what I personally believe the Republican party should stand for and the course it should take. What I try to do, and what I believe every good Republican or every good Democrat should do, is work within my party for the adoption of those views.

I believe that, once the majority within a party makes a decision, the best interest of the party and the nation is served if the party unites in support of that decision. I recognize there should be exceptions. Some individuals, as a matter of principle, feel so strongly on certain issues that they would be going against everything they stand for if they supported the position of the administration or the party majority. I understand and respect that point of view. But not the view of those who say, "I can't follow my party on this issue because it is politically inadvisable."

Anyone who attacks his own party will get publicity at the moment. But in the end, if his party or his administration goes down, he will go down with it. There are very few Borahs, Norrises or Hiram Johnsons in American political history. Though it may appear, in the heat of the moment, that one who bucks his party represents and is attuned to current public sentiment, history shows that most candidates are saddled with the records of their party and its administrations whether they like it or not. The man who deliberately weakens his party almost invariably ends up by weakening himself.

If there is more than one bona fide candidate for a nomination, the only way you can find out which is the strongest is to test them in a field of battle. That is preferable to having the bosses pick the candidate. Primary contests can be kept on a constructive basis if opponents for the party's nomination direct their fire against the program of the prospective nominees of the other party, instead of against each other.

We have not done nearly enough to encourage rank-and-file union members and local union leaders to participate and join in the party. I recognize the fact that at the national level the situation offers very

(296)

little promise. I certainly don't intend to tailor my position on labor-management legislation to meet what I regard as the extreme position taken by the national leaders because I think it is not in the public interest. On the other hand, I don't think the Republican party can make a greater mistake than to write off organized labor. It would be bad for the party and bad for the country. We could not survive as a national party. We already start each election by virtually conceding a hundred House seats and twenty-two Senate seats to the Democrats in the South. Therefore we have to win overwhelmingly in the North and West to catch up. Those are the areas where organized labor and also unorganized labor are very potent political forces. Too many Republicans do not realize that in politics unorganized workers tend to justify themselves with the same issues and same causes as the organized workers. A candidate who gets tagged as being antilabor thereby incurs the opposition of both organized and unorganized labor which, on a national scale, can mean sixty-five million people. There was a time when the Republican party was known as "the party of the full dinner pail." Unfortunately, the depression served to change that picture and to paint Republicans as "the party of the rich and privileged interests." The Democrats have very studiously continued in every election to charge Republicans with responsibility for the depression. But that issue is receding. In 1956 we got a substantial portion of the labor vote for the same general reason that we got the vote of other segments of the population. In 1958 we lost it because of the recession and because the much-publicized "right-to-work" issue created in the minds of wage earners generally the impression that the Republican party was anti-labor, both organized and unorganized. It harmed us not only in California and Ohio and other states where it was on the ballot but also in many states where it was not.

The trouble with most politicians is that whenever they talk to labor leaders they only talk about labor. This is a great mistake. When I talk with Jim Carey or Dave McDonald or others, we talk about the world struggle. We talk about the economy in general. I don't agree with some of their ideas. But there are areas of agreement, and I find this group which represents a very large segment of our society can contribute to solving these problems. I believe that an administration in developing its policy, even though you don't have the support of labor leaders, should call them in and say, "Boys, let's talk this thing over."

I think both labor and business have a right to get into politics. Rather than complain about the political activities of labor leaders, businessmen should devote the same amount of effort to politics to see that their views are also adequately represented.

I believe that the hundreds of thousands of dollars that were spent in trying to pass the right-to-work initiatives in Ohio, California and other states in the 1958 campaign could much better have been spent in support of candidates for Congress and the state legislatures who could take an independent, courageous and fearless attitude toward the right kind of labor legislation.

Technically speaking, it should be referred to as the Democrat rather than the Democratic party.[1] But I don't think any election is going to be determined by semantics, and I think it is rather silly to spend so much time and effort over whether we are going to say "Democrat" or "Democratic." I consistently use the term "Democratic" and after every speech I get letters from around the country from good Republican friends telling me what a terrible mistake I made. I doubt if I lost any votes for the Republican side by referring to the Democrats as Democratic. And I doubt if those who refer to the Democratic party as Democrat party have gained anything for the Republicans.

I realize that many in the Southern wing of the Democratic party and some more conservative elements of the Republican party believe all conservatives ought to get into one party, and all liberals or radicals, depending on which term you apply to the opposite economic philosophy, ought to get into another party, so we could have a clear-cut fight on the issues. I believe in the two-party system, and also that there should be room for differing opinions in both parties. This avoids violent swings from one extreme to another after elections. For the extremists to take over our two parties would encourage such trends. Furthermore, the price of such a coalition to the Republicans would be that we would have to abandon the position that we have traditionally taken on the civil rights issue. That is too great a price to pay, morally and politically, even though generally speaking we can make common cause with Southern conservatives on many economic issues.

[1] The Greek adjective is *demokratikos,* which becomes in English "democratic." There is no Greek source for the adjective "democrat." E. M.

The bright Republican hope for making a major breakthrough in the South has been greatly dimmed by the strong position we have taken on civil rights. I believe that this is a temporary setback. It means we cannot expect to crack the South on a broad scale in the near future. But over a period of time I believe responsible Southern leaders will come to recognize that there are other issues which are more important to the best interests and to the future of the South than that one. They will also come to realize that their extreme position on civil rights is, in the long run, untenable, and it would be best for all to have a two-party system. But even now we should certainly make an effort to attract into the Republican party Southerners who find our economic philosophy closer to theirs than the philosophy which has been imposed upon the Democratic party by its National Committee, the ADA, and certain national labor leaders—a philosophy which both the President and I have properly described as radical rather than liberal.

Television is not so effective now as it was in 1952. The novelty has worn off. There is a very early point of diminishing returns in using television. Both parties did too much of it in the 1956 campaign. People probably got tired of seeing favorite programs thrown off for political speeches. I believe in personal appearances and think the personal touch is still the most effective way of campaigning. I believe in a campaign of motion. I also think the most effective appearances of a candidate are before nonpolitical forums where he has a chance really to make converts.

Public opinion polls are having an increasing effect each year on elections and on the selection of candidates. There is no question but that a great number of what we call "swing voters" vote for the person they think is likely to win. Once this bandwagon psychology starts, it is very difficult to stop. That's why public opinion polls can have a very devastating effect on the course of campaigns. In the 1958 Congressional campaign one of our biggest problems was that the polls consistently showed Democrats all over the country leading Republicans. There's no question but that a great number of people simply believed that and paid very little attention to the issues. I should point out that polls do not affect the great majority of voters. But the people they do affect—the ten per cent minority who are swing voters—are the ones that frequently control an election.

It is obvious that people like to play winners, they like to be with winners. Winners get favorable treatment. Losers are scorned. I mean, of course, the great mass of people. Only a few, who are students of government, bother to find out "Why did he lose?" Nothing in politics succeeds like success, and nothing hurts more than failure. But it does not last in either case. A person in political life must expect that he will succeed sometimes and fail other times. Franklin Roosevelt, one of the master politicians of all time, suffered a major defeat in his Supreme Court fight. Truman was hurt terribly by what was probably one of the worst losses in recent history—the Democratic loss of Congress in the mid-term election of 1946. Everybody wrote him off; all the experts agreed that he was finished. In 1948 he was elected president on his own. Winston Churchill in 1939 was completely discredited as far as the voters were concerned. Look how he came back and then later lost again.

While the "win" psychology is very important, I always have had the feeling that where the Presidency is concerned, men who eventually come to the top in both parties are those who best understand the issues and best fit the needs of the times. I never felt that a lightweight, an individual with only a superficial understanding of the great national and international issues, could get the nomination. I don't think one will in either party next time—but, of course, it could happen. The people who nominate at conventions invariably select the man they think has the best chance to win. Those who say that Taft's supporters in 1952 were for him whether he could win or not are wrong. The Taft people were not just for Taft. They also were for him because they thought he could win.

INDEX

Acción Democratica party, 241
Accra, West Africa *Daily Mail*, 204
Acheson, Dean Gooderham, 7, 8, 114
Achilles, Theodore C., 210, 212
Adams, Sherman, 1, 7, 111, 115, 116, 121, 123-125, 149, 151, 160 n, 164-167, 170, 176, 177, 183, 185, 190, 192, 197-199, 201, 288
Adams-Goldfine issue, 197-199, 201
Adelson, William, 25
Africa, 204, 205, 206
Aiken, George D., 118
Albright, Robert C., 252
Alcorn, Hugh Meade, 199
Algeria, 205
Alhambra *Post-Advocate*, 48
Almadaospina, Raoul, 209
American Bar Association, 280
Americans for Democratic Action, 117, 179, 299
Anderson, Robert, 186, 254
Andreas Bello High School, Venezuela, 236
Andrews, Bert, 57-58, 59
Aragon, Ernest, 228
Army-McCarthy hearings, 147-148, 150
Arvey, Jake, 99
Asia, good-will tour of, 149
Associated Press, 109

Baker, Robert G., 259, 260
Baltimore *Sun*, 200, 250
Barkley, Alben, 99, 278
Barnes, Stanley, 43, 107, 111, 126, 132, 149

Batten, Barton, Durstine and Osborn, 122, 155, 266 n
Beauty and the Beast, 34
Becky Sharp (film), 32
Behrens, Earl, 96
Bejar, Hector, 214
Benson, Ezra, 202
Bentley, Elizabeth, 51, 52, 55, 62
Berle, A. A., Jr., 52
Berle, Milton, 122
Berlin crisis, 254, 258 n
Berryman, Jim, 10
Betancourt, Dr. Romulo, 241
Bewley, Thomas, 29
Bird in Hand, 23
Boddy, Manchester, 74-75, 76, 77
Bogotá, Colombia, 217
Bohlen, Charles E., 145
Bolívar, Simón, 221, 230, 235
Bolivia, 207-208
Bonfires, Whittier College, 23
Borah, William E., 296
Boston, 1951 speech at, 85-87
Boston *Globe*, 35, 252
Brandeis, Louis D., 280
Breasher, Ernest, 107
Breckinridge, John C., 138
Brennan, Bernard, 102, 104, 106
Bricker, John, 68, 202
Bridges, Styles, 165, 182
Briggs, Dean, 16
Brock, William, 23-24
Brown, Edmund G. (Pat), 78, 168
Brownell, Herbert, Jr., 25, 84, 89, 94-

97, 115, 116, 135, 153, 174, 267-268
Burns, Dr. Arthur, 257
Butler, Paul M., 2, 168, 196, 251
Byrnes, James F., 102

Caldera, Dr. Rafael, 241
California
    1945 campaign, 44-49
    1950 campaign, 71-83
    Democratic party in, 72, 74-75
    Republican party in, 43-44, 73
California Democratic Women's League, 75
"California Democrats for Nixon," 78-79
California Republican Central Committee, 99
"California Volunteers for Good Government," 72
Campaigns
    (1940), 41
    (1945), 44-49
    (1948), 53, 71
    (1950), 71-83
    (1952), 66, 84-137, 197
    (1954), 7, 10, 138, 152-157
    (1956), 70, 158-187
    (1958), 186, 199-202, 267, 299
    (1960), 186-187, 268-270, 276-277
Caracas, Venezuela, 218, 219-246, 248, 249, 251, 252
Carey, James, 297
Carnegie Foundation for International Peace, 53, 57, 58, 62, 64 n, 69
Case, Clifford P., 153
Catholic University, Peru, 210, 212, 214
Celler, Emanuel, 8, 66
Central American tour (1955), 247-248
Central Intelligence Agency, 58, 146
"Challenge of 1952, The," 85-87
Chambers, Whittaker, 50, 51-70
"Chapman, Mr.," 126-127
Checkers (dog), 4, 124, 130, 135
Chicago Daily News, 94, 200
Chicken Luncheon, 148
China, 200, 250, 295

China, McCarthy boycott against, 145-146
Chotiner, Murray M., 43, 45, 46, 73-74, 76, 79, 81, 82, 94, 95, 97, 99, 102, 104, 109, 111, 114, 116, 120, 121, 124-128, 131, 133-135, 141, 156, 157, 168
Christian Socialist Party, 241
Churchill, Randolph, 4, 249
Churchill, Winston, 205, 300
CIO, 118
CIO Political Action Committee, 46-47, 99
Circulo Militar, Venezuela, 237, 244-245
Citizens for Eisenhower, 115, 135, 138, 167
Citra-Frost Company, 29-30
Civil Service Commission, 156
Clay, Gen'l Lucius D., 10, 115
Clement, Frank G., 180
Cleveland, Grover, 192
Coca-Cola Company, 126
Collins, Thomas E., Jr., 229, 238 n, 244
Colonialism issue, 205-206
Colombia, S. A., visit to, 208-209
Committee on Government Operations, 142
Communism, issue of, 7, 8, 11, 39, 43, 46, 47, 51-70, 74-76, 78-80, 85-87, 89, 98, 108, 113, 116, 118, 119, 130, 131, 140-141, 143-153, 155, 156, 157, 160, 200, 205-210, 212-216, 219-222, 224, 225, 229, 230, 233, 235, 236, 239, 240 n, 241, 242, 248 n, 249, 250, 255, 256, 257, 287, 289, 294
Conant, James, 145
Congressional Quarterly, 49
Coolidge, Calvin, 255
Cox, Lewis, 18-19
Creel, George, 78
Cronin, Rev. John F., 51
Crosley, George, 60, 63
Crossfiling system, California, 45, 75-76
Crusade for Political Purity, 101, 108, 114, 119

(302)

Daily, Col. Gerald M., 236
Daily Mail (Accra, West Africa), 204
Davies, Lawrence E., 80
Davis, John W., 25
Day, Roy O., 44, 45, 72
Del Sesto, Christopher, 185
Democratic National Conventions, 99, 180
Democratic party in California, 72, 74-75
Democratic Senate Campaign Committee, 10
Dennis, Eugene, 233
Denver, Col., 154, 188-193, 196
Denver Post, 135, 147
Depression (1930's), 24, 26, 202, 297
Dewey, Thomas E., 3, 9, 25, 53, 58, 76, 84, 85, 89, 90, 91, 96, 120, 121, 124, 126-128, 133, 151, 155, 159, 160, 162, 178, 185 n, 194, 257, 262, 266, 267, 274
Dexter, Dr. Walter F., 24, 44
Diario del Ecuador, 217
Dillon, C. Douglas, 58
Dixon-Yates issue, 152
Dodson, Leonidas, 22
Dollard, Charles, 62
Dominican Republic, 251
Donovan, Richard, 107
Dorn, Evelyn, 28
Douglas, Helen Gahagan, 40, 70, 71-83, 278-279
"Douglas-Marcantonio Voting Record," 80-81
Downey, Sheridan, 71, 72, 74, 75
Drinkwater, John, 23
Drown, Jack and Helene, 35, 122
Duke Bar Assosiation, 26
Duke University, 24-27, 139
Dulles, Allen, 58
Dulles, John Foster, 1, 26, 53, 57, 58, 63, 64 n, 68, 69, 76, 146, 150, 152, 164, 175, 176, 192, 194, 195, 200, 201, 238, 240, 250, 255, 257, 258, 264, 289
Dumbarton Oaks Conference, 53

"Dump Nixon Movement," 169-186, 255

East Whittier Friends Meeting House, 20-21
Ecuador, 216-217
Edson, Peter, 107-109
Eisenhower, Dwight D., 1, 4-8, 10, 23, 66, 68, 76, 84, 85, 87-99, 101, 102, 106-121, 123-128, 130-136, 138-140, 143-156, 158, 160-200, 203, 204, 219, 220 n, 238, 239, 243, 246, 247, 249, 251, 253-258, 260, 265, 268, 274-275, 280-281, 287, 288, 289
   disability agreement, 194-195
   heart attack, 188-193, 196, 198, 200
   ileitis attack, 169-171, 193
   1957 memorandum to Nixon, 247
   stroke, 193-194
Eisenhower, Mrs. Dwight D., 97, 126, 131
Eisenhower, Dr. Milton, 151, 155, 167, 175, 188
Eisenhower Trophy, 154
Eisler, Gerhard, 233
El Colombiano, 215
El Comercio, 217
El Tiempo, 215
Elizabeth, Queen of England, 4
Emerson, Thomas I., 35
"End Poverty in California" program, 42
England, visit to, 205, 249
Estrada, Pedro, 223
Eugene, Oregon, 117-118
European trip (1951), 87
Evening Star, 189
Exceptional Civilian Service Medal, 220 n
Export-Import Bank, 248

"Fair Deal," 101
"Fair Play Amendment," 93
Fala (dog), 124
Falkenburg, Jinx, 225
Farm issue, 202
Fascism, 79-80

FBI, job application, 26, 27
Finch, Robert H., 191
Fine, John S., 98
Finletter, Thomas K., 25
Flemming, Arthur S., 10, 193
Foreign policy advisory board, proposed, 76
Frankfurter, Justice Felix, 56
Franklins, The, 21
Freda, 279
Fronte Liberal del Pueblo, 209
Fulbright, J. William, 260-261
Fullerton High School, 15

Gabrielson, Guy George, 91
Gallup Polls, 100, 180-181, 252
Garcia, Señora, 234
Geneva, Big Four meeting at, 188
Gerrymandering, in California, 43
Ghana, Africa, 205
Gibbons, Boyd, 44
Gibson, Dunn and Crutcher, law firm, 115
Goddard, Judge Henry W., 66
Goldfine, Bernard, 197
Goldsmith, Arthur J., 162, 171
Goldwater, Barry, 270
Government Contracts Committee, 256
"Great Crusade," 98
Greek-Turkish Aid Bill (Truman Doctrine), 75, 76, 287
Green Island, 37
Grubb, Dale, 228, 230, 234
Guatemala, 155
Guylay, L. Richard, 173, 192

Hagerty, James C., 111, 126, 149, 167, 169, 170, 175, 183, 189, 191, 193, 196, 253
Hall, Leonard W., 140, 148, 149, 152, 165, 169, 170, 172, 173, 174, 177, 178, 181, 182, 183, 184, 185, 191, 192, 198, 266 n
Halleck, Charles E., 154, 170
Harding, Warren G., 14, 255
Harriman, Averell, 266
Harris, John, 35
Harvard Club of California Prize, 16

Harvard Law School, 54
Havana, Cuba, 35
Hebert, F. Edward, 54, 55
Herblock, 10, 263
Herter, Christian A., 58, 162, 169-178, 181, 185, 186, 200, 238
Herter, Mrs. Christian A., 185
Herter Committee, 49, 204
Hillings, Patrick, 124, 126, 179
Hillman, Sidney, 45
Hiss, Alger, case of, 7, 50, 51-70, 71, 76, 77, 84, 86, 97, 130, 135, 144, 151, 152, 287
Hiss, Mrs. Alger, 57
Hoffman, Paul G., 90, 96, 105, 115, 123, 151
Holmes, Justice Oliver Wendell, 54
"Honest Deal," 101
Hoover, Herbert, 66, 72, 76, 84, 118, 164, 202, 287, 289
Hoover, J. Edgar, 26, 27, 252
Horack, H. Claude, 26, 27
"Hounds tooth" cleanliness, 118-119
Hughes, James D., 227, 228, 229, 234, 237, 238, 244, 245
Humphreys, Robert, 110, 121, 125, 173, 184-185
Huse, Captain, 236

"I Love Lucy," 122
"Ike and Chris" buttons, 185-186
"Iklopedia" (notebook), 2
In the Court of Public Opinion, 59
Indo-China conflict, 255-256
Inter-American Highway, 248
Ives, Irving M., 201

Jackson, Don, 267
Javits, Jacob K., 162, 168
Jessup, Philip, 86
Jiménez, Pérez, 219, 221, 223, 229, 237, 241, 242, 244
Johns Hopkins University, 53
Johnson, Hiram, 296
Johnson, Lyndon, 9, 246, 254, 259-261, 292
Johnston, Vic, 165
Jones, Elizabeth Jensen, 132 n

Jorgensen, Frank E., 43, 44, 72

Katcher, Leo, 107
Kaufman, Judge Samuel H., 65-66
Keating, Kenneth, 10, 265
Kennedy, John F., 6, 49-50, 283
Kent, Roger, 8
Kersten, Charles J., 58
Key, William, 218
Khrushchev, 205
King, Rev. Martin Luther, Jr., 251
Knight, Goodwin J., 174, 180, 181, 191, 278
Knight, John S., 94
Knowland, Helen, 94-95
Knowland, William, 23, 45, 71, 72, 73 n, 81-82, 91, 94, 95, 97, 98, 106, 115-116, 134, 148, 178
Korea, 250
Korean War, 78, 80, 85, 108, 143, 254, 287
Kroll, Jack, 99
Kuest, Frank, 134

La Habra, Calif., 29
Labor Committee, 6, 49, 142
Labor legislation, 283-284, 298
Langlie, Arthur, 181
Larrazabal, Adm. Wolfgang, 219, 241, 243-245, 249
Latin America, see South America
Latty, E. R., 24
Leathers, Harlan, 25
Lebanon crisis, 6, 254
Leyvictos, 208
Liberal party, Paraguay, 250-251
Lima, Peru, 209-216
Lincoln, Abraham, 124, 286
Lippmann, Walter, 8, 136, 252
Little Rock desegregation issue, 162 n, 227
Lodge, Henry Cabot, 94, 160, 161, 174, 181, 186
Logue, Robert, 15
London, England, 205, 249
London Daily Worker, 249
"Look Ahead, Neighbor" Special train, 111, 116

Los Angeles Daily News, 74, 107, 123
Los Angeles Mirror, 107
Los Angeles Times, 159
Luce, Mrs. Clare Boothe, 97

MacArthur, Gen'l Douglas, 88 n, 91
MacKinnon, George, 159
Macmillan, Harold, 205
Maine, 1954 elections, 152
Mar Vista Lane, Whittier, Calif., 139
Marcantonio, Vito, 75, 76, 79, 80, 81
Marin, Luis Muñoz, 244
Marshall Plan, 49, 287
Martin, Joseph W., Jr., 44, 68
McAtamney, James W., 228
McCarthy, Joseph, and McCarthyism, 2, 7, 8, 76, 138-152, 157, 159, 255, 266
McClellan, John L., 146
McClure, John, 154
McDonald, Dave, 297
McDowell, John, 55, 62-63
McElroy, Neil, 238
McKeldin, Ted, 174, 181
Medford, Oregon, 116
"Meet the Press," 64, 107
Mendoza, Eugenio, 244
Mikoyan, Anastas I., 11
Milhous, Elmira, 13, 17, 19
Milhous, Hannah, see Nixon, Mrs. Hannah Milhous
Mitchell, James P., 254, 257
Mitchell, Stephen, 110, 114, 118
Montgomery (Ala.) Advertiser, 136
Morgan, Gerald D., 192
Morhouse, L. Judson, 265
Morse, Wayne, 261
Moskowitz, Sam, 228
Mundt, Karl E., 55, 110
Mundt-Nixon Communist Registration Bill, 153 n, 160
Murphy, Robert G., 6, 254
Mutual Security Agency, 145

Nasser, Gamal Abdel, 206
National Security Council, 5-6, 10, 191, 192, 193, 203, 254, 258, 261
National Youth Administration, 24

NATO conference, 194, 289 n
NBC El Capitan Theater, Hollywood, 126
Nelson, Rockwood, 44
New Deal, 24, 36, 48, 66
New Hampshire primaries, 161, 165-166
"New Nixon, The," 136
New Republic, 8, 48 n
New York City, 1952 speech at, 85
New York *Daily News*, 120 n
New York *Herald Tribune*, 57-58, 116, 126, 135, 179
New York *Journal American*, 135
New York *Post*, 107, 109, 111, 120 n, 187, 252, 265, 266
New York Times, 80, 178, 200
Newsome, Roy, 15
Newspaper Enterprise Association, 107
Newspaper Publishers Association, 11
1958 (magazine), 216
Nixon, Arthur, 18, 20
Nixon, Donald, 14, 16, 18, 19, 21
Nixon, Edward, 18, 19
Nixon, Francis A. (Frank), 12, 14, 17, 18, 20, 44, 139, 184, 186
Nixon, Hannah Milhous, 13, 14, 16, 18-20, 44
Nixon, Harold, 13, 18, 20
Nixon, James, 17
Nixon, Julie, 98, 262
Nixon, Patricia, 45, 98, 130, 262
Nixon, Richard Milhous
    ancestry, 16-18
    birth, 12-13
    childhood, 13-15
    election to House, 48-49
    election to Senate, 83
    election to Vice-Presidency, 138
    entry into politics, 41
    financial status, 38-39
    law studies, 24-25
    marriage, 4, 34
    Navy service, 36-38
    nomination for vice-presidency, 66, 96-98
    as president of the Senate, 259-260
Nixon, Thelma Ryan (Pat), 4, 30-35,

41, 95, 100, 107, 112, 113, 117, 119, 122, 125, 126, 130, 131, 134, 137, 139, 153, 157, 185, 186, 189, 203-205, 210, 214 n, 225-229, 232, 234, 235, 237, 240 n, 243, 244-246, 251, 258, 262-263
"Nixon Fund," 4, 23, 26, 93, 100, 101-121, 122-137, 161, 197, 262
"Nixonland," 8
Nixon's Hamburger Stand, 37
"Nixophobia" (notebook), 2
Norris, George W., 296

Oakland *Tribune*, 72
O'Brien, Dr. Robert W., 132 n
OPA, 35-36, 255
"Operation Poor Richard," 238-239, 249
Order of Coif, 24
"Order of the Hound's Tooth, The," 134
Orthagonians, 21-22, 23, 24
Overseas missions, 203-252

PAC (CIO), 46-47, 99
Panama, Inter-American Chiefs of State meeting, 171, 175, 176
Paraguay, 250-251
Pearl Harbor, 35
Pearson, Drew, 141-142, 167
Peaslee, Amos J., 160, 167
Peaslee, Dorothy, 167
Pepper, Claude, 78
Perdue, William, 25
Peress, Dr. Irving, 148
Perry, Herman L., 44, 72
Persons, Gen'l Wilton B., 125, 145, 146, 153, 165, 167, 173, 191, 192
Peru, 209-216
Philip, Prince of England, 4
Phillips, John, 44
"Pink sheets," 81
Pittini, Archbishop Riccardo, 251
Pamona, California, 108
Porter, Charles O., 117
Portland, Oregon, debate in, 160
Potter, Charles E., 9

Powell, Adam Clayton, 49
Price, Waterhouse, accounting organization, 115
Protestant clergy, Communist influence on, 146
Public opinion polls, 100, 180-181, 252, 299
Puerto Rico, 244
Pulgarvida, 209
"Pumpkin Papers," 65

Quakers and Quakerism, 2, 17, 18, 20-21, 35, 37, 57, 65, 142, 280
Quemoy-Matsu issue, 200-201
Quigley family, 16
Quito, Ecuador, 217

Radio speech, on McCarthy, 149-150
Rankin, John, 49, 54
Rayburn, Sam, 9, 154-155, 254, 267
Recession (1950s), 152, 201, 257, 297
Reporter magazine, 107
Republican party
    in California, 43-44, 73
    future of, 268-270
    and Hiss case, 66, 70
    National Committee, 130-131
    National Conventions, 9, 91-98, 106, 159, 166
    in the South, 299
    State Convention, Columbus, Ohio, 152
Rhee, Syngman, 250
"Richard M. Nixon Chair of Public Affairs, The," 23
Right-to-work issue, 202, 283, 297, 298
Rockefeller, Nelson, 3, 5-6, 186-188, 252, 264-268
Rodham, Wade, 228, 232, 233
Rogers, Ted, 122, 126, 131
Rogers, Tony, 190
Rogers, Will, Jr., 73 n, 77, 81-82
Rogers, William P., 1, 57, 108, 109, 120, 121, 122, 124, 126, 145, 146, 147, 150 n, 174, 181, 182, 184, 185, 189-192, 194, 195, 257
Rogers, Mrs. William, 190
Roosevelt, Eleanor, 279

Roosevelt, Franklin D., 9, 43, 53, 124, 138, 143, 149, 150, 286, 288, 291, 300
Roosevelt, James, 78, 82
Roosevelt, Theodore, 286, 288
Roosevelt, Theodore, Jr., 279
Rubottom, Roy R., Jr., 240
Russia, see Soviet Union
Ryan, Thelma (Pat), see Nixon, Thelma Ryan

San Francisco Chronicle, 97
San Marcos University, 208-214, 215, 248
Santa Fe Railroad, 13
Santa Fe Springs, Calif., 14 n
SCAT, 37, 159
Schiff, Dorothy, 266
Scliris, Louis, 235
Scott, Hugh, 270
Seaton, Fred A., 111, 114, 186
Senate Investigating Committee, 57, 168
Senate Office Building, 259
Senatorship, 1950 campaign for, 71-83
Shanley, Bernard M., 160
Shannon, William V., 252
Sherwood, John, 211, 213, 228, 232, 233
Shockney, Henrietta, 12-13
Shroyer, Thomas, 88-89
Sinclair, Upton, 42
Slippery Gulch Rodeo, 15
Small Town Girl (film), 32
Smathers, George A., 10, 78
Smith, Gen'l Bedell, 256
Smith, Dana C., 101-108, 116, 119, 120, 123, 135
Smith, Grant, 17
Smith, Margaret Chase, 97, 142, 174
Smith, Dr. Paul S., 22, 124
South, Republican party in, 299
South America, goodwill trip to, 9, 11, 206-252
Soviet Union, 10-11, 53, 65, 79, 205, 206, 295, see also Communism, issue of
Sparkman, John, 99, 110 n, 124

(307)

Sparks, Edward J., 220, 240
Sputnik, 194, 201
Stassen, Harold E., 5, 7, 72, 76, 87, 88, 91, 93, 119, 120, 134, 140, 145, 151, 155, 158-187, 255, 265, 277, 285
State of the Union Message, 196
Stevens, Robert, 147, 148
Stephens, Thomas S., 267
Stevenson, Adlai E., 2, 3, 8, 10, 67-70, 86, 99, 101-102, 108, 110, 112, 114, 123, 130, 136, 137, 139-140, 144, 149, 156, 157, 168, 251, 273, 274, 289 n
"Stevenson Fund," 123
Stripling, Robert, 55, 64
Stroessner, Gen'l, 251
Student Exchange Program, 248
Suez issue (1956), 249
Summerfield, Arthur, 110, 112, 116, 121, 125, 126, 133, 134, 153
Susan, 279
Symington, Stuart, 146

Taft, Robert A., 68, 76, 84, 88-96, 106, 114, 161, 166, 178-179, 268, 277, 285, 300
Taft-Hartley Labor Law, 6, 49, 77, 88
Taylor, Robert, 231
Tax reform issue, 254, 284
Teapot Dome Scandal, 14, 287
Television, Army-McCarthy hearings, 150
Television program (1952) on Nixon Fund, 4, 23, 26, 115, 120, 121, 122-137, 262; see also Nixon Fund
Thompson, Frank, Jr., 205
Thornton, Dan, 174, 181
Time magazine, 52
Tipton, Harold, 80
Tribuna Popular, 220-223
Trujillo, 251
Truman, Harry, 2, 6, 8-10, 53, 54, 66, 70, 76, 79, 84, 85, 88, 98, 99, 108, 111, 147, 150, 153, 197, 254, 264, 287-291, 300
Truman, Margaret, 291

Truman Doctrine (Greek-Turkish Aid bill), 75, 76, 287
Trysting Place, The, (play), 21
Twining, Gen. Nathan, 238
Tydings, Millard, 143
Tydings Committee, 150 n

Un-American Activities Committee, 7, 49, 50, 51-70, 76
United Nations, 53
United Press, 109
United Republican Finance Committee of Los Angeles County, 104-105
University of Oregon, 117
University of Southern California, 32, 33
Upton, Dr. Albert, 21, 22-23, 30, 124

Van Buren, Martin, 274
Variety, 136
Venezuela, see Caracas, Venezuela
Ventuni, Oscar Garcia, 228, 229
Veterans' loans vote, 260-261
Volunteers for Eisenhower, 102
Voorhis, Jerry, 39-49, 158

Wallace, Henry, 47, 75, 165, 208, 289
Walters, Vernon, 213, 225-226, 228, 233-234
Warren, Earl, 43, 73, 76, 81-83, 88-94, 99, 106, 108, 119, 159, 161, 255, 262
Washington, D.C., 17
Washington Post, 6 n, 10, 252, 263
Washington Star, 10, 187
Watkins, Arthur V., 151
Watkins Committee, 151
Waugh, Samuel C., 217, 232
Weinberg, Sidney J., 167-168
Westinghouse Company, and Nixon television program, 120
Wheeling, West Virginia, 133-134, 140-141
White, Harry Dexter, 59, 62
White House Stag Night, 7
Whitener, Basil, 25
Whittier, Calif., 17-18, 28, 39, 40, 41, 99, 139, 184

Whittier Alumni Association, 30
Whittier College, 21-22, 23, 24, 30, 39, 44, 99, 124, 132 n
    Commencement Address (1954), 39-40, 139
Whittier High School, 14-15
WHO, 87
Willkie, Wendell, 41, 273
Wilson, Glen, 112
Wilson, Woodrow, 78, 192, 286
Wingert and Bewley, law firm, 28
Winster, Lord, 250

Woods, Rose Mary, 108-109, 133, 154, 173, 235
Wray, Merton G., 21
Wroble, Lester, 37, 38

Yalta, 53
Yorba Linda, Calif., 12, 13, 16, 40
Young Republicans, Boston speech to, 85-87

Zanuck, Darryl, 131
Zuazo, Hernán Siles, 208
Zwicker, Gen'l Ralph W., 148

Set in Linotype Fairfield
Format by Marguerite Swanton
Manufactured by The Haddon Craftsmen, Inc.
Published by HARPER & BROTHERS, New York